ANTHROPOLOGICAL PAPERS OF
THE UNIVERSITY OF ARIZONA
NUMBER 79

Seventeenth-Century Metallurgy on the Spanish Colonial Frontier: Pueblo and Spanish Interactions

Noah H. Thomas

THE UNIVERSITY OF
ARIZONA PRESS
TUCSON

The University of Arizona Press
www.uapress.arizona.edu

© 2018 The Arizona Board of Regents
All rights reserved. Published 2018

Printed in the United States of America

23 22 21 20 19 18   6 5 4 3 2 1

ISBN-13: 978-0-8165-3858-4 (paper)

Editing and indexing by Linda Gregonis
InDesign layout by Douglas Goewey

Library of Congress Cataloging-in-Publication Data are
available at the Library of Congress.

♾ This paper meets the requirements of ANSI/NISO
Z39.48-1992 (Permanence of Paper).

About the Author

NOAH THOMAS received a B.A. from the University of
California at Santa Cruz, an M.A. in Anthropology from
New York University, and a Ph.D. in anthropology from the
University of Arizona. He lives in Ventura, California, and
currently works as a consultant in historic preservation and
environmental compliance and as a freelance jazz musician
and coffee roaster.

Cover

Perforated and stamped copper disk and overview of the
metallurgical facility at Paa-ko. Photos by the author.

Contents

Acknowledgments vii

1. **Introduction** 1
   Ethnohistorical and Historical Sources 5
   Archaeological and Ethnographic Data 6
   Technological Analysis 6
   Integrating the Evidence 6

2. **Technology, Value, and Identity** 8
   Representation, Style, or Choice 8
   Acculturation, Creolization, and Transformation 10
   Agency and Practice 12
   The Construction of Value 13

3. **Puebloan Mineral Use and Exchange** 15
   Color Symbolism 16
   The Role of Minerals in Exchange 17
   Colonial Transformation of Value and
   Signification 18
   Conclusion 19

4. **The Historical Record of Mineral Exploitation
   in New Spain and on the Northern Frontier** 21
   1521 to 1550: Conquest, Labor, and
   Congregation 21
   1550 to 1650: Expansion of the Mining Frontier 25
      Zacatecas 25
      Parral 28
   Late Sixteenth-Century Expeditions 29
   Oñate and the Establishment of the Colony 30

The Periodicity of Mining Communities 32
Referencing Value: A Comparison of Assays 36

5. **History of Excavations at Paa-ko** 37
   Early Research 37
   University of Chicago Field Studies Project,
   1996 to 2005 40
   The Metallurgical Facility 40
   Dating the Workshop 41

6. **Construction and Use History of the
   Metallurgical Facility: The Archaeological
   Evidence** 43
   Eastern Terrace Excavations, Features,
   and Surfaces 45
      Combustion Feature and Associated
      Ventilation System: 97E/-172N/F1 47
      Furnace and Associated Ventilation System:
      Feature 101E/-170N/F1 49
      Ventilation Shafts: Features 102E/-170N/F1
      and 103E/-170N/F1 51
      Masonry Bin: Feature 99E/-169N/F1 52
      T-shaped Masonry Furnace:
      Feature 100E/-168N/F2 52
      Base of Eastern Terrace Deposits 53
   Western Terrace Excavations and Features 53
      Masonry Construction of the Terrace 53
      Interior Surfacing Episodes 55
      Furnace Feature 90E/-168N/F1 and
      Interior Surfaces 2 and 3 56

Interior Surfaces 4, 5, and 6 and
Associated Features...................................... 59

Furnace: Feature 90E/-169N/F1................. 59

Furnace or Fore Hearth:
Feature 89E/-170N/F3 62

Accumulation of Heat-Altered Adobe:
89E/-170N/F1.. 62

Charcoal Accumulation: 89E/-168N/F1 63

Heat-Altered Adobe Accumulation,
Ore Roasting Feature: 88E/-172N/F2.......... 63

Features Associated with Interior Surface 7....... 63

Pit and Furnace Collar: 88E/-170N/F3......... 64

Pit Feature: 90E/-170N/F1 64

Western Exterior Area 64

Northern Exterior Area................................. 65

Combustion Feature: 90E/-163N/F1 66

Northern Terrace Excavations......................... 66

Comparison of Metallurgical Features 67

Furnaces.. 67

Charcoal Preparation and Ore-Roasting Features .. 68

Summary 68

**7. Metal Smelting, Refining, and Copper
Working at Paa-ko: Materials Analysis**........... 69

Analysis Methods.. 69

Ore Samples 71

Samples LA162-211 and LA162-338............... 72

Sample LA162-206................................. 72

Sample LA162-214................................ 72

Samples LA162-23, LA162-209, and
LA162-212 72

Slag 73

Fayalitic Copper Slag: Samples LA162-16,
LA162-24, and LA162-85........................... 73

Melilite-Fatyalite Copper Slag:
Samples LA162-72, and LA162-105............... 74

Magnetite-Delafossite Copper Slag:
Samples LA162-54 and LA162-109 74

Lead Slag: Samples LA162-55 and
LA162-74... 75

Metal Refining 75

Samples LA162-15, LA162-17, LA162-337,
and LA162-339.. 75

Refractory Materials 76

Copper Working.. 78

Lead- and Copper-Isotope Analysis 79

Discussion 81

**8. Material Value and Personal Value:
Creating Wealth within Colonial
Systems of Appropriation**......................... 86

Early Colonial Negotiations of Value 87

Shifting Contexts of Production....................... 88

West Mexican Metallurgists............................ 89

Wealth and Value.. 90

Conclusion 92

References Cited.. 93

Index 103

Abstract 109

Resumen 109

-- **TABLES** --

4.1. Colonial Period Mines in Northern New Spain 33

4.2. Colonial Period mines in the Los Cerrillos area,
New Mexico.. 36

5.1. Radiocarbon Samples from the Metallurgical
Workshop... 42

6.1. Strata Description of Figure 6.17,
Feature 90E/-169N/F1............................... 61

7.1. Characteristics of Samples Discussed
in the Text 70

FIGURES

1.1.   Paa-ko (LA 162) and its regional setting............. 2

1.2.   Historical mining districts in the vicinity of Paa-ko (LA 162) 3

4.1.   The mining centers of Parral and Zacatecas in relation to the New Mexico Colony 26

5.1.   Historical features at Paa-ko........................ 38

5.2.   Calibrated dates range for radiocarbon samples recovered from the workshop 42

6.1.   Southern Terrace 44

6.2.   Eastern Terrace, lower surface and associated features 45

6.3.   Eastern Terrace, base of deposits and associated features 46

6.4.   Overview of Eastern Terrace: furnace features 97E/-172N/F1 and 101E/-170N/F1 47

6.5.   Feature 97E/-172N/F1, combustion feature and associated ventilation system....................... 48

6.6.   Profile of combustion Feature 97E/-172N/F1 49

6.7.   Kiva II ventilation system........................... 49

6.8.   Feature 101E/-170N/F1 with late glaze ware ceramics 50

6.9.   Plan view of ventilation system associated with Feature 101E/-170N/F1 51

6.10. Feature 100E/-168N/F2 and associated features 52

6.11. Western Terrace interior, upper surface............ 54

6.12. Interior of Western Terrace, Surface 6 and posthole alignment................................... 55

6.13. Western Terrace, interior Surface 3 and furnace Feature 90E/-168N/F1 56

6.14. Western Terrace, interior Surface 5 and furnace Feature 90E/-169N/F1, bowl 2 57

6.15. Western Terrace, interior Surface 7................. 58

6.16. Western Terrace, Feature 90E/-169N/F1, Surface 5.. 60

6.17. Profile of Feature 90E/-169N/F1 61

7.1.   Color and consistency gradients of refractory material... 77

7.2.   Sheet copper thicknesses 78

7.3.   Blank exhibiting chisel marks and perforation 79

7.4.   Perforated and stamped disk 79

7.5.   Foot-shaped pendant................................ 79

7.6.   Lead-isotope ratios of various Paa-ko materials... 80

7.7.   Copper-isotope ratios in relation to lead-isotope ratios.. 81

COLOR PLATES

1.   Copper ore: Sample LA162-211

2.   Copper ore: Sample LA162-338

3.   Copper ore: Sample LA162-206

4.   Copper ore: Sample LA162-214

5.   Galena in calcite gangue: Sample LA162-212

6.   Slag: Sample LA162-72, in transmitted, plain polarized light

7.   Slag: Sample LA 162-72, in transmitted, cross-polarized light

8.   Fayalitic copper slag: Sample LA162-16

9.   Fayalitic copper slag: Sample LA162-85

10. Melilite-fayalite copper slag: Sample LA162-105

11. Magnetite-delafossite copper slag: Sample LA162-109

12. Lead slag: Sample LA162-55

13. Lead slag: Sample LA162-74

14. Litharge and glass: Sample LA162-15

15. Litharge: Sample LA162-17

16. Adobe sample recovered from furnace Feature 90E/-168N/F1

17. Cold-worked sheet copper

18. Annealing twins in sheet copper

19. Sulfur from the interior of the Western Terrace

Acknowledgments

This publication would not have been possible without the support of many individuals and institutions. I would particularly like to thank Mark T. Lycett for taking a gamble on me as an unaffiliated graduate student by hiring me, introducing me to the archaeology of New Mexico, and providing me the opportunity to engage in the study of Paa-ko Pueblo. His guidance in methodology, theory, and collaborative field work have made this publication possible. I owe a debt of gratitude to Diane Gifford Gonzales, who twisted Mark's arm to hire me in the first place and for her inspiration, mentorship, and example as a scholar. This work would not have been possible without the help and advice of David J. Killick; his patience and guidance in the material analysis was invaluable, as was his challenge to keep me both rooted in the material and open to fresh perspectives. I also thank David for his perspicacious reviews of multiple drafts of the manuscript and his tireless pursuit of funding opportunities for the project. Similarly, I would like to thank Barbara J. Mills, Judith Habicht-Mauche, Kathleen D. Morrison, and Thomas E. Sheridan for their insightful comments, suggestions, and conversations surrounding the late prehistoric and early historical Pueblo world, colonialism, and the Spanish Colonial borderlands. Special thanks to Judith Habicht-Mauche and Alyson Thibodeau for conducting isotope studies of the Paa-ko materials, and to Phillip O. Leckman for providing the regional and site overview maps and for many hours of engaging conversation over bowls of green chile.

The research underpinning this publication was generously funded by grants and fellowships from the National Science Foundation, the Mellon Foundation, and the American Council of Learned Societies. Additional funding was provided by research grants from the Emil Haury Scholarship Fund; the William Shirley Fulton Scholarship Fund; the Reiker Grant, School of Anthropology, University of Arizona; and the Arizona Archaeological and Historical Society.

I gratefully acknowledge the insightful comments offered by the anonymous reviewers. Deepest thanks to T.J. Ferguson, Allyson Carter, Linda Gregonis, Maren Hopkins, and the editorial staff of the University of Arizona Press. Thank you for pursuing the publication of this research and for your perseverance and patience with the author. Many thanks to the student excavators, staff, and crew of the University of Chicago Summer Field Studies Program. Thank you for your dedication in the field, careful observation, insight, humor, and camaraderie.

CHAPTER ONE

Introduction

Located on the east side of the Sandia Mountains in Bernalillo County, New Mexico, the pueblo of Paa-ko (LA 162) is one of three large, pre-Hispanic settlements occupied during the Classic period (AD 1350–1600) in the area (Figure 1.1). The other two communities are Tijeras Pueblo (LA 581) and San Antonio (LA 24). Each of these pueblos are typical aggregation-period settlements that supported fairly large populations at their peak of occupation. They are composed of multiple room blocks arranged around a series of plazas.

Paa-ko, the largest of the three pueblos, is significant archaeologically because of its history of occupation, which spans the late prehistoric and early colonial periods, and due to its location, which suggests ties to both the Rio Grande and the Galisteo Basin. In her assessment of precolonial Pueblo settlement patterns, Barrett (2002) suggests that the East Mountain area where Paa-ko is located may have had a history of successive occupations by different linguistic groups. This led Spanish officials to be uncertain about the region's linguistic affiliation in the seventeenth century. The East Mountain area may have functioned as both a corridor of population movement and as a refuge in times of stress for Keres, Tano, and Tewa speakers (Barrett 2002; Lambert 1954; Nelson 1914).

Spanish interest in Paa-ko in the early colonial period had two foci—the incorporation of the population within the Catholic Church and the exploitation of mineral resources located in its vicinity. Both interests are evident archaeologically at the site, with the foundation of a chapel (*visita*) in its historical period plaza and the establishment of a metallurgical workshop adjacent to room blocks exterior to the plaza. These imposed cultural forms are evidence of Spanish attempts to channel Pueblo productive action

to the benefit of the New Mexico colony. Archaeologically, Paa-ko is significant in that it offers an opportunity to investigate a fairly isolated community that was directly linked to Spanish interests yet was distant from the centers of early seventeenth-century colonial power. The metallurgical facility must be understood in this context, namely, that Paa-ko was a place on the frontier where people were engaged in an extractive technology important for Spanish colonial interests. The pueblo's location offered both the benefits and detriments of marginalization.

The industrial facility at Paa-ko is situated within a region with a long history of mineral exploitation. Five mining districts are located in proximity to the site: Cerrillos, centered on the mines of the Cerrillos Hills; Old Placers in the Ortiz Mountains; New Placers in the San Pedro Mountains; Placitas on the Northeast side of the Sandias; and Tijeras Canyon to the south and west (Figure 1.2). The New Placers District is the closest to Paa-ko (approximately 4 miles northeast) and shares the historical place name of San Pedro. The Cerrillos District, as discussed in Chapter 4, was mined during the historical period, from the late sixteenth century through mid-twentieth century. The Old Placers and New Placers districts were the site of placer gold booms in the early nineteenth century, with the New Placers District becoming a significant source of copper in the territorial period of the late nineteenth century. The Placitas and Tijeras Canyon districts may have seventeenth- and eighteenth-century mining roots, but they were primarily developed in the late nineteenth and early twentieth centuries as copper, lead, and silver mines (Ferguson and others 1999).

Precolonial mineral exploitation in the region has been documented archaeologically and ethnohistorically. The

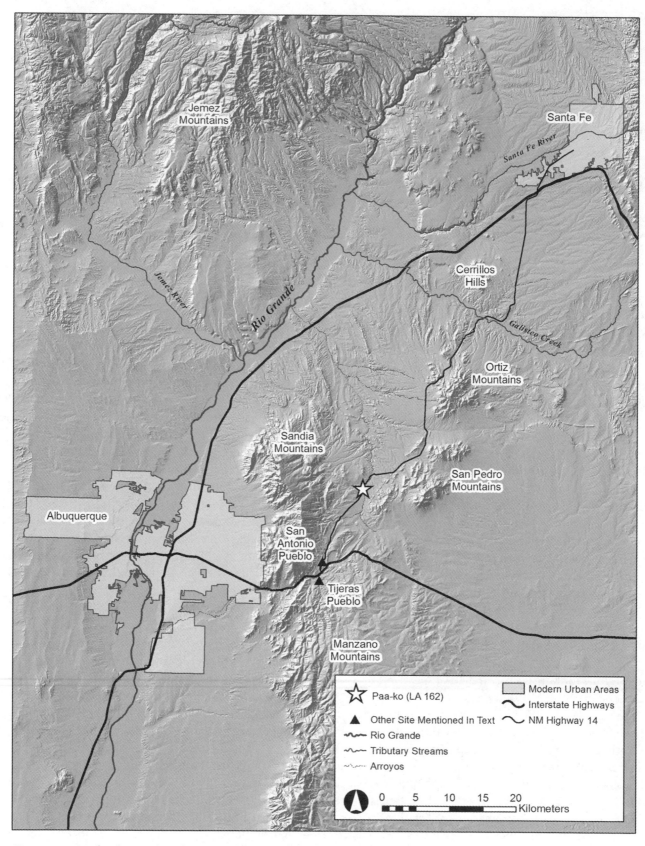

Figure 1.1. Paa-ko (LA 162) and its regional setting. Map courtesy of Phillip Leckman.

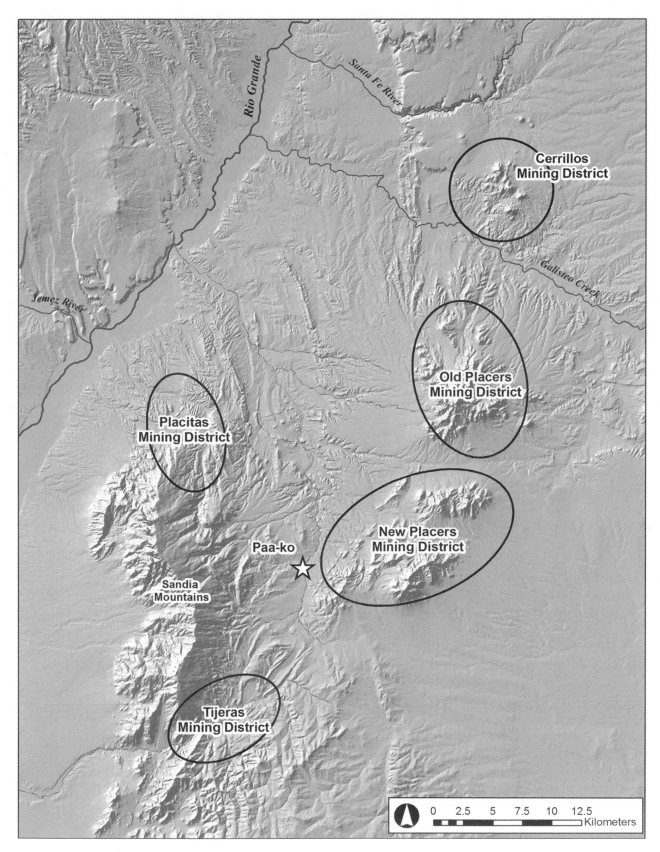

Figure 1.2. Historical mining districts in the vicinity of Paa-ko (LA 162). Map courtesy of Phillip Leckman.

Cerrillos Hills played a central role in the procurement of lead minerals for use in glaze recipes from the thirteenth through seventeenth centuries. Turquoise from Cerrillos was most likely mined and exchanged from the ninth century to the time of contact (Habicht-Mauche and others 2000; Milford and Swick 1995; Thibodeau and others 2015). The Sandia region, more generally, played a part in mineral procurement strategies across the Pueblo Southwest as recently as the late nineteenth and early twentieth centuries (Ferguson and Hart 1985). From a regional perspective, Paa-ko is situated centrally to these districts, and ore from at least two separate mining localities were recovered during excavation.

Access to wood resources for charcoal production was a major concern for the mining industry in New Spain (Bakewell 1971; Flores 1994). In the copper mining centers of Michoacán, for example, Spanish colonial authorities would often move indigenous populations closer to wood or water resources in order to facilitate production (Barrett 1987). Paa-ko was ideally situated for the exploitation of wood resources suitable for smelting. Macrobotanical analysis of wood charcoal from features within the metallurgical facility suggests that a broad range of wood resources were used. Historically, hardwood species were preferred fuel sources for smelting technologies. An unidentified species of oak was used in some of the metallurgical features, but ponderosa pine (*Pinus ponderosa*) was the predominant taxon encountered (Lycett 2004). The availability of wood and water near Paa-ko, coupled with a sedentary labor source, may have been a major factor in the decision to situate the metallurgical facility at that pueblo.

Although Paa-ko has a long history of archaeological interest and study, the metallurgical facility was not discovered until 1996, when researchers from Northwestern University's Summer Field Studies Program worked at the site. Subsequent summer excavations by the University of Chicago Field Studies Program continued until 2005 under the direction of Mark Lycett. These excavations revealed an extensive facility of more than 165 square meters that occupied two terraces bounded by masonry construction. The data recovered from the excavations and subsequent analyses provide a rare perspective on seventeenth-century metallurgical practices and the shaping of such practices in the isolated context of colonial New Mexico.

The pueblo's location on the east side of the Sandias and west of the Galisteo Basin made it ideally suited to be a refuge, first from people escaping Plains-Pueblo conflict and later from Spanish colonial control. Spanish prospectors may have built upon Tano connections to the area to establish the facility at Paa-ko. The excavation data available for the pueblo suggest that it was occupied at the time of Spanish colonization. The population of Paa-ko was most likely incorporated into the functioning of the facility, providing labor and knowledge of local resources. The Spanish probably organized the pueblo under the *encomienda* system. This may have led to labor displacement from subsistence activities and other traditional practices involved with the functioning of the pueblo both economically and socially.

The facility at Paa-ko represents an early introduction to New Mexico of metal smelting and forging, as no metallurgy was practiced in the U.S. Southwest until the Spanish arrived. As with many aspects of Spanish colonialism, the mining practices in New Spain were built from a base established by precolonial indigenous labor, skill, and knowledge about mineral use (Flores 1994; West 1994b). West Mexican metallurgists, who had been working with metals since at least the ninth century AD, were among the groups exploited by the Spanish for their knowledge and skills (Hosler 1994). In New Mexico, the Spanish relied on Puebloan groups to show them local mineral resources. The workshop at Paa-ko, then, is at the intersection of Puebloan mineral use and Spanish colonial mining as filtered through West Mexican metallurgical practices.

With that intersection in mind, this study integrates historical data on the development of Spanish colonial mining with ethnohistorical research on mine laborers, studies of colonial production practices in New Mexico, and observations on precolonial Puebloan mineral acquisition and ritual production. At the core of the research that led to this volume is an understanding of technological practice generated from a program of material analysis. Observations of the material composition and structure of artifacts related to production processes revealed by the archaeology were used to reconstruct the technological choices made by the metallurgists at Paa-ko. The products and byproducts of production found at the facility are quite varied and include evidence for copper smelting and copper sheet-metal production, the smelting of lead ores and production of lead metal, and the recovery of precious metals through cupellation and other refinement technologies. This suite of technologies has some unusual aspects that are explored here as products of the particular social and historical context in which they played a part.

Paa-ko and its metallurgical facility are situated in a particular historical moment of Spanish colonialism in New Mexico, a context within which social relations and cultural structures of meaning and value were negotiated, reformulated, and developed anew. The facility operated within colonial structures of power but incorporated Pueblo and possibly West Mexican labor and productive practices. This nexus is explored with attention to the situated agency of practitioners of the technology and their engagement in the construction of value, both in terms of material wealth and social significance.

Individual agency, modeled as practice (Bourdieu 1977), shapes technology and the larger social and economic spheres in which it operates. In turn, agency is situated in historical contexts that form the basis for the interpretation of practice as indicated by the archaeological and technological data. In this regard, it is important to consider that any given historical context (especially under colonialism) is composed of complex intersections of multiple historical trajectories and individual and collective agencies. To that end, efforts were made in this study to capture as much of the underlying diversity of historical processes that influenced the technology at Paa-ko as possible. This approach falls under the under the common archaeological premise, articulated by Wylie (2000), that convergent lines of independent evidentiary sources allow for the generation of robust and plausible accounts of archaeological phenomenon.

The contextual approach adopted here is used to historically situate the technological choices. This is made possible by the use of material analytical methods and approaches and the archaeological analysis of the facility. The material analytical methods included optical and electron microscopy and chemical-composition data generated through X-ray fluorescence (XRF) analysis and energy dispersive spectroscopy (EDS). These materials analyses and the archaeological data allowed for observations about the technology used at Paa-ko including furnace operation and temperature regimes, choices in mineral acquisition and processing, and techniques of metal processing and refining. These analyses detail practice, but not the evaluative contexts within which they were engaged. Therefore, recourse to historically situated and socially contextualized frameworks is necessary.

ETHNOHISTORICAL AND HISTORICAL SOURCES

The social and historical contexts of metallurgical production at Paa-ko can be understood by surveying ethnohistorical and historical sources pertaining to Puebloan production practices, Spanish colonialism in the Southwest, the development of the Spanish colonial mining industry,

and the history of metallurgical practice more generally. As with all evidentiary sources used in archaeological analysis, the premise of their production should be understood, and inherent biases identified. This is particularly true for documentary evidence pertaining to the colonization of New Mexico, where documents were often used as proxy agents and should be read with colonial politics in mind.

Among the historical sources consulted were translations of entrada records and the records of the establishment of the New Mexican colony, especially Bolton (1963), Hammond and Rey (1953, 1966), Scholes (1930, 1942), Hodge and others (1945), and Marrow (1992). Also consulted was a translation of the 1598 Farfan expedition to the mines near Hopi, which provided additional mineral characterization data not present in earlier translations (Sheridan and others 2015). The historical material presented here on the mining industry is a synthesis of a variety of secondary sources and analyses, but primarily relies upon the excellent work of Bakewell (1971) and West (1949) for Mexico and Milford and Swick (1995) and Vaughan (2006) for New Mexico. Also consulted were Baragallo (1955), Barrett (1987), Blanchard (1989), Flores (1994), Grinberg (1996), Maldonado (2006), Mayer (1974), Motomura (1997), Platt (2000), Probert (1969), Pruna (1989), Salazar-Soler (1997), Stein and Stein (2000), and Vaughan (2001).

Ethnohistorical research concerning the structure of the mining industry plays an important role in this analysis, especially in regard to how mining intersected with other Spanish colonial economic practices. Central to this discussion is an assessment of how indigenous free labor played a role in the development of mining practices on the northern frontier (Bakewell 1972; Sheridan 1992; West 1949). Barrett's (1987) discussion of the colonial copper industry and its organization during the sixteenth century provides a historical perspective on the persistence of metallurgical practice in communities that specialized in copper and copper alloy production in the precolonial period. Other ethnohistorical work developed by archaeologists, such as Hosler's (1994) work on West Mexican metallurgy before the Spanish conquest and Maldonado's (2006) discussion of mining and metal production under the early colonial period Tarascan state, were important for developing an understanding of the influence of indigenous metallurgists in the formation of the Spanish colonial mining industry.

The historical record of sixteenth- and seventeenth-century metallurgical practices as depicted in the works of Agricola (1556), Barba (1640), Biringuccio (1540), and Ercker (1580) were also consulted in order to provide a background on the technological repertoire of seventeenth-century metallurgists and to formulate possible technological analogues present in the archaeological remains of the facility (Barba 1923; Hoover and Hoover 1950; Sisco and Smith 1951; Smith and Gnudi 1959). In particular, Barba's (1923) description of Spanish colonial metallurgy was useful, in part because his observations were the most comprehensive and were contemporary with the operation of the facility at Paa-ko. His technical descriptions and philosophical treatise were particularly informative for this analysis.

ARCHAEOLOGICAL AND ETHNOGRAPHIC DATA

The Paa-ko facility was excavated over a period of 10 years under the direction of Mark Lycett, first by Northwestern University and then by the University of Chicago. These excavations and subsequent analyses focused on the economic practices that were introduced during the early colonial period. In addition to the metallurgical facility, the University of Chicago archaeologists investigated the historical plaza and the floodplain of the Arroyo San Pedro.

In addition to excavation data for the facility at Paa-ko, this study relies on archaeological, ethnographic, and ethnohistoric data concerning the Pueblo IV period (AD 1300–1600). In addition, ethnographic data concerning ritual paraphernalia production, mineral procurement, and color symbolism were consulted (Cushing 1979; Ford 1992; Ortiz 1969; Parsons 1966). Most important to this study are archaeological data concerned with mineral procurement and processing strategies that were part of the ceramic glaze ware tradition and the katsina cult, as well as patterns of exchange related to those traditions (Adams 1991; Crown 1994; Duff 2002: Ferguson and Hart 1985; Habicht-Mauche, Eckert, and Huntley 2006; Habicht-Mauche and others 2000; Huntley and others 2007; Lycett 1995; Mills 2002; Nelson and Habicht-Mauche 2006; Preucel 2002; Snow 1981; Spielmann 1998; Ware and Blinman 2000). The production of glaze during the Pueblo IV period offers an avenue into a production process that used mineral sources, pyrotechnology, and forms of exchange predicated on ritual production that provides a baseline from which to observe the impact of colonial appropriations of similar resources. Discussions concerning the nature of exchange in the Pueblo IV period have also been informative and the models that various researchers have proposed are weighed against notions of commodity exchange under systems of ritual production (Kohler and others 2000; Snow 1981; Spielmann 1998, 2002).

Ethnographically, the work of Parsons (1966), Cushing (1979), Ortiz (1994), and Ford (1992) have been particularly informative. Parsons' work offers a comparative perspective of Pueblo ritual practices that is useful for looking at the possible range of past practices. Her work offers a set of suggestions as to how minerals were incorporated in Pueblo exchange systems. Ortiz and Ford offer an additional perspective, documenting the interrelationship between the economic and political with the religious and meaningful. Their work provides an overall framework for placing the use of minerals in various contexts within the construction of multiple regimes of value. The combined use of ethnographic and archaeological sources is not without its problems, as extrapolating past behavior from ethnographic records is at best conjectural and at worst assumes a vision of indigenous societies as static and unchanging. The ethnographic is used here to provide a basis for thinking about the ways in which minerals may have been incorporated in various value constructions, how they fit in different classes of material objects, and, more broadly, how color may have played a part in constructing value and meaning across spheres of action and materiality.

TECHNOLOGICAL ANALYSIS

Samples of metal, slag, refractory materials, and ores from the facility were analyzed using a variety of techniques. These included optical microscopy, scanning electron microscopy with energy dispersive spectroscopy (SEM-EDS), X-ray fluorescence (XRF), and stable lead isotope analysis. Refractory materials were experimentally refired. Copper sheet artifacts were photographically documented, weighed, and measured. Samples of the copper were examined in reflected light with a metallographic microscope. For a more complete discussion of the methods used to analyze these artifacts, see Chapter 7.

INTEGRATING THE EVIDENCE

In this study, historical, anthropological, and archaeological approaches are integrated to understand the mining and metallurgical technology of the seventeenth-century facility at Paa-ko. This follows similar approaches to studies of mining communities that focus on the social construction of mining and metallurgical practices and not solely on techniques of production (Killick and Fenn 2012; Knapp, Pigott, and Herbert 1998). At its core, the analysis presented here describes and defines the practices used at the facility, so its focus is necessarily material. But rather than the describe the technology solely from the perspective of its technical construction, the material culture produced is considered as the product of a specific history, materiality, and semiotics of production.

In this regard, Wylie's (1989) discussion of the utility of the metaphor of "cables" (as opposed to chains) as linking arguments between diverse sources and "tacking," both within (vertical tacking) and between (horizontal tacking) sources, to build robust arguments, are appropriate for this analysis. Within the historical and ethnohistorical data sets, this study tacks vertically between local colonial interactions and colonial processes on a broader scale, documenting the development of the mining industry in New Spain with its incorporation of indigenous labor while exploring various contexts of production under seventeenth-century colonialism in New Mexico. Similarly, the research looks at broad trends in the use of minerals for ritual production within the Pueblo world from the fourteenth century to the advent of colonialism, with reference to ethnographic documentation. It tacks between these sources and the archaeological and material specifics of the development of glaze ware traditions and their semiotics.

The inferences generated are cabled to archaeological and material observations (both field and laboratory). The continuities and discontinuities of each are explored. This limits the interpretation of the material record of the facility by embedding it within the range of social contexts of production possible for its historical context. Similarly, the broad overlay of historical data is limited by the constraints imposed by the material record of production. In the resulting technological analysis, the social context and historically situated contextualization of practice take precedence over assessments of the technology's successes or failures from a twenty-first century viewpoint. The observed technological practice is evaluated not in terms of productive rationality or efficiency, but rather as the situated agency of practitioners that is both socially and historically referential and potentially transformative.

CHAPTER TWO

Technology, Value, and Identity

With its concern for historical processes and the negotiative contexts of social action, this study dovetails with the general trend in nonbehavioralist archaeologies to emphasize the analysis of practice, or the generation and maintenance of cultural forms through creative action (Pauketat 2000, 2001). As Pauketat (2001) suggests, such approaches entail a general acknowledgment that historical processes are central to the understanding of past and present social action. Furthermore, such processes are, to a large extent, shaped by the embodiment and creative transformation of historical experiences through the actions of people (de Certeau 1984).

In addition, the direct technological analysis of specific production practices used here incorporates a series of concepts and methods of analysis derived from the Social Construction of Technology (SCOT) approach of Bijker (1995), the Technological Style approach of Lechtman (1977), and Lemmonier's (1993) Technological Choices approach. These central tendencies are linked through an overall interest in practice theory and its relation to technological analysis, but have deeper, historical roots in Marcel Mauss's (1979) exploration of the link between socially and historically constructed body gesture and technique (see also Bourdieu 1977; Dobres 2000; Dobres and Hoffman 1994). In dealing with the specific historical, ethnohistorical, and technological data concerning the development of the metallurgical facility at Paa-ko, particularly in the context of Spanish colonialism, it became clear that many of the approaches to technology based on a Maussian understanding of technique failed to address how power relations affect technological constructions.

Power dynamics are often subsumed or displaced by an over-emphasis on technology as a representation of ethnicity, rather than being indicative of a practitioner's creative action in the negotiation of often competing frameworks of meaning.

It is argued here, for example, that the introduction of the mining industry in colonial New Mexico owed much to precolonial exchange practices involving mineral pigments. Spanish wealth extraction involving these materials was prefigured by Puebloan practices of ritual production. The role of minerals in both Spanish colonial and Puebloan regimes of value placed the exchange or appropriation of these materials at a critical nexus for cultural construction during the early colonial period. This highlights the importance of understanding the resultant technology at Paa-ko in terms of relevant theories of exchange, materiality, and value. In particular, (following another foundational concept from Mauss) the literature concerning theories of gift exchange, the play between inalienable and alienable objects within such exchanges, and the relationship to the construction of self and society through transactions encompassed by gifts and commodities, monetary transactions, and symbolic exchange, are particularly salient (Beidelman 1989; Graeber 2001; Keane 2001; Miller 1987; Myers 2001; Thomas 1991, 2002; Turner 1989; Weiner 1985).

REPRESENTATION, STYLE, OR CHOICE

Derived from the pioneering metallurgical work of Cyril Stanley Smith, the Style and Technology approach to artifact analysis was primarily developed by archaeometallurgists, particularly through the work of Heather Lechtman, who succeeded Smith at MIT. The analysis of technological style builds from Smith's (1981) recognition that technologies appear to have organizing principles that are culturally proscribed, what he described as an aesthetic experience of their making. Smith's ideas are rooted in the strong structuralist and modernist approaches to cultural theory and art history in vogue when he began exploring ancient technology in the 1950s, through the modernist concern with media and aesthetic and the structuralist insistence on primacy of meaning in the composition of form. This legacy has continued, particularly in the stated link between the material composition of artifacts, their visual appearance, and what Lechtman (1977, 1984) and Hosler (1994) have termed "material metaphors."

The value of this approach has been in the renewed emphasis on the importance of cultural meaning over functionalist interpretations of artifact variability and composition. The interpretive potential of the approach is limited by its over-emphasis on form, because of its reliance upon object-oriented studies (often from museum collections that lack adequate archaeological provenience data) and the inseparable link that the approach establishes between form and meaning. These aspects downplay contextual relationships and tend to offer technological analyses that are rich in metaphoric associations, but lacking in any sense of the practitioner as a social actor, particularly in terms of social agency.

Often the culmination of analysis is in the exposition of what Lechtman (1984, 1999) has termed "ethnocategories," linked to a larger sense of ethos suggested by comparisons with other technologies present within the culture or through reference to ethnohistoric or ethnographic literature. Practitioners of past technologies take on an apolitical stance in Lechtman's (1999:223) work, strangely paralleling normative views of the practice of science: "People understand and manage the physical and social world in which they live by creating ethnocategories of things, events, behaviors and relationships that help render the world intelligible." Technological choice is revealed by an analysis of the constraints imposed on action by the physical limits of materials and by the "culturally bound" nature of practice (Lechtman 1999). Individual action is limited by the confines of cultural structure and, to a certain degree, the approach tends to deny political action in past social systems within which technology played a part.

This critique is best articulated by Marcia-Anne Dobres (2000:131):

Meaning does not miraculously hover above everyday material practices any more than it exists as some intangible substrate structuring action from below. Rich though they are, what is curiously missing from symbolic studies of technologies past and present is explicit discussion of how agents *make* meaning through their non-discursive, everyday technological practices enacted in particularly structured social settings. There is a disturbingly normative quality to this body of work that often leaves the reader with the sense that these world views float above or below the practical consciousness of those faithfully adhering to them, and that technological practice is little more than the routinized, traditional, and thus patterned material behaviors of unconscious agents obliviously (but faithfully) going through the motions.

As Dobres suggests, such approaches to technology tend to hold a normative and restrictive view of culturally embedded action without reference to social agency.

Despite these limitations, the analysis of technological style is an enticing approach because of its effective use of pattern recognition and its ability to discern broad, archaeologically significant patterns across a wide range of material classes. Yet the benefits of the approach are lost when the social and historical context of practice are not taken into account. Few studies of technological style exist that deal with periods encompassing dramatic cultural change, such as under colonialism (for an exception, see Epstein 1991). This attests to the inability of the approach to move beyond delimitating style to adequately address the underlying and more salient theme of cultural production, namely the creative tension between cultural structures and individual action or agency.

Other studies of technology have attempted to integrate the contextual and historical approaches to analysis. Lemmonier's (1993) discussion of technology, although wary of analyses based on individual agency, concludes that technologies are ultimately representations of unconscious and conscious tendencies for action or schema held by practitioners. These representations can establish social differences in between-group and within-group interactions. Similarly, Bijker (1995), a sociologist and historian of technology, focuses on the influence of "relative social groups" in the creation of technological systems, suggesting that technology develops in relation to the needs of user groups as defined ethnographically or historically. These approaches tend to position technology in relation to what could be called operational schema shared by members of a social group. Such mental maps or sets of needs could be in conflict with those of other groups, but, in general, technologies are conceptualized as arising from successfully satisfying the social or mental preconditions to their existence (Bijker 1995: Lemmonier 1993:64–84).

What is strangely missing from these approaches is a concern for political or social power in the construction of technology. This is despite the fact that the competition among relevant social groups ultimately results in the success or failure of a particular technology. Bijker (1995:263) attempts to integrate power into his analysis, yet he defines power relationships so narrowly (as micropolitics) that he tends to deny the importance of larger society-wide structures of power as an influence in the development of technology. In failing to address larger social and cultural power dynamics, Bijker's technological analysis is confined to the politics of the boardroom, while ignoring other power relationships, particularly that of labor.

The social relations of power are central to the construction of technology and to the kinds of cultural or social representations that Lemmonier's and Lechtman's approaches emphasize, as well as in the construction of the perceived needs of Bijker's "relevant social groups." As Eric Wolf (1990:91) succinctly states, "power is implicated in meaning through its role in upholding one version of signification as true, fruitful, or beautiful, against other possibilities that may threaten truth, fruitfulness, or beauty." This is particularly true in colonial interactions where basic modes of production are in conflict.

> When one mode enters into conflict with another, it also challenges the fundamental categories that empower its dynamics. Power will then be invoked to assault rival categorical claims. Power is thus never external to signification – it inhabits meaning and is its champion in stabilization and defense [Wolf 1990:92].

The syncretic technologies of the colonial period cannot be understood without reference to the institutions of power enacted by the colonizers such as those that organized indigenous labor under *encomienda, repartimiento,* and the labor and doctrinal requirements of the mission system. In early colonial interactions, indigenous institutions of social power were important for structuring the conditions within which novel forms of production were instituted; they should not be overlooked. These are perhaps less evident due to the dominance of the historical record, which frames colonial institutions of power

as pervasive. Ethnohistorical and archaeological research plays an important role in elucidating such institutions and practices.

ACCULTURATION, CREOLIZATION, AND TRANSFORMATION

Material culture in colonial contexts is not usually approached from a technological perspective. Instead, materials have more often been analyzed following the legacy of culture-contact studies from the late nineteenth- and early twentieth-century American anthropology, with its focus on artifact pattern analysis as a proxy indicator of "acculturative" consumption patterns. The divide between an approach to analysis based on technological style or representation and one based on the development of culture-contact studies appears to follow what Lightfoot (1995) has observed as a false dichotomy between prehistoric and historical archaeology. This split in research approaches could also be a product of the history that Rubertone (2000) details concerning the ambivalence towards the inclusion of Native American history under the rubric of historical archaeology. Technology studies and artifact pattern analysis share many common themes and problems, particularly in the way in which they tend to view material culture as an indicator of a static view of ethnic identity.

This common thematic content derives from a set of foundational concepts within which both an understanding of cultural style and ethnic identity were formulated in American anthropology, namely the blurring of semantic boundaries between concepts of *diffusion, acculturation,* and *assimilation,* as well as the related concept of *tradition.* As Herskovits (1958: 12–13), following Kroeber (1931), states:

> The problem of terminology with which we are presented may be simplified if the relationship between the words "acculturation," "diffusion," and "assimilation" be further analyzed. In his discussion of diffusion, Kroeber defines it as a "process . . . by which elements or systems of culture are spread, by which an invention or a new institution adopted in one place is adopted in neighboring areas . . . in some cases . . . until it may spread over the whole world." Diffusion, this process by means of which culture spreads in space, is contrasted by Kroeber with tradition, which represents the means by which a given culture persists in time; that is, how the content of a culture is handed down from one generation to another within the same society. And though both "rest

largely on the same psychological basis: imitation," yet "as technical and . . . semi-popular term" the word diffusion has "come to be nearly restricted to its intercultural meaning" so that one almost never speaks of the diffusion of culture from one generation to another, but only from one people to another.

"Assimilation," on the other hand, is defined as "the name given to the process or processes by which peoples of diverse racial origins and different cultural heritages, occupying a common territory, achieve a cultural solidarity sufficient at least to achieve a national unity." Its significance, we are told, lies deeper than the superficial adoption of similar traits of a common culture by a number of groups of different origin; fundamentally, assimilation is not achieved until a people have attained a *unity of thought* that underlies the "veneer" of acceptance of traits of a material nature [emphasis mine].

The reliance upon psychological understandings of cultural process in American anthropology of the 1930s tended to reify culture and stress ethos as an explanatory concept. Such developments run parallel to the historical formation of the mental template model, or *milieu intérieur*, a foundational concept for Lemmonier's (1992:83–84) approach to technological analysis, developed from the work of Leroi-Gourhan (1993). Both approaches suggest that prehistoric societies were largely organized around shared beliefs or cultural dispositions, as articulated in the culture-history approach dominant at the time. Leroi-Gourhan's approach can be perceived as an outgrowth of Durkheim's concept of mechanical solidarity as well (via Mauss), emphasizing the distinction between the socially cohesive power of shared belief versus the socially binding nature of economic interdependence present in modern nation-states.

The history of culture-contact studies in the Americas was compromised by its early use of assimilation models, often suggesting an inevitable dissolution of indigenous culture due to the unquestioned assumption of the efficacy and superiority of Western cultural forms. The often state-driven applied anthropological focus of assimilation studies was developed in part to justify early twentieth-century administrative policies that included forced relocation and education of tribal groups (Rubertone 1989, 2000). Despite this early history, assimilation models were challenged in the mid-1930s. Models were developed that incorporated a concept of the interrelationships of power and the effect of tribal and individual choice in regard to acceptance

or rejection of imposed cultural forms. In particular, Melville Herskovits (1958) recognized the importance of understanding the history of social relations prior to contact as well as the social context of contact situations (Herskovits 1958). This was in part made evident to him through his work on African American culture and the need to recognize social power dynamics in the context of American slavery. Recent work within American historical archaeology builds on Herskovits's legacy, and has developed notions of the material culture of contact as syncretic, embodying multiple ethnic or identity expressions, and reflecting the multiethnic composition of early colonial communities (Armstrong 1998; Cusick 1998; Herskovitz 1958; Singleton 1998). The result of such research has been to redefine acculturation in terms of the dynamic interplay among multiple ethnic components, reflected in the terms such as "transculturation" (Deagan 1998) and "creolization" (Ferguson 1992).

As I have argued elsewhere, terms of hybridity, of which these are a part, have conflicting uses and are as much tied to colonial discourses on the nature of ethnic difference as they are to postcolonial appropriations celebrating that difference (Thomas 2007). Although archaeologists have tended to use such concepts to explore the development of nonconformist identities among the colonized or subaltern, such terms often play a part in current political discourse that emphasizes national unity ideologies based on the erasure of ethnic difference. As Alonso (2004) has discussed, these often mask political and economic inequalities faced by indigenous peoples through a nationalist discourse that emphasizes the value of a hybridized national identity as modern. This is contrasted with a sense of an indigenous identity as something backward (Alonso 2004; Dean and Leibsohn 2003). The fact that terms of hybridity can so easily embody seemingly opposite meanings is related directly to the overlap of meanings discussed by Herskovitz between such foundational anthropological concepts as tradition and the nationalist overtones of assimilation as indicative of a unity of thought.

Singleton (1998) has suggested that rather than rely on the determination of ethnic markers, research should shift away from acculturative models and towards the contextualization of interaction in terms of hegemony. She suggests that an emphasis on the analysis of domination and resistance, and a focus on power more generally, allows for a nuanced understanding of cultural interrelationships, particularly under the institution of slavery. Included within this continuum are acts not only of domination, control, and resistance, but also accommodation, negotiation, and the construction of alliances (Scott 1990; Wolf 1990). By focusing on power dynamics, archaeologists can attempt to define underlying cultural tensions expressed in material culture assemblages:

> Viewed in this way, archaeologists can move beyond interpretations of "ethnic markers" or "grammars" to understand the signs and symbols that enslaved African Americans used to take some control of their world. This perspective allows archaeologist[s] to treat material culture of slavery as part of a system of control, part of a system of resistance, and simultaneously part of both systems [Singleton 1998:182].

Singleton's focus on the expression and resistance of power in the context of African American slavery may be more broadly applied to other forced labor contexts in the Americas. More generally, a focus on agency, within which resistance may be encompassed, shifts material culture analysis from static culture concepts towards understanding how objects and technologies were used under colonialism to engage dynamic social processes including the development of new economic strategies as well as novel forms of representation and signification (Capone and Preucel 2002; Lomawaima 1989; Mills 2002; Mobley-Tanaka 2002).

AGENCY AND PRACTICE

Material culture studies benefit from incorporation into contextual frameworks that focus on agency, either as intentional political action or as a habitual kinesthetic action rooted in socialized practice. This is evident in the strong analysis presented by Ehrhardt (2005) on the development of Illinois copper-base metal working in early colonial contexts, which derived from an analysis rooted in the investigation of technological style. It is also evident in studies of culture contact that were developed from artifact pattern analysis. For example, Deagan (1983, 1995) contextualized consumption and use patterns as a reflection of ethnic identity in public and private spaces under Spanish colonialism, while Lightfoot, Martinez, and Schiff (1998) discuss the relative influence of materially expressed social identity at different spatial scales of analysis within the colony at Fort Ross.

In her analysis of the incorporation of European metals within the copper-working tradition of the Illinois, Ehrhardt (2005) combines a stylistic approach to technology with a concern for situating technology within a larger context of practice that she terms the "technological system," as defined by David Kingery (1993). Ehrhardt documents the incorporation of European metals into Illinois systems of representation. But rather than observing degrees of acculturation or a truncation of indigenous frameworks for meaning, she emphasizes the practitioners' creative responses to new materials and networks of distribution. She documents how such materials were removed from European contexts of exchange and value and made meaningful within Illinois society through their incorporation within new spheres of indigenous social and material exchange and expressions of worth. Ehrhardt's approach departs from traditional analyses focused on the definition of cultural norms to a concern for the agency of practitioners. She adopts "a view of technology in which all technological activity is viewed as potentially innovative, creative, and imbued with multiple levels of social and ideological significance which can be revealed through detailed, fine-grained, finely textured analysis" (Ehrhardt 2005:197).

Deagan's (1983, 1995) artifact pattern analysis reveals categories of social choice based on divisions in public or private space in her work at colonial St. Augustine and Puerto Real. Her contextualization of choice reveals available spheres of social action for individuals within the colonial community. Specifically, she is able to address how gendered associations with public and private space allowed for certain expressions of indigenous identity and their synthesis within colonial society. Attention to the spatial context of social agency allows Deagan to construct a nuanced view of social interaction with the colonial communities she researches. Ultimately, Deagan argues that private spaces offered an acceptable context for the inclusion of indigenous practice within colonial life, primarily through the incorporation of indigenous women within colonial households.

Lightfoot, Martinez, and Schiff (1998) offer an interesting synthesis of what could be termed a study of the technological style of midden deposition and recycling patterns at colonial Fort Ross. Through attention to the spatial contexts of social action, the authors detail the social expression of identity from the structuring of household refuse and consumption patterns to village site structure within the pluralistic society of Fort Ross, which was composed of Russian administrators, Alutiiq Alaskan sea-mammal hunters, and Kashaya Native Californian women.

Of particular interest for this study is the way in which the authors link the structure of economic relations between colonizer and colonized with the expression of indigenous practices at the household level. Similar to

Deagan, Lightfoot, Martinez, and Schiff (1998:216) document a maintenance of local Native Californian food processing and trash deposition practices within the household. This suggests the strong influence of Native Californian women within such contexts, in contrast to the structuring of village neighborhoods more generally, which tended to follow practices associated with Alutiiq village structure. They argue that the lack of economic support from Russian administrators in times of resource stress facilitated cultural connections between Kashaya women and their home communities, thereby necessitating a maintenance of traditional practices. The flow of materials recycled from European contexts (earthenware and porcelain sherds, bottle glass and scrap metal) into refuse deposits within households at Fort Ross and into local indigenous communities demonstrates an incorporation of such goods through practices rooted in indigenous production contexts.

These studies situate practice within economic and political spheres of action. It is from this perspective that it is possible to address colonial technological practice in its historical context of social relations. Of particular influence for this study is Ehrhardt's emphasis on the potential innovative and creative aspects of technological action and her tracing out of the pathways within which an appropriated material was assigned value outside of its original use context. Issues concerning the construction of value, particularly the ways in which appropriated materials enter new social contexts of production, use, and distribution, are central to understanding the development of technology at Paa-ko. Observations of technological choice as practice situated within the social context of value construction, rather than the construction of identity per se, is a more informative approach for the Paa-ko materials.

THE CONSTRUCTION OF VALUE

The metallurgy at Paa-ko can be considered as a place where mineral wealth was extracted and a site where mineralogical and metallurgical knowledge was exchanged between practitioners of a Spanish colonial industry and the inhabitants of the pueblo. The technologies used at the site reference a construction of value. This study explores this construction in terms of the establishment of Spanish colonial value systems and how those systems impacted Puebloan exchange. It also examines the overlapping and variously intersecting regimes of value surrounding Pueblo use of minerals and Spanish appropriation of metallic ores (Appadurai 1986). Such constructions included the

negotiation of the relative value of minerals and pigments in early colonial interactions; the relative exchange values and the social value of gift giving within such interactions; and acts of value assessment, assay, and the calculation of specie value in relation to the cost of industry and mining. In pursuing how value was constructed and negotiated within these various contexts this study follows Myers (2001) and Keane (2001) in their call for renewed emphasis on the materiality of objects in the understanding of social contexts of production. From an archaeological standpoint, this may seem like a moot point. But as Keane (2001:70) cogently suggests:

> the very materiality of objects means that they are not merely arbitrary signs. Their materiality makes a difference both in the sources of their meanings and in their destinations, such that they are subject to shifting physical, economic, and semiotic contexts. . . . Insofar as objects often *seem* to carry their values and meanings on their sleeves, as it were, they can play critical roles at the intersections among these shifting contexts. Their power and value emerge at the intersection of their character as conventional signs and their potential roles in a possibly unlimited range of contacts.

From a more archaeologically and regionally specific perspective, Habicht-Mauche (2006) has articulated the need to situate the technological analysis of Puebloan glaze ware within multiple contexts of social action. Following Appadurai's (1986) notion of the importance of objects in human life, Habicht-Mauche argues for uncovering the "social histories" of objects, as a kind of meta-history that reveals the embeddedness of objects in social action. As she states:

> We cannot divorce discussions of resource selection and production from those of distribution or from those of use, since each of these processes represents potential arenas of social action where cultural meanings may be inscribed and social relationships and identities may be negotiated. Thus, this approach dissolves the false distinction that is sometimes made between technological and economic approaches to the study of material culture, on the one hand, and social and symbolic (or "stylistic") approaches on the other [Habicht-Mauche 2006:10–11].

This dissolution is due to the underlying role of material culture in the construction of various regimes of value within which aspects of economy and social signification are circumscribed.

Kopytoff's notion of the biography of objects revealing their relationship to the construction of value within acts of exchange is of central importance here. As he notes in regard to culture contact situations,

> [b]iographies of things can make salient what might otherwise remain obscure. For example, in situations of culture contact, they can show what anthropologists have so often stressed: that what is significant about the adoption of alien objects—as of alien ideas—is not the fact that they are adopted, but the way they are culturally redefined and put to use [Kopytoff 1986:67].

His notion of the shifting associations of objects through their individual histories is directly relevant to the discussion of the transformation of material values under colonial appropriation. As discussed in more detail in Chapter 3, Puebloan mineral pigment procurement and exchange established a distinct set of meanings between the production of inalienable (or nearly inalienable) objects and the exchange necessary for ritual production. This differed from the valuation determined by colonial spheres of exchange and that held by prospectors seeking wealth.

It is the interaction among these regimes of value that structured the technology used at Paa-ko. The metallurgical facility fits Kopytoff's notion of a case study that bridges the extremes of commodity production on the one hand, and his "forces of singularization" on the other.

> [T]he most interesting empirical cases to be studied, with ultimately the highest theoretical returns, are the cases in between. It is from these cases that we can learn how the forces of commoditization and singularization are intertwined in ways far more subtle than our ideal model can show, how one breaks the rules by moving between spheres that are supposed to be insulated from each other, how one converts what is formally unconvertible, how one masks these actions and with whose connivance, and, not least, how the spheres are reorganized and things reshuffled between them in the course of a society's history [Kopytoff 1986:88].

The Spanish term *metales* is a good focal point for the discussion of the construction of value in the context of production at Paa-ko, due to its dual reference to ore and its potential metallic wealth. Determination of the wealth value of minerals in a newly encountered landscape was a process that involved intersecting regimes of value and practice that included indigenous Puebloans and the multiethnic colonial miners. *Metales* were defined within this interactive context. The extraction of wealth, from the identification of minerals, the mobilization of labor, and colonial administrative power associated with this endeavor extended from these regimes. The workshop at Paa-ko was a product of this process and therefore a site of new forms of cultural production.

The materials analyses and historical data presented here inform a central issue concerning how equivalencies of value (both in terms of exchange and cultural meaning) were established in the negotiative contexts that surrounded the appropriation of *metales* in New Mexico. This is really an issue of the enactment of social power. As Myers (2001:7) argues, "the making of equivalence between different objects, between objects or wealth . . . is hardly a given; equivalence is, rather, commonly imposed through the application of social power." At Paa-ko, who wielded this social power was very much in question. Although the establishment of the colony was coercive, particularly in its appropriation of Pueblo labor, colonists were dependent upon Pueblo resource knowledge and skill for survival. Puebloan categories of value had the potential to underpin the veneer of colonial dominance, creating syncretic cultural forms, and offering opportunities for the enactment of opposing cultural meanings. This historical context places Pueblo agency centrally in the production of the New Mexico colony's early economy.

CHAPTER THREE

Puebloan Mineral Use and Exchange

Metallurgy was not practiced in the U.S. Southwest before the Spanish colonists arrived, although copper bells (crotals) were traded into the region from West Mexico as early as AD 900, and native copper from Mississippian cultures may have been incorporated into deposits at Chaco Canyon (Judd 1954; Vargas 1995). Vargas identified two phases of trade based on bell typology that corresponded with known types and phases of production in the West Mexican metal-working zone identified by Dorothy Hosler (1994). Phase I trade (AD 800 to 1200 or 1300) was centered on a distribution node in the Hohokam region, with the sites of Gatlin and Snaketown figuring prominently. Phase II bell trade (AD 1200 or 1300 to 1500) centered on Gila Pueblo within Hohokam-Salado exchange, with an additional center of consumption, if not trade, at Paquimé. The volume of exchange for both periods was most likely never very substantial, and Vargas (1995:71) suggests that it was not "regularized or systematic." Instead, bells are thought to have been special items that were exchanged among elites with ties to West Mexico. In comparing accounts from the Cabeza de Vaca entrada with the known archaeological distribution of copper artifacts in the greater Southwest, Epstein (1991) concluded that the only metal artifacts in circulation during the mid-sixteenth century were heirloom pieces and objects removed from archaeological sites such as Paquimé.

There is no substantive evidence for the occurrence of metals other than copper in the prehistoric Southwest, even though copper, tin, silver, and gold alloys were all being produced in West Mexico during this time (Hosler 1994). The fact that copper artifacts do not appear to have been exchanged to any great degree compared to materials such as turquoise, shell, and macaw and turkey feathers, indicates that although knowledge of metal may have existed in pre-Hispanic times, it was not particularly associated with ritual production or other regimes of value in the Southwest.

That is not to say, however, that metallic ores or mining activity were unknown to southwesterners (Thomas 2011). Turquoise, which often co-occurs with metallic ores, was valued and mined over many generations (Hedquist 2017; Hedquist and others 2017; Thibodeau and others 2015). Lead, copper, iron, and manganese oxide were used extensively as components in ceramic glazes and as pigments. Glaze paint recipes for ceramic vessels included these ores from their earliest use in the latter half of the thirteenth century through the late seventeenth century (Fenn, Mills, and Hopkins 2006; Herhahn 2006). In the Southwest, glaze was applied as a painted decoration to parts of a vessel, rather than being applied to the whole vessel in the style typical of Old World glazed ceramics. Glaze recipes included the use of lead and copper as fluxes that lowered the melting point of their admixture with silica and produced a glossy finish. Copper, iron, and manganese also acted as colorants (Habicht-Mauche 2006). Glaze recipes varied among various Puebloan communities. Fenn, Mills, and Hopkins (2006) have documented a complex interplay between glaze recipes and firing practices, suggesting that potters manipulated mineral components to produce a desired color under both oxidizing and reducing atmospheres. Herhahn (2006) suggests that regional traditions of glaze production developed over time, with an emphasis on copper colorants among the Western Pueblos and manganese in the Eastern Pueblos.

Specific minerals were also included as temper within Eastern Pueblo glaze wares. The persistence of this practice from precolonial times to the late seventeenth century has led Capone (2006) to suggest that it was a component of inter-Pueblo identity signaling. The use of glaze and paint design and mineral inclusions as temper played various roles in inter- and intra-community and regional exchange, particularly through ceramic use in ceremonial feasting and the expression of regional identity (Adams 1991; Crown 1994; Duff 2002; Graves and Eckert 1998; Habicht-Mauche 1993; Mills 2002). In her stylistic analysis of Pueblo IV ceramics, Habicht-Mauche (1993:96) has argued that this shift away from an emphasis on local production and consumption commodified production for use in trade.

Nelson and Habicht-Mauche (2006) argue that glazed ceramic forms may have circulated in more locally significant exchange spheres and were important inter-community social signifiers. They contrast this with the role of glaze minerals in regional exchange patterns. Based on lead isotope studies of glaze paint and archaeologically recovered galena, it has been determined that minerals from mines in the Cerrillos Hills of New Mexico were widely distributed across the Southwest (Habicht-Mauche, Eckert, and Huntley, 2006). They suggest that the two different trajectories of exchange "denote the presence of multiple, crosscutting exchange networks that functioned within different social and economic contexts and at different geographic and social scales" (Nelson and Habicht-Mauche 2006:198). The broader regional exchange of minerals may be linked to patterns of exchange regulated by ritual production.

Snow (1981) suggests that the trend toward community specialization (for example, the production of specific ceramic forms, cotton production at Hopi, etc.) was driven by the need to obtain materials for ceremonial paraphernalia. Researchers have interpreted this phenomenon to be related to the functioning of the katsina religion or the Southwest Regional Cult (Adams 1991; Crown 1994), which linked communities at a regional level. Many of the design elements on early Rio Grande Glaze Ware may reflect aspects of one of these religious movements, particularly in the emphasis on polychrome design and the vitreous, light-scattering quality of the glaze. These characteristics of Rio Grande Glaze Ware and their possible symbolic associations contrast with other contemporary ceramic wares of the northern Rio Grande, which may have referenced more localized ideologies (Graves and Eckert 1998).

Mineral procurement and processing for ceramic production may also have been associated with the creation and maintenance of community and place. Place is a significant structuring concept in southwestern indigenous ideology (Lycett 2002; Rubertone 2000). Andrew Duff's (2002) analysis of the production and consumption of several different wares in the Little Colorado region suggests that migrant households during the Pueblo IV period maintained historical associations to place through the crafting of specific wares. Such associations are related technologically to the locations of mineral resources within the landscape, thus creating metaphorical associations with ancestral places through the practice of resource procurement. Pueblos stopped producing glaze wares after the 1680 Pueblo Revolt.

Ethnographic documentation of mineral use has centered on the use of mineral pigments in ritual production, particularly for their use in the creation of katsina masks. Parsons (1966:352–353) suggests that, due to the spiritual significance of pigments, mineral procurement and processing were proprietary rights of kiva societies and were conducted in a manner similar to parties that were conducted for the grinding of prayer-meal. Pigments were created from a variety of minerals including kaolin clay, malachite, azurite, hematite, and pyrolusite (a manganese-dioxide ore). Cushing (1979:92) notes that the Zuni obtained lead and zinc minerals, as well as specular hematite, to create pigments associated with warfare. The importance of pigment was stressed by Parsons (1966:341) in her claim that "the pigments are what make the mask sacred" citing Bunzel's (1932) remark that it also made them "valuable."

COLOR SYMBOLISM

Much of the meaning of minerals is conveyed through their associated colors. Alfonso Ortiz's (1969) classic ethnography on San Juan (Ohkay Owingeh) Tewa social organization reveals the importance of color in expressing basic social organization and core cosmological concepts. Moiety divisions are indicated by distinct color combinations that define the basic cosmological division between summer and winter. The summer moiety is indicated by the colors blue/green, yellow, and black, whereas the winter moiety is referenced through the use of red and white. These color distinctions symbolize the summer moiety's association with new plant growth, sunshine, and rain clouds, while the winter moiety's association is with snow and the hunting season. White Corn Maiden and Blue Corn Maiden, the two origin mothers of Ohkay Owingeh, are also associated with these moiety color distinctions. In turn, colors are linked to a sacred geography based on six cardinal directions. They refer to the four sacred mountains surrounding Ohkay Owingeh, as well as zenith and nadir directions. In the Tewa world view, colors are rooted to the origin of socialized people; they are linked to the creation of six pairs of brothers who explored and defined the boundaries of the universe from the place of origin (Ortiz 1969).

Ortiz also documents the color association of minerals with the qualities inherent in each moiety, particularly the distinction between "hot" and "cold" natures. Metals are generally thought to be cold in nature, but minerals can take on either hot or cold natures. Black minerals, such as jet, are associated with warmth due to their color association with the summer moiety. Silver, in particular, is a cold substance and is not supposed to be worn during summer rituals least it bring cold weather. The distinction between hot and cold is also extended to other substances, particularly in the division between domesticated and wild taxa, with domesticated, ripe substances deemed hot and wild and unripe substances as cold. Most European domesticated animals are considered hot substances, whereas wild animals, associated with the hunting activities of the winter moiety, are considered cold (Ortiz 1969:118, 178–179).

Internal qualities such as hot and cold, sometimes linked with the external display of appropriate colors, play a part in healing practices as well. Ford (1992:132–133) documents the use of red coral and jet amulets worn to protect infants from harm. Similarly, medicinal plants are thought to possess either cold or warm properties and are used to treat ailments that possess the opposite internal quality: ailments caused by an overabundance of cold are treated by substances classified as hot. These practices are part of a larger suite of behaviors believed by the Ohkay Owingeh people to be useful in shaping natural processes in order to re-establish the correct flow of seasonal events (Ford 1992:144–150).

THE ROLE OF MINERALS IN EXCHANGE

Mineral pigments were important for their use in decorating katsina masks. Acquisition of pigments for katsina rituals may have spurred the regional mineral trade in the late precolonial period. Adams (1991) suggests that the widespread acceptance of the katsina cult in the fifteenth century, found in communities from the Hopi mesas to the Galisteo Basin, Salinas, and Humanas areas, was due to its association with rainmaking. Among the Rio Grande pueblos, elements of katsina cult imagery may have been borrowed from a similar masked tradition of the Jornada style that is thought to have been associated

with warfare (Adams 1991:142–143). The overlapping imagery may also have been the result of incorporating katsina ceremonialism into ritual sodalities such as war or healing societies (Ware and Blinman 2000). Adams (1991:159) notes that, ethnographically, the performance of katsina ritual is accompanied by the redistribution of food and wealth within pueblos. This redistribution extends to individuals from other pueblos or tribes, thus creating an informal market exchange. Adams (1991:159) argues that this exchange may have been a key component of the success and widespread distribution of the katsina cult throughout the Pueblo world.

Other researchers have hypothesized the existence of markets in the precolonial Pueblo world based on similar observations of the exchange of ritual material and the apparent commodification of ceramics during the Pueblo IV period. Kohler, Van Pelt, and Yap (2000:199) propose that markets are the most efficient way to distribute goods over large areas. Market distribution involved many non-related individuals and made use of plazas and large-scale public events.

The application of market concepts to explain widespread artifact distributions may, however, mask other social formations that would result in similar patterns. The link between large-scale public events and the distribution of glaze ware ceramics may have been more closely associated with the social strategies of individuals or sodalities within pueblos, either as aggrandizing behavior in the context of ritual feasts, or as a political process of intra- and inter-pueblo alliance formation (Graves and Spielmann 2000; Spielmann 1998). The fact that many of the objects involved in widespread exchange during the Pueblo IV period were used in the production of ritual paraphernalia associated with the katsina cult suggests the importance of exchange in the maintenance of a moral economy rather than market exchange.

The dichotomy between markets and contexts of exchange that assume a foundation of reciprocity may reflect a conflation of the context of exchange with the meaning of exchange. Although exchange appears to have been conducted around the peripheries of ritual events, no abstract system of pricing or establishment of equivalencies of value appears to have been formalized, as suggested by Nelson and Habicht-Mauche's (2006:213) analysis of glaze mineral distribution:

> When we examine the acquisition and distribution of Cerrillos lead from the perspective of individual glaze ware potters or potting groups within communities

we see the result, not of an abstract, overarching organizational system, but of choices and strategies made in response to local needs and individual interests, as constituted within culturally defined realms of value and meaning.

The fact that so much of the exchange documented archaeologically and ethnohistorically involved the production of semiotically dense objects (either as glaze-painted ceramics or ritual paraphernalia) suggests that the overall context of exchange took place within the frames of value mediated by these material objects and dictated by the needs of various pueblos.

Parsons' observation that ceremonies and important ritual knowledge could be shared, borrowed, exchanged, or purchased among historic Puebloans also provides a sense of the possible dynamic of ritual exchange that is distinct from commodity exchange in a market system. Parsons stressed that political processes were embedded within such exchange and were dominated by negotiations designed to integrate foreign or inter-Puebloan influences. In this regard, she thought the act of masking had a particular importance in giving value to new ceremonials, in that the mask, being valuable in itself, also bestows value (Parsons 1936:1162). This is different from market exchange, in that the biography of objects and the political associations of ritual goods play a major part in the establishment of exchange value rather than the establishment of an equivalency of value based on price.

Although the goods necessary for making ritual paraphernalia were often traded or exchanged, the paraphernalia themselves were usually not exchanged and were held in restrictive contexts. Like other materials used in ritual production, then, the value of pigments comes from their association with objects that rarely entered exchange relationships, such as katsina masks or ancestral places. The exchange of objects that refer to the un-exchangeable may be referred to as the practice of "keeping-while-giving" (Weiner 1985). The value of such exchange practices may be more nuanced than the notion of social solidarity suggested by Adams regarding katsina ceremonialism. As Weiner (1985:224) suggests:

> An individual's role in social life is fragmentary unless attached to something of permanence. The history of the past, equally fragmentary, is concentrated in an object that, in its material substance, defies destruction. Thus, keeping an object defined as inalienable adds to the value of one's past, making the past a powerful

resource for the present and the future. The dynamics surrounding keeping-while-giving are attempts to give the fragmentary aspect of social life a wholeness that ultimately achieves the semblance of immortality, thereby adding new force to each generation.

Mills' (2004) discussion of inalienable objects in the context of Puebloan ritual paraphernalia suggests that such objects could have both collective and individual identities, thus establishing and at the same time undermining attempts at political hierarchy through their use and ritual deposition. Rather than representing social solidarity in a broad sense, the use of inalienable objects creates meaningful historical associations that may establish social distinctions and claims to authenticity between ritual sodalities and individual participants within such societies. Following Ruth Bunzel's (1932) ethnographic work at Zuni, Mills suggests that the regular production of katsina masks as inalienable possessions reflected an individual's value and social standing within the community. The possession of a mask and the right to impersonate a katsina were directly related to an individual's social value and the value of his household. These values were associated with place and history as conferred through katsina impersonation. They also reflect the high cost of producing a mask through food payments and feast sponsorships. This highlights the inextricable and culturally meaningful links among Puebloan subsistence economy, exchange, and ritual production (Spielmann 2002).

Mills suggests that such practices have a deep antiquity in Puebloan history, predating the advent of katsina ceremonialism in the fourteenth century. The intensification of ritual production and the social hierarchies associated with the possession of inalienable objects may have historical connections to the frequent destabilization of communities and subsequent migrations in the Southwest that have occurred since the twelfth century (Mills 2004; Ware and Blinman 2000). The attempt at establishing inalienable goods created a conceptual basis for evaluating materials through their involvement in ritual production. Such practices were part and parcel of the way that social value was constructed, both collectively and individually.

COLONIAL TRANSFORMATION OF VALUE AND SIGNIFICATION

Minerals entered a new system of value designation when the Spanish began their mining ventures. Spanish production of wealth contrasted sharply with the concept of the inalienable that was present in precolonial exchange. The negotiation and contestation of mineral value during this period would have impacted the way that Puebloans exchanged minerals and may have disrupted the production of ritual paraphernalia.

The intersection between Puebloan mineral use and Spanish mining has relevance for the way in which metallurgy was structured at Paa-ko, both in the initial introduction of metalworking and in its subsequent transformation. The metallurgy of Paa-ko, situated within the historical moment of the establishment of the colony of New Mexico, can be viewed in multiple, competing notions of value. Ultimately, Spanish miners sought to create wealth through the workshop by producing specie with monetary value, the foundation of commodity exchange. Pueblo intersection with this system of production entailed not only an introduction to a new suite of pyrotechnological techniques, but also to a new relation of value between minerals and wealth.

Ceramic technologies were impacted by colonialism in several ways. Glaze ware vessels became the colono ware of New Mexico, replicating European forms including soup plates, pitchers, and candle sticks, which probably became true commodities in a newly established market exchange system. The meanings signaled by glaze ware also became increasingly complex. Potters played with ideologically potent images in design fields by juxtaposing Catholic religious imagery and traditional designs. There was also a general trend toward the obliteration or concealment of design through the use of runny glaze.

Glaze wares were reintroduced into the Zuni area in the 1630s when the mission at Hawikuh was established. Glaze ware designs found at Zuni included an increased use of warfare motifs and semiotically potent feather imagery, perhaps referencing powerful religious sodalities (Mills 2002). Katsina iconography often appears on the interior of these vessels, suggesting an attempt at concealing ritually significant imagery that was perhaps recognizable, and persecuted, by the Catholic Church (Mills 2002:91).

Mobley-Tanaka (2002) similarly documents the simplification and abstraction of ritually significant designs on Rio Grande glaze pottery associated with mission communities. At the same time, vessels made in non-mission communities retained elaborate and explicit designs. In addition, semiotic substitutions appear to have been made. For example, explicit bird imagery was replaced with more abstract cross images on the same design fields, in effect using Christian iconography in either a duplicitous or syncretic way to continue a pre-Christian symbolic context.

The tendency to obliterate design by using runny glaze could indicate a disruption of traditional mineral procurement strategies or a change in learning frameworks during the colonial period. The mining interests of the new colony were centered on the mineral deposits of the Cerrillos Hills, the primary source for glaze minerals in the Pueblo IV period. Other lead-based substances produced as byproducts of the Spanish mining industry could have been substituted in glaze technology. Litharge (lead oxide), a product of the refining of silver through cupellation, would have created a less viscous glaze if substituted in equal portions for galena in glaze recipes, due to a higher lead content per volume than what galena would produce. Alternatively, with the disruption and contraction of communities during this period, knowledge of glaze recipes may have faltered, or the available time allowed for craft production may have diminished, leading to inconsistencies in recipe preparation as has been observed for temper preparation (Capone 2006).

Missions increasingly became the focus of indigenous settlement as Pueblo communities were disrupted by disease and the subsistence demands of the colonizer (Lycett 2005). Missions became the contexts within which food and material production took place. As settlement contracted around such communities, perhaps the semiotic contexts of production and signification and the context of raw material acquisition also shrank. Within mission communities the associations among different individual and collective constructions of value, linking the acquisition of materials with ritual production, may have been displaced by community production in which Church symbolism and the mission economy dominated. Ceramics and glaze paint would have become commodities within the mission system, and signification would have taken on the dual role described by Mobley-Tanaka (2002) of expressing identity with the Church as well as providing hidden transcripts of resistance.

CONCLUSION

Inter-Pueblo exchange during the Pueblo IV period included the construction of value associations for materials, based on their acquisition for ritual production and their use in the production of inalienable objects that identify the owner's place in individual and collective social hierarchies. During the colonial period, mission communities subsumed much of the productive capacities of formerly autonomous pueblos. Earlier contexts for the construction of value were displaced by the imposition of new production processes and new regimes of value associated with mission life. Mineral exploitation by Spanish colonial miners disrupted traditional procurement and use strategies for ritually valued materials such as mineral pigments. Although the physical extent of this disruption is not known, from the perspective of Pueblo economic relationships, mining interests must have significantly displaced the construction of value through ritual production, replacing it with a new construction based on wealth acquisition.

The people of Paa-ko felt the impact of both colonial contexts of production, through incorporation into the *visita* system and through the operation of the metallurgical workshop adjacent to the historical plaza. Paa-ko was a site of intense cultural production during the colonial period. From the incorporation of domestic animals to the reorganization of extramural space including the placement of a chapel within the historic plaza, to the introduction of novel technologies, the Pueblo inhabitants of Paa-ko felt the brunt of Spanish colonial economy and ideology. Despite this, their creative action shaped the resultant technologies and subsistence practices in unexpected ways, creating novel economic strategies that redefined that interaction at least partially on Pueblo terms.

The Historical Record of Mineral Exploitation in New Spain and on the Northern Frontier

The metallurgical facility at Paa-ko is an anomaly in the Santa Fe-Albuquerque region. No other seventeenth-century metal production facility of its scale has been found in New Mexico. But the site looks less anomalous if placed in the context of mining enterprises developed in the late sixteenth and early seventeenth century in Northern New Spain. No archaeological documentation of such mining facilities in Northern New Spain had occurred by the time of this writing. But abundant historical documentation and secondary historical analyses provide a perspective from which to compare the material record of metallurgy at Paa-ko with roughly contemporary activities in this larger region. In addition, recent archaeological work in West Mexico may provide analogs for the development of the technology present at Paa-ko both in terms of its material representation and the influence of Spanish colonial culture on indigenous pyrotechnology.

For this study, the historical literature was approached in two ways. First, following Peter Bakewell's (1971:114) lead, an analysis of the "*structures* of mining" is presented, with a particular concern for how the perception of the productivity of landscapes described by various colonial officials, soldiers, and miners reflected not only their hopes toward turning a profit, but also how they envisioned a successful mining operation. How the landscapes of New Mexico were envisioned changed from the initial entrada through the early colonial period, a shift that parallels certain developments of the mining industry in New Spain and New Galicia.

Second, the historical literature was assessed in order to define the scale of mining operations and the types of technologies utilized in geological and social landscapes

that were similar to those found in seventeenth-century Paa-ko. The mining industry expanded through Northern New Spain in the decades before the colonization of New Mexico and the colony was founded by members of this industry. Labor relationships, material resources, and available technology from this period provide strong analogues for understanding the development of the technology at Paa-ko. Mining and metallurgical processing in New Mexico encountered many of the difficulties already overcome by mining operations in Northern New Spain and New Galicia by the middle of the sixteenth century. New Mexican mining endeavors may have been hindered by the colony's remote location relative to supply lines from New Spain. Coupled with other social and historical factors, New Mexico's isolation kept mining development in the region to a much smaller scale than the development of similar deposits in other areas of the northern frontier.

1521 TO 1550: CONQUEST, LABOR, AND CONGREGATION

The historical assessment of mineral wealth in New Mexico was in part conditioned by the changing ways in which individuals in early Spanish colonial society sought to gain material wealth. The potential for gaining social and material rewards for individuals participating in the expansion of the northern frontier changed over the course of the sixteenth century. The Spanish mining industry in Mexico began when colonial elites appropriated tribute networks of metallic goods that had been produced and amassed during the precolonial period by indigenous miners and metallurgists. This period of exploitation was short-lived but consisted of the "mining" of ceremonial objects from temple structures, shrines, and tombs (West 1994b). Throughout this early period, Spanish colonists identified mineral resources by observing the ways in which local indigenous populations adorned themselves using mineral and metal products. The use of materials such as turquoise pendants and mineral pigments for adornment is frequently mentioned in expedition narratives and was a common theme running through the speculation surrounding New Mexico before the Coronado entrada of 1540 to 1542.

Knowledge of metal resources was often equated with the possible existence of metal-using, state-level societies. Such speculation contributed to the political maneuvering that made the Coronado entrada possible. As governor of Nueva Galicia, Francisco Vázquez de Coronado played a significant part in perpetuating the myth of New Mexico's wealth through statements to his superiors in Mexico City. Hearsay about the nation of Topira was conveyed to Coronado by the indigenous community around San Miguel de Culiacán, who claimed that Topirans wore gold, emeralds, and other precious stones; that they covered their houses with silver and gold; and even served meals in vessels of the precious metals (Flint and Flint 2005).

Such descriptions echo earlier conquest descriptions of the Valley of Mexico, suggesting similar occurrences of the types of political and productive systems that could be appropriated under the conquest rights of *encomienda,* a legal grant from the Crown for the right to obtain indigenous labor and tribute goods. These statements also indicate an early recognition of indigenous people as repositories of knowledge about landscape resources. Throughout the Coronado entrada a persistent line of questioning posed to indigenous individuals encountered in the new lands concerned mineral resources. Members of the expedition tried to assess indigenous knowledge concerning mineral resources in specific ways, such as probing their ability to recognize the qualities of different metals and alloys (Flint and Flint 2005:400).

In the 1530s, exploitation of the mineral resources of Central and West Mexico was built on the foundations of precolonial mines and depended on the skill, technology, and labor of Tarascan and other West Mexican metal workers. Metal smelting and smithing traditions in West Mexico had a 600-year history before the Spanish arrived. These traditions were focused on precious metal extraction and specific qualities of sound and color produced by copper, gold, and silver alloys (Hosler 1994). In colonial Mexico, all subsurface minerals legally belonged to the Crown. Rights for the development of mines were granted to individuals, but a percentage of the metal produced had to go to the royal treasury. Claims could be held indefinitely, almost as private property, as long as the claimant continued to work the mine (Barrett 1987; Couturier 2003; Stein and Stein 2000).

In order for Spanish colonial society to maintain economic forms developed from its Old World roots, a number of metal products beyond gold and silver were necessary for the functioning of basic technologies. Iron, copper, and tin became valuable resources that were also regulated by the Crown. Due to Spain's attempt to dominate the European iron industry, iron production was limited to Spanish foundries, and most of the iron used in New World colonies was produced in Spain. Limited local production of wrought iron appears to have been undertaken in areas where supply was a problem (Baragallo 1955; Simmons and Turley 1980; Vaughan 2006).

Copper and copper alloys such as brass were produced in Europe, and a trade in copper vessels played a significant part in the colonization efforts by European powers on the West Coast of Africa and northeastern America (Ehrhardt 2006; Herbert 1981; Rothschild 2003; Rovira 1995). In the Spanish colonial world, copper was produced in Cuba and New Spain, but the Cuban source appears to have not been effectively utilized until the seventeenth century (Barrett 1987; Pruna 1989).

Copper-arsenic and copper-tin bronzes were produced by indigenous smiths in the precolonial and early colonial period in West Mexico. Tin and bronze were essential for the production of armaments in New Spain and were exploited by the Spanish very soon after colonization (Hosler 1994). Brass, a fairly high-tech material for its time, was probably not produced in New Spain in the precolonial period (although see Grinberg 1996 for a different assessment) or during the sixteenth or seventeenth century. West Mexican copper was sent to foundries in Spain for that purpose (Barrett 1987).

Barrett's (1987) comprehensive historical study on the copper industry of New Spain highlights the importance of this industry for the colony and its reliance upon Native American skill and labor in the early years of its development. New Spain's copper was used in a variety of industries, among them armament production, as an alloy with silver in coinage, and in the production of utilitarian goods, copper kettles, *comales,* and chocolate pots (Barrett 1987:1–4). *Comales* and chocolate pots represent the direct incorporation of indigenous foods and cooking technologies into colonial society.

This incorporation can also be seen in the development of the copper industry itself. Developing from the Tarascan precolonial industry, New Spain's copper production continued to be under the technological control of indigenous metal workers until the seventeenth century. Copper metal and goods were produced for the colony by Tarascan metal workers under *encomienda*. Their *encomendero* was under contract to provide a certain amount of either ore or smelted metal for the Crown. This relationship changed with increased demand in the seventeenth century when the Crown took over production directly (Barrett 1987). Metal workers from the traditional indigenous background continued to play a major role in the development of New Spain's metal resources and formed the core of skilled labor used in the mining industry of the northern frontier in the latter half of the sixteenth and throughout the seventeenth century (Bakewell 1971).

Maldonado's (2006) survey and analysis of archaeological remains and historical documents relating to metal production in the Itziparátzico region of Michoacán details the technological knowledge possessed by Tarascans in the early colonial period. Using survey data accumulated in the region coupled with a material analysis of slag and ore samples, Maldonado was able to characterize the technology of mining and metal processing of copper ores. Due to the lack of stratigraphic deposits and adequate chronological markers, the dating of the metallurgical material at Itziparátzican has not been established. By the time of the conquest, however, we know that Tarascan metallurgists were exploiting copper carbonates and the more difficult to process copper sulfides. Maldonado (2006) suggests that some sort of forced or natural draft system was established for the smelting of copper sulfide ores during either the late protohistoric or early colonial period, although it is conceivable that the industry represents a technology from later in the colonial period.

If the industry dates to the early colonial period, the familiarity with draft systems that were either forced or wind-powered would explain the ready incorporation of Tarascan metallurgists into Spanish colonial metal production systems, which commonly used *hornos castillanos*, which required a high volume, directed blast of air. A similar incorporation of indigenous, wind-driven smelting technology occurred in the initial stages of silver ore processing at Potosí, which today is in Bolivia (Bakewell 1984). The ability of West Mexican metallurgists to effectively exploit copper sulfide ores also required ancillary pyrotechnical operations including charcoal production, the roasting of ores, and multiple smelting regimens. With such a wide breadth of knowledge and a probable development of specialized labor for different sectors of the industry under some control from the Tarascan state (Maldonado 2006), it is understandable that Spanish colonial elites would attempt to maintain the functioning of the industry without dramatically changing its structure. Analysis of early Spanish colonial mining industries gives a sense of the structure of the industry in the first decades of the colony of New Spain. This, in turn, puts into perspective the way in which New Mexico's resources were assessed by the Coronado expedition (Baragallo 1955; Barrett 1987; Burkholder and Johnson 1990; Flores 1994; Hu-DeHart 1981; Lockhart and Schwartz 1983; Reff 1991; Sanchez-Crispin 1994; Spicer 1962; Stein and Stein 2000; West, 1949, 1994a, 1994b). One of the pivotal legal institutions for labor appropriation in the sixteenth century, *repartimiento*, was derived from earlier, unofficial appropriations of indigenous labor for the gold mines of Hispañola shortly after the founding of Spain's first New World colony by Columbus. Columbus initially framed the expedition as a monopoly company where members were paid for their services. Failure to compensate the colonists triggered a near rebellion in 1497, with colonists abandoning the eastern half of the island, disregarding the governorship, and developing their own institutions of labor and wealth accumulation that were later legalized by the Crown. The labor appropriations that they claimed eventually formed the basis of the Crown's mechanisms for compensating participants in the conquest under the *encomienda* system (Lockhart and Schwartz 1983; West 1949).

Just as the foundation of the *encomienda* system was tied to the historical development of mining interests in the New World, so other major policies were geared toward the control and resocialization of Native American populations. Coupled with the right to appropriate labor was the development of the forced congregation of indigenous populations into communities modeled after Iberian towns. This policy was initially developed in the Caribbean to gather a population that was severely reduced by disease in an attempt to maintain a viable labor pool for *encomenderos* and the exploitation of placer gold deposits.

Social policies of enculturation and Catholic incorporation were at times in conflict with *encomienda* labor claims and were often given priority over such claims (Lockhart and Schwartz 1983). For example, in the communities around the copper mines of Inguarán and La Huacana, initial colonial interests in congregating labor closer to the mines was deemed of secondary importance to the need to congregate the indigenous population near a mission community. As a result, the traditional indigenous communities were actually moved farther away from the mines in order to accommodate religious instruction (Barrett 1987:24).

A key theme of many of the early expeditions into the northern frontier of New Spain was concern for the viability of *encomienda* grants. Richard Flint and Shirley Cushing Flint's (2005:381) recent retranslation of the documents pertaining to the Coronado expedition stresses this fact, recognizing that

> the Coronado expedition and scores of others like it that took place during the 1500s were not primarily exploring parties bent on simply charting the unknown. Empty land was of little interest to them, regardless of its mineral or agricultural potential. Instead, they sought out people—specifically, people who possessed or produced high-value goods that might be appropriated by means of a kind of taxation.

In the disappointment that followed the arrival of the Coronado entrada, more tempered assessments of New Mexico's potential were given in subsequent accounts of the expedition. Although potential mines and mineral resources were not specifically identified in the documents of the 1540s entrada, evaluation of sources of wealth, in terms of both physical and social geography, are present.

This search for an integrated landscape of producers, goods, and products placed a priority on the value of Native American labor as a source of tribute. The *encomienda* system was initially formulated to provide a labor and subsistence base for the exploitation of mineral resources in the Caribbean. It radically reorganized traditional settlement systems where tribal hierarchies were weak and indigenous populations were dispersed. Rather than reorganize existing extractive systems, Spanish colonial elites sought to replace indigenous elites as the recipients of tribute. This developed into a reliance upon Native American labor and productivity, even in regions of the colony where tribute systems had not existed before colonization. Indigenous productive skill at turning local resources into commodities extracted through tribute became the primary means for wealth extraction engaged in by colonial elites during this early period (Burkholder and Johnson 1990).

The link between possible *encomienda* systems, landscape, and mineral resources is specifically addressed in the documents of the Coronado entrada. Castañeda de Nájera, whose chronicle is one of the most detailed records of the Coronado expedition (although written years after the expedition), assessed the lack of value in both the social and physical geography of New Mexico:

> I state that in a space of seventy leagues across that settled land and of a hundred and thirty leagues lengthwise along the Rio de Tiguex, no more peoples or settlements were seen or found than those already related. There are *repartimientos* in Nueva Espana with a greater number of people, and not just one but many. In many of those pueblos along the Rio de Tiguex there was a silvery metal, which they had in order to glaze pottery and paint their faces [Flint and Flint 2005:422].

It is interesting that in his negative assessment of the possibility of establishing *encomienda* rights, Castañeda de Nájera links mineral resources with the poverty of settlement along the Rio Grande in comparison to the densely populated areas of central Mexico. Rather than an indication of wealth, this passage suggests the improbability of an *encomienda*-based mining industry. In the decade following the return from New Mexico, Castañeda de Nájera was one of Coronado's most articulate detractors, claiming that he was misled into believing that there were profitable *encomienda* grants available in the new lands (Flint and Flint 2005).

In summary, during the first half of the sixteenth century, the incipient mining industry in New Spain was built as an extension of the tribute economies of the precolonial period in Central and West Mexico. The organization of labor under *encomienda* and *repartimiento* attempted to replicate precolonial practices when possible. The very recognition of the resources was tied to indigenous uses of precious metal sources in ceremonial objects and other items of value. This complete reliance on indigenous knowledge and labor structured the way in which new territory was assessed.

When the exploitation of metal resources in New Spain and New Galicia shifted from the appropriation of tribute goods to the production of metal in the 1530s, technologies of production were also reliant upon Native American knowledge, skill, and labor (Flores 1994; West 1994b). The structure of the industry changed dramatically in the latter half of the sixteenth century due to the discovery of major silver ore deposits in places like Zacatecas and the introduction of a new production system centered around mercury amalgamation, along with the decoupling of *repartimiento* and mine labor through the development of skilled Indian wage labor.

1550 TO 1650: EXPANSION OF THE MINING FRONTIER

By the last decades of the sixteenth century, the nature of the mining industry in New Spain had changed. The discovery of new silver ore deposits and the development of large-scale mercury amalgamation recovery methods after 1550 increased the scale and productivity of silver mining in New Spain (West 1994b). The abundant silver mines of Zacatecas (discovered in 1546), Guanajuato (1557), and Santa Barbara (1567) had pushed the mining frontier beyond central and west Mexico into the arid regions of northern New Spain (Sanchez-Crispin 1994). By 1600, many of these mines had grown into large multiethnic settlements that drew resources from a wide area (Bakewell 1971; Mayer 1974; West 1949). This change in the nature of the mining industry is reflected in the renewal of claims of mineral wealth in New Mexico and the expeditions that followed.

The mining communities of Zacatecas and Parral deserve particular attention because of the role of these communities in the colonization of Northern New Spain and because of their connection to the New Mexico colony (Figure 4.1). The technological and social structures developed in these centers played a significant role in the development of mining in the region and are important to understand as a baseline for creating a general picture of the full extent of the Spanish colonial mining industry in the late sixteenth and early seventeenth centuries (Vaughan 2006).

Zacatecas, in particular, is closely connected to the initial interest in New Mexico. Juan de Oñate and Juan and Vincente de Zaldívar were colonial elites based there and tied by ancestry to the founding of the city. In addition, the suite of technologies that would make mining in New Mexico potentially profitable were developed in Zactecas.

Zacatecas

The mines of Zacatecas were discovered by Juan de Tolosa in 1546 after a concerted effort to locate new mineral resources, possibly under the direction of the lieutenant governor of New Galicia, Cristóbal de Oñate. Ore obtained from local Zacatecos Indians triggered interest in the area. The minerals were subsequently determined to be economically marginal, but with an influx of capital provided by Oñate, a mining town was established and much more profitable deposits were discovered. This eventually led to the discovery of one of the greatest silver strikes of the Spanish colonial world (Bakewell 1971). This sequence of

events (minerals presented by local indigenous communities, the establishment of settlements, and the influx of capital by landholding elite) clearly structured the subsequent colonization of New Mexico in the late sixteenth century.

In the decade following the founding of Zacatecas, a major development in silver-production technology occurred that ultimately made the deposits in the Zacatecas mining district profitable. This was the invention of the patio process, an industrialization of the assay technique of mercury amalgamation. It was introduced to New Spain in 1554 and reached Zacatecas by 1557 (Bakewell 1971:138). This process made low-grade ores profitable, even for ores with as little as 1 ounce of silver per quintal (100 lbs). The rival technology of charcoal-fueled smelting followed by cupellation was still employed in the district for ores with a higher lead content, such as galena. Smelting and cupellation technology was generally used for ores with more than 8 ounces of silver per quintal (Milford and Swick 1995).

The silver ores of Zacatecas were primarily of a low lead content and consisted of deposits produced through the supergene enrichment of silver sulfide ores. This produced a zone of enrichment close to the water table, which was around 300 feet below the surface. The ores retrieved from this type of deposit, considered to be "dry" and hence difficult to smelt, were most amenable to the patio process. Rates of return for these types of deposits were hypothesized to be about 70 percent of the ores' silver content using mercury amalgamation versus a 40 percent rate of return using traditional cupellation (Blanchard 1989). Lead ores such as galena that contained some silver were also present in the area, particularly at the mines of Sombrerete. These were successfully exploited using smelting and cupellation technology.

The application of these two technologies (smelting versus the patio process) also reflected differences in social and economic structures within the industry. The smelting technology of the period utilized furnaces of small capacity, keeping production facilities to a fairly small size in relation to mercury amalgamation patios (Probert 1969). Materials needed for furnace operation (charcoal, bone ash, adobe, and carbonate or ferrous fluxing material) were available in the local area or were produced by the silver-mining industry itself (e.g., litharge and hearth lead). The technology was also less time intensive compared to mercury amalgamation. Processing could often be accomplished in a few days, with the major reduction phase lasting 8 to 10 hours. Smelting could also be undertaken on a small scale and was often used by mine laborers to refine ore that was obtained as a wage bonus, a *pepena* (Bakewell 1971:145).

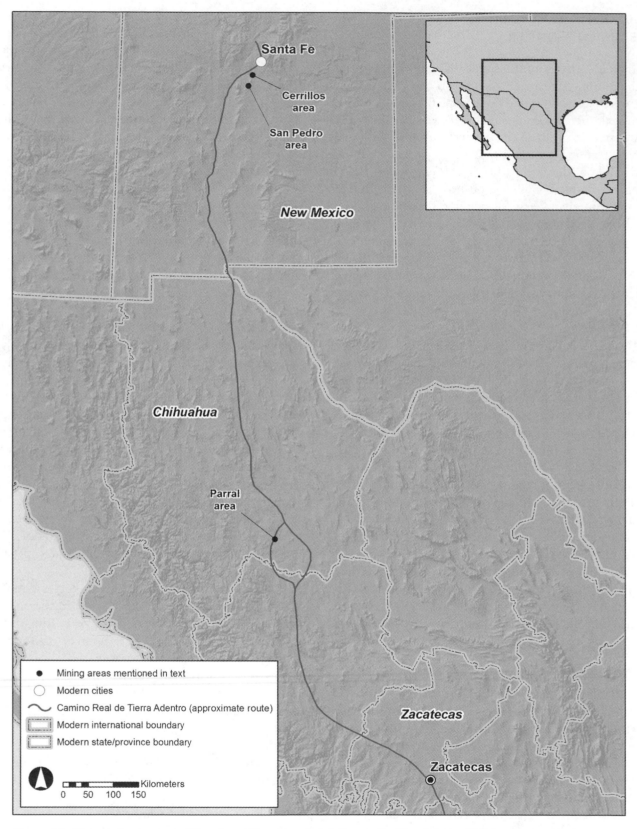

Figure 4.1. The mining centers of Parral and Zacatecas in relation to the New Mexico Colony. Map courtesy of Phillip Leckman.

In contrast, mercury amalgamation using the patio process was capital intensive, involving the construction of machinery necessary to grind the ores to a fine powder and to wash the amalgamated mass. In Zacatecas, such machinery involved the use of large numbers of draft animals. A larger labor force was also needed for the mixing of amalgam and for processing the large amounts of ore necessary for the technology to be profitable. The greatest expense in the patio process was the intensive use of mercury, obtained from mines in Peru, which was an expensive commodity controlled by the Crown. Like smelting, the process used additional mineral resources such as copper sulfate (*magistral*), procured locally or from as far away as Michoacán (Barrett 1987), and salt. Salt was obtainable from sources in the Zacatecas region but, like mercury, was a commodity controlled by the Crown.

Crown control of mercury and salt significantly structured the economics of the industry, not because those resources necessarily equated with higher costs for the miner, but because miners often resorted to credit mechanisms offered by brokers or Crown officials. Mercury was often obtained in advance of projected silver production, putting miners at risk of excessive debt when mining profits did not materialize (West 1949). The Crown sought to profit from both the sale of mercury and its tax on silver, leading many miners to try to circumvent the system by selling silver directly to merchants in order to pay off accrued debts. This often led miners into a cycle of debt-credit extension that could result in the complete loss of fortunes for once wealthy families (Bakewell 1971:118). Other commodities necessary for the patio process could often be obtained through local exchange systems or as bulk bids under contract (Borah 1992).

The patio process was also time intensive. After mining and sorting the ore, the technology consisted of an 11-step process spread out over a period of months. The first step was to grind the ore to a flour-like consistency with large stamps and grinding mills driven by mules or horses. The resulting *harina* (flour) was gathered on the open-air amalgamation patio in large piles and mixed with water, 2.5 to 3 pounds of salt per quintal of ore, and *magistral*. West (1949:32) suggests that other materials were often added. Among these additives were lime or iron filings, perhaps a practice that developed from the similar inclusion of these materials into blast furnaces to aid in the smelting of iron-rich or iron-poor ores respectively (Craddock 1995). To this mixture, 10 to 12 pounds of mercury were then added to each pile. These materials were then spread into a thin layer, or *torta*, on the patio and mixed for days by

hand or through the treading of mule teams. Depending on the ambient temperature it could take up to two to three months for the mercury to be completely incorporated or amalgamated with the ore. The resulting material was then washed in a series of tanks to separate the amalgam from gangue material by gravity separation. The subsequent material was then placed in coarse cloth bags, and excess (unamalgamated) mercury was squeezed out of it to be reused. The remaining amalgam was then beaten into triangular molds, placed in a reverberatory furnace, and heated to decompose the amalgam. The mercury vapor was recovered by condensation onto the furnace chamber, and refined silver was recovered from the molds (Bakewell 1971; Baragallo 1955; Flores 1994; West 1949). Mercury losses were fairly high and may have contributed significantly to local environmental degradation. Nriagu (1993) has argued that these losses in the patio process are a significant portion of high background mercury levels still cycling in the global environment today.

The lack of water on the northern frontier made water-driven machines such as stamp mills, bellows, and whims unusable. This problem was overcome through the use of draft animals on a large scale, and by incorporating indigenous technologies (Flores 1994). In Zacatecas *haciendas de minas*, typical three-ore grinding machines used 100 mules (Bakewell 1971:117). All machines used in the process were powered by draft animal or human labor, as the water resources available in Zacatecas could not support water-powered machinery (Bakewell 1971:142–143). This situation lead to the development of large ranching establishments that were often owned by the miners. Along with large agricultural haciendas, the ranches formed the supporting pillars for the mining industry and economy of the northern frontier in the seventeenth century (Sheridan 1992; West 1949).

Native American labor was essential to the industry. Because of the lack of a stable sedentary population in this region, (as well as legal restrictions to its use) *repartimiento* labor was not used in any frequency in Zacatecas. Forced labor and free wage-labor provided the bulk of the work force for the mines (Bakewell 1971:122–129). This appears to be true in general for the northern frontier (West 1949). Slaves of African descent, together with a minor component of slaves from the Philippines, were coupled with Indian captives from the Chichimec Wars to form the forced labor pool (Mayer 1974). Cycles of slave raiding and warfare also played a part in the development of the Parral mines, particularly when labor shortages were encountered (West 1949:52).

As Bakewell has detailed, most of the laborers at Zacatecas were free wage workers who were drawn from indigenous groups in Central and West Mexico. The ethnic identities of Indian laborers were emphasized in the establishment of individual barrios within the city. Bakewell identifies five distinct barrios at Zacatecas that were associated with four different tribes: Tlaxcalans, Mexicas, Texcocos, and Tarascans. These identities were maintained until at least the 1680s. Tarascan and Tlaxcalan barrios even maintained separate governing bodies (Bakewell 1971:56). Tarascan mine laborers settled in two barrios and Bakewell (1971:128) suggests that, at least during the early seventeenth century, a majority of the incoming labor force was from Michoacán, the area of the former Tarascan state, presumably because of their knowledge of metallurgy and mining practices.

Outside of the barrios, Bakewell suggests that some of the indigenous wage laborers used in the *hacienda de minas* were housed within the facilities. These facilities may have had structural parallels with the facility at Paa-ko. A typical hacienda that focused on smelting technology consisted of a *casa de morada*, or owner's house; *apostentos* or workers' quarters; a chapel; stables; and *galeras*, or sheds used to house furnaces; bellows mechanisms; and charcoal (Bakewell 1971:145, 126). Although Bakewell's sources do not distinguish between skilled and unskilled labor, the association of wage laborers with the machinery of the hacienda suggests some division of labor along occupational specialties. The influx of workers from Michoacán suggests the incorporation of a workforce already accustomed to task specialization within the metallurgical industry, as Maldonado (2006) has suggested for the precolonial copper industry of that region. The possibility that many of these workers lived within the *hacienda*, in proximity to the technology and to owner's families, provides an analog from which to understand the situating of smelting facilities within the occupied pueblo of Paa-ko. Haciendas functioned as nearly self-sufficient economic units whose closest parallel economically in the newly colonized north would be the pueblos.

Parral

West's (1949) historical analysis of the Parral district provides an additional perspective on the social and technological conditions of mining. The rich deposits at Parral were discovered in 1631, although mining had occurred in the region since the 1570s. The bonanza had a large influence on the development of New Mexico's extractive industries. The salt beds in the Estancia Basin and the hide and textile industries of New Mexico were important, both as raw materials used in the mercury amalgamation process dominant at Parral, and as a means to outfit miners more generally (West 1949:81–82). Chronologically, the rich deposits of Parral frame the latter part of the occupational history of the metallurgical facility at Paa-ko, thereby providing a useful point of comparison and a sense of the general trend of the silver mining industry in the latter half of the seventeenth century. Similarly, the early mining in the Parral district, particularly the lead-silver deposits of Santa Bárbara, are contemporaneous with both the initial foundation of the New Mexico colony and the facility at Paa-ko. Santa Bárbara is also significant because the colony departed for New Mexico from this community and some of the miners from the area joined the company (Hammond and Rey 1953).

The early mines of Santa Bárbara yielded a lead-rich ore, probably galena, and were only marginally profitable in terms of silver extraction. The district became a major supplier of lead and litharge for use in cupellation operations for the silver-bearing galena mines of Zacatecas and Sombrerete in the last decades of the sixteenth century (West 1949:10, 105). The mining and production of materials used in silver processing (such as lead, litharge, and *magistral*) have received little treatment in the historical literature on mining in New Spain. Yet without the contribution of materials from these sources, silver production would not have been possible. Besides mines in the Santa Bárbara area, the mines of Mapimí, 150 miles southeast of Santa Bárbara, and the mining settlement of San Gregorio in Nuevo León, produced lead products (Gerhard 1993; West 1949). The development of these resources provides another possible economic model for the exploitation of lead-based minerals in New Mexico.

The bonanza ores of Parral were similar to the lead-free silver ores of Zacatecas, namely deposits produced through the supergene enrichment of silver sulfide ores. Deposits at Parral also included an extensive zone of oxidized ores such as silver chloride, present near the surface (Bakewell 1971; West 1949:13, 18). These two types of deposits were exploited using the patio process. A major difference between the Zacatecan deposits and those of Parral was the proximity of the major ore bodies in Parral to a source of water, the Río San Gregorio. The use of water-powered machinery was possible at Parral in contrast to the situation at Zacatecas (West 1949:27).

West (1949:84) suggests that with the development of the deposits at Parral one of the key economic partnerships that drove the mining industry throughout the latter Spanish colonial period was established, namely the involvement of merchants in mining through capital financing and credit mechanisms. This relationship developed as a profitable goods distribution system, but toward the latter half of the seventeenth century merchants became increasingly involved in the financing of mining operations. In the late seventeenth and early eighteenth centuries, merchants often became miner owners through debt collection processes (Couturier 2003).[*]

The Crown facilitated the large-scale distribution of goods as well as transportation of bullion back to Mexico City by establishing road systems. Roads initially founded by merchants supplying the mines in the north were eventually maintained by the Crown. The system linked the major ports of Veracruz and Acapulco as well as communities throughout Central and West Mexico to Zacatecas and Parral. The first extension of this distribution network into New Mexico occurred with the arrival of the first supply caravan from Mexico City in the first few years of the New Mexico colony's existence (Scholes 1930). This exchange became more frequent as the Crown took over the responsibility of supplying New Mexico's missions. The roads soon became a target for banditry and Indian raiding (Bakewell 1971; Mayer 1974; West 1949). This tended to limit the flow of goods to large caravans that could afford armed escort, although small-scale trading probably played a significant role. The indigenous communities of West Mexico may have played an additional role within these trading networks, as some became specialized in the transportation of goods by foot, an extension of precolonial trade patterns (West 1973).

Labor at Parral was structured in a similar way to the mining industry in Zacatecas and was heavily reliant upon the availability of Indian labor. Although West (1949) and Bakewell (1971) emphasize the diminished role of slave labor in the industry as a whole, slavery or other forms of forced labor seems to have been preferred by mine owner over the wage system. This is evidenced by their repeated requests for the reinstitution of *repartimiento* and the high prices that they would pay for African and Indian slaves (Bakewell 1971:121–124; Mayer 1974:13–16; West 1949:52–53). The desire for slave labor reflects the attempt by mine owners to control the mobility of the workforce, one of the major problems affecting the profitability of

mining endeavors. The Parral boom of the 1630s and 1640s exacerbated an already depressed mining industry in Zacatecas by drawing free labor to the north, forcing the closure of many haciendas (Bakewell 1971).

LATE SIXTEENTH-CENTURY EXPEDITIONS

Late sixteenth- and early seventeenth-century assessments of the value of mineral deposits in New Mexico differed from Coronado-era accounts in their evaluations. The first detailed assessment dates to the 1580s, nearly 40 years after the founding of Zacatecas and well into the development of the colonial silver mining industry. Unlike the Coronado entrada, expeditions of the late sixteenth century saw opportunity in mineral deposits based on their assay worth, rather than the availability of *encomienda* labor.

The Gallegos *relación* of the 1581 Rodríguez-Chamuscado expedition describes the first assays conducted on minerals from New Mexico, probably from the Cerrillos Hills. It also describes mineral deposits in other locations along the Rio Grande, most likely from the Socorro area. The assays were conducted on ores given to them by inhabitants of the pueblos in the vicinity of the Cerrillos sources, and possibly on ores extracted from the veins themselves. The assays were conducted after the expedition arrived back in Mexico City. The most profitable assay mentioned by Gallegos came from ores associated with the Pueblo of San Marcos (here described as San Mattheo):

> While we were at the pueblo which we named Malpartida, a league from the discovery that was found and which was called San Mattheo, we asked if there were many metals, showing them the samples we brought for that purpose and asking them to take us where the metals were. They immediately brought us a large quantity of metals of different kinds. They brought samples of a copperish steel-like metal. This mineral was rich, as it appeared. It assayed about twenty maravedis per hundred-weight. The other metals assayed less. We asked them where-from they brought those metals. They gave us to understand that close by, near the province and pueblo, were many metals, and they thought that part of them came from there. We went to see them, and mines of different metals were discovered [Hammond and Rey 1966:28–29].

Twenty maravedis, equivalent to 20 marks, would be about 160 ounces per quintal, a fairly rich assay. Phillipe de Escalante, a participant of the expedition, most likely

---

[*] The Zaldívar family was one of those affected by debt accretion. Hit hard by the mercury supply crisis of the mid-seventeenth century, the family was forced to sell most of their land holdings around Zacatecas (Bakewell 1971).

laid claim to the mines at Cerrillos and recounted the assay totals in his brief narrative:

> We also discovered in the said country eleven mine prospects, all having great veins of silver. From three of them ore was brought to this city and given to his Excellency. He sent it to the assayer of the mint to be assayed; he assayed them and found one of the samples to be half silver; another contained twenty marks per quintal, and the third five marks [Bolton 1963:157].

Following Milford and Swick's (1995) conversion of these values into modern equivalents, the ores assayed (most likely veins of galena, not native silver) were rich, with 3,200 ounces of silver per ton and 800 ounces per ton respectively. Milford and Swick (1995:19) suggest that, although these reported values may be exaggerations, ores recovered from Spanish workings in the Cerrillos Hills that were re-opened in the early twentieth century assayed close to 200 ounces per ton, suggesting a potentially higher yield at their initial discovery.

As they returned to their starting point in Santa Bárbara, Chihuahua, the Rodriguez-Chamuscado expedition encountered additional mineral deposits:

> On leaving the said Pueblo of Puaray and having gone twenty leagues from the said province, six settlements and mineral deposits were discovered. These are in a very fine place with abundant water and timber. [They had] very good veins, rich in contents, and many enclosures which, in the opinion of all of our men, were and are very good, for nearly all were miners who knew about mines, veins, and metals [Hammond and Rey 1966:53].

Hammond and Rey suggest that these mines were near where the Rio Salado drains into the Rio Grande, as the expedition traveled along the west bank of the river. Recent lead-isotope studies of glaze ware vessels from the Salinas Pueblos suggest that some of the galena used in the production of these glazes originated from a source in the Magdalena or North Magdalena mining districts, which are west of the Rio Grande near Socorro (Huntley and others 2007). These sources may have been the same as the deposits visited by the Rodriguez-Chamuscado expedition, as the prospects were indicated by local knowledge of previously exploited sources. The Gallegos *relación* is also the first indication of the mineralogical knowledge held by members of the expedition, as they are identified as miners. The mention of water and timber also suggests that Gallegos knew the economic and technological requirements for mining.

The Espejo expedition of 1582, sent to New Mexico to recover two Franciscan priests who went to evangelize the southern Tiwa as part of the preceding Rodriguez-Chamuscado foray, also provided a fairly detailed assessment of mineral resources in the region (Hammond and Rey 1966). Diego Pérez de Luján, the chronicler of the expedition, appears to have had both a working knowledge of the mining industry and a familiarity with mineral deposits. His connection to mining endeavors is suggested by the biographical note included in the Hammond and Rey (1966:39) translation of his account, which stated that after the expedition Luján went to Nuevo León in order to prospect. As other researchers have noted, one of the great values of Luján's account is that it was written in a diary form, with entries made throughout the course of the expedition. During the journey, Luján weighed in on the availability and quality of potential ores, making note of the proximity and availability of labor and wood. He made these comments about the potential in the Zuni region: "Having received news of mines, God willing, we are going to discover them. I shall give an account of whatever takes place. At present I merely wish to say that if there are good mines this will be the best land ever discovered, because the people of these provinces are industrious and peaceful" (Hammond and Rey 1966:184).

From Hopi, the expedition was led to mines west of the mesas, most likely in the Verde Valley, Arizona, sources for the blue-green pigments noticed at Zuni and Hopi. Upon being assayed, according to Luján's account, they were shown to have no silver content and interest in the area waned. This contrasts with Espejo's account, which states that silver was recovered from these sources (Bolton 1963). In Luján's account, the recognition of a possible labor source that was both "industrious and peaceful" was given as much weight at the potential discovery of ore sources. This reveals a working knowledge of the industry and a historical knowledge of the development of mining challenged by the Chichimec Wars, as well as revealing a template for the colonization of the region.

OÑATE AND THE ESTABLISHMENT OF THE COLONY

The connection between the Spanish settlement of the north and the development of mining interests began a generation earlier with the efforts of Juan de Oñate's great uncle Cristobal de Oñate, and through the pacification and colonization efforts of Francisco de Ibarra who established the community at Santa Bárbara. The New Mexico colony was organized and administered by the Oñate and Zaldívar families, who in the late sixteenth century were tied by marriage and business partnerships. They wielded a significant political influence in Zacatecas and the northern frontier (Bakewell 1971; Vaughan 2006). The initial colony assembled in the 1590s drew heavily from the mining center of Zacatecas for personnel, as well as from other mining communities in the north such as Sombrerete and Santa Bárbara.

The colony was well equipped for mining and smelting operations. Supply inventories list large bellows for use in furnaces as well as smaller bellows for silver refining. Five hundred pounds of mercury, probably for amalgamation assay rather than for use in the patio process, were also listed. Other reagents in the supply inventory included greta, or litharge, and lead for use in the smelting and cupellation processes. Other minerals brought to New Mexico included sulfur, alum, and verdigris, most likely for use in medical treatments, although they could have also been incorporated in assay technologies as well (Hammond and Rey 1953). Sulfur recovered from the Paa-ko excavations could be representative of this latter practice (see Chapters 6 and 7).

After the establishment of the colony in 1598, expeditions were sent to areas reported to have mineral resources. The area visited by Luján was re-examined by an expedition led by Marcos Farfan de los Godos, the captain of the guard of the New Mexico colony. The expedition headed west, proceeding from Zuni to Hopi, over the Little Colorado and past the San Francisco Peaks, into the hills west of the Verde Valley, an area that became an important American copper mining district. Relying on Hopi guides, the expedition encountered rancherías of non-Pueblo people, probably Yavapai, who processed minerals for pigments to be used in ritual and for trade with the Western Pueblos (Braatz 2003). After establishing contacts with leaders from each group, Farfan's group proceeded from settlement to settlement. As they traveled, they were presented with "powdered ores of different colors," along with other gifts of food and animal hides. They were subsequently led to a mine "from which the Indians extracted the ores for their personal adornment and for the coloring of their blankets, because in this mine there are brown, black, water colored, blue, and green ores," and that some of these ores were "so blue that it is understood that some of it is enamel" (Bolton 1963:244).

A recent retranslation of the Farfan document has been undertaken by ethnohistorians at the Arizona State Museum as part of a project under the guidance of the Hopi Tribe to compile all available historical documents relating to the tribe. This retranslation suggests that Farfan actually claimed the mineral to be the European colorant known as smalt. One of the first synthetic colorants, smalt was derived from cobalt ore (Harley 1982). The ores that Farfan encountered, however, were most likely azurite, a copper carbonate, and not a cobalt mineral. In his mis-identification of smalt, which Farfan identified as a natural ore, he may have been suggesting that the ore he found was an indicator of the presence of silver, as cobalt was often associated with silver deposits in Europe.

The Farfan and the Luján documents reveal the extent to which Spanish prospectors used Native American informants to identify the location and assessed value of minerals. The Farfan document, in particular, echoes the official history of the founding of Zacatecas, in which silver ores were presented to Juan de Tolosa by Zacateco Indians. As an official account of the colony, one of Farfan's objectives may have been to establish a parallel history for his intended audience. The fact that minerals were exchanged as gifts suggests the development of a relational value for minerals among the Yavapai, Hopi, and Spaniards, at least in the context of Spanish prospecting expeditions.

Properties of color and luster seem to have played a major part in the determination of ore value prior to their assay. In the 1580s, the Rodriguez-Chumuscado expedition carried a comparative collection of ores in order to obtain information on the occurrence of similar minerals from Pueblo inhabitants. It is apparent from the routes of exploration and descriptions in the Farfan document that ore bodies were located based on the mineral procurement and processing techniques of the Pueblos and Yavapais. As discussed in Chapter 3, this exploration strategy formed the institutional basis for the development of technological syncretism both in the establishment of the mining industry and in the intersection with, and disruption of, indigenous economic and social networks involved with pigment production.

At the time of colonization, lead- and copper-glazed wares were no longer being produced by the Western Pueblos. It is interesting that the Hopi area drew so much attention, as the predominant ores they were exploiting were copper-bearing, and copper minerals were not usually associated with silver in New Spain.

Spanish mining interests were, however, quick to map onto Puebloan mineral procurement strategies for the production of lead glaze in finding ore bodies to exploit (Ramenofsky and Vaughan 2003). They established mining and smelting operations in proximity to the primary sources of the minerals used for the Eastern Pueblo glaze ware traditions—the Galisteo Basin, the Cerrillos Hills, and the Ortiz, Sandia, and San Pedro mountains. Two excavated archaeological sites in this area contain evidence for the continuity from protohistoric Puebloan mineral procurement to processing strategies appropriated by Spanish mining practices: the Bethsheba Mine (Bice, Davis, and Sundt 2003) and San Marcos Pueblo (Vaughan 2001). The Cerrillos Hills sources, including the Bethsheba Mine, have been recognized as one of the primary sources for the lead ore used in glaze paint recipes in both the precolonial and early colonial periods (Habicht-Mauche and others 2000). An additional source of lead has been identified in the Soccoro area as well (Huntley and others 2007). Excavation and survey of the Bethsheba Mine have indicated that the deposit was worked along the same vein from precolonial times through the early colonial period, where Spanish-influenced mining proceeded from the exposure of ores created by precolonial Puebloan mining practices (Bice, Davis, and Sundt 2003). San Marcos Pueblo, the closest pueblo to the Cerrillos Hills, most likely played a large role in the distribution of this material in both periods. During the colonial period it became one of the major Spanish mission sites in the Galisteo Basin. The smaller Puebloan community of La Cienega, to the north of the Cerrillos Hills (as yet unidentified archaeologically), may have been a community forcibly incorporated into the early mining industry of the colony through *encomienda* demands (Milford and Swick 1995).

Historical records, summarized by Milford and Swick (1995) and Vaughan (2006), suggest that there were two mining foci for the initial colonial mining industry—in the Cerrillos Hills of the Galisteo Basin and either the San Pedro/Ortiz Mountains or the Manzano Mountains. Interest in these localities was due to their purported mineral value, as well as the relatively beneficial social and geographical position of these resources. During the early seventeenth century, Juan de Zaldívar established two mining and ore-processing operations in pueblos adjacent to the mineral resources, one at San Marcos and the other at the pueblo of Tuerto. Tuerto Pueblo has not been identified archaeologically, but Paa-ko may be a good fit as the Tuerto and San Pedro drainages are contiguous, and Paa-ko contains the most extensive archaeological evidence for early seventeenth-century ore processing and metal production yet excavated. The works at Tuerto were established in order to process ores recovered from Zaldívar's mine of Annunciacion. The location of this mine is unknown but is thought to have been in the vicinity of the intersection of the Tuerto and San Pedro drainages (Milford and Swick 1995).

THE PERIODICITY OF MINING COMMUNITIES

The longevity of the mining centers of Zacatecas and Parral was unusual for mining communities in New Spain in the sixteenth and early seventeenth century. Most mines functioned for only a brief period, with bonanzas being exploited until they ran out, or the mining was disrupted by other social and cultural factors. Some mines were profitable for only for a few years, while others produced for a few decades. Mines were abandoned and revisited over the course of the colonial period, when social conditions were favorable for their exploitation and as new technologies such as explosives and steam power became available. As mines became unproductive, the colonial communities that supported them were either abandoned or turned their attention to other pursuits, such as agriculture or providing goods for cattle ranching (Gerhard 1993). As can be seen in a cursory review of mining settlements described in Peter Gerhard's compilation of historical information on the northern frontier of New Spain, the small scale and periodicity of New Mexican mining follows a general trend for the industry in Northern New Spain (Table 4.1).

The mines of Santa Bárbara and Mapimí in Nueva Viscaya are interesting in this regard. Santa Bárbara's fortunes were tied to the quality of ores exploited, whereas Mapimí's intermittent periods of exploitation were due primarily to increased warfare during the seventeenth century. Santa Bárbara's first period of exploitation began in the late sixteenth century and ended in the first decade of the seventeenth century due to the poor quality of the ores. Mining and extractive metallurgical techniques were originally focused on the silver content of ores, but due to their poor quality and high lead content, the industry shifted to the extraction of lead for use in cupellation in the Zacatecas region mines. Interest in the Santa Bárbara mines did not resume until the 1680s and then only for a few decades. Mining resumed in the late eighteenth century with the discovery of gold deposits (Bakewell 1971; Gerhard 1993). Mapimí had several periods of exploitation. First developed as a silver mine, focus soon shifted to the production of lead and lead products for use in the silver industry in Zacatecas and Parral (Bakewell 1971). Mining at Mapimí was repeatedly interrupted by Indian raids and rebellions; the settlement was rebuilt at least six times (Gerhard 1993:210).

Both mining locations used nonlocal Indian skilled labor within the industry, as in the mining communities of

Table 4.1. Colonial Period Mines in Northern New Spain (compiled from Gerhard 1993)

Mine(s), Location	Period(s) of Exploitation	Characterization/ Reason for Abandonment	Labor	Resource
Acaponeta, Nueva Galicia	1587-late 18th century	None	Spaniards, non-Indian	Silver
Aguas Calientes, (Los Asientos de Ibarra), Nueva Galicia	1704–1716	None given	Not mentioned	Silver
Colotlán (Los Reyes, Tepec), Nueva Galicia	1550; 1622-1689; 1784	Indian raids; not profitable	Mestizos	Silver
Charcas, Nueva Galicia	1590-1605, 1690s-?	Poor ores	Not mentioned	Silver
Ojo Caliente, Nueva Galicia	1597-1605(?); 1690s-?; 1780-1781	Poor ores; bonanza quickly exploited	Not mentioned	Silver
Ramos, Nueva Galicia	1608-1630s (?)	Bonanza finished	Not mentioned	Silver
Catorce, Nueva Galicia	1778-1800(?)	Boomtown	Not mentioned	Silver
Fresnillo (San Demetrio), Nueva Galicia	1570-1609	Silver content dropped	Tarascans, Tecuexes, Negro slaves	Silver
Guachinango, Nueva Galicia	1540-1605	Mining activity shifted westward	Nonlocal Indians, African slaves	Silver
Hostotipac, (Los Reyes, La Resurrección, San Sebastián), Nueva Galicia	1597-late 18th century	None	"Many Spaniards and Indians"	Silver
Hostotipaquillo (Xocotlan, Guaxacatlan, Amaxaque, Xora), Nueva Galicia	1540s; 1583-late 18th century	None	Nonlocal Indians, African slaves	Silver
Juchipila, (Mezquital)	1737-?	None	Not mentioned	Silver, gold
Lagos (Comanja), Nueva Galicia	1560-1649	Warfare, poor ores	Not mentioned	Silver (?)
Mazapil, Nueva Galicia	1569-1573; 1590-1608	Warfare; miners moved to other areas	Indians from the south, African slaves	Silver
Nayarit (Santiago del Espada, Tenamachi, Naguapan), Nueva Galicia	1580-1582; 1590s	None given	Unreduced Indians, African slaves, mulattos	Silver(?)
Nieves (San Joaquín, San Miguel del Mezquital), Nueva Galicia	1564-1604	"Not of great importance"	Not mentioned	Silver
Purificación, Nueva Galicia	1530s-1540s	Placers depleted	Repartimiento	Gold
Sierra de Pinos (Nuestra Señora de la Concepción de Cusco, La Pendencia, Espíritu Santo)	1594-1622; mid-17th century	None	Tlaxcaltecans, Otomis, others	Silver
Sombrerete, Nueva Galicia	1555-1590s; 1646-1700; 1791-1800	Ore value	Tlaxcaltecans, African slaves	Silver

continued

Table 4.1. (continued)

Mine(s), Location	Period(s) of Exploitation	Characterization/ Reason for Abandonment	Labor	Resource
Tepic, Nueva Galicia	1540–1550s	Labor shortage	Local Indian labor	Silver
Tequepespan, Nueva Galicia	1570s(?)–1600	Not profitable	"The original [Indian] settlement of Sta Maria Acuitlapilco seems to have been moved, …the old site being converted into a mining camp"	Silver
Tequila (San Pedro Analco, Santa Cruz de las Flores, Brasiles) Nueva Galicia	late 18th century	None given	Not mentioned	Silver(?)
Nuevo León (San Gregorio, Ciudad de León, San Pedro Boca de Leones, Santiago de las Sabinas, San Antonio de la Iguana, San Carlos del Vallecillo), Nueva León	1577–1580s(?); 1690s on	Warfare, slave raids; poor ores	Tlaxcaltecans	Silver, lead
Batopilas (Urique, San Joaquín de los Arrieros), Nueva Vizcaya	1690–1753; 1769 – (?)	Ore body worked out, none	Not mentioned	Silver
Ciénega de los Olivos (Tónachic), Nueva Vizcaya	1570(?); 1803	None	Not mentioned	?
Cosihuiriáchic (San Francisco Saguaríchic, San Juan, Santa Rosa), Nueva Vizcaya	1678; 1683–1686; 1686–?	Mine collapse; richer veins in region	Not mentioned	Silver
Cuencamé, (San Antonio de Padua), Nueva Vizcaya	1601–1652	Indian raids, disease	Zacatecos, Tarascans, Mexicanos, Tecuexes	Silver
Chihuahua (Santa Eulalia), Nueva Vizcaya	1707–1760; 1790–1820	Indian raids	Not mentioned	Silver(?)
Guanaceví, Nueva Vizcaya	1570s(?)–1616; 1640–1763	Warfare	Spaniards, African slaves, Indians from Central Mexico	Silver
Guarisamey (San José de Basis), Nueva Vizcaya	1761–1778; 1784–?	Principal veins were exhausted	Not mentioned	Silver, gold
Mapimí, Nueva Vizcaya	1589–1616;1617–1654; 1662–1683; 1688–1703; 1712–1715; 1716–1777; 1778–	Warfare, Indian raids	Skilled Indian and African miners	Lead
Mezquital, Nueva Vizcaya	1588	Mines discovered, not worked	None	?
Papasquiaro, Nueva Vizcaya	1590s(?); 1761	None given	Not mentioned	Silver
Parras y Saltillo, Nueva Vizcaya	1600s(?)	Indian raids, mining sporadic	Tlaxcaltecans, Tarascans, Chichimecs	?

Table 4.1. (continued)

Mine(s), Location	Period(s) of Exploitation	Characterization/Reason for Abandonment	Labor	Resource
Real de Oro (Indehe, La Victoria), Nueva Vizcaya	1567–1573; 1581–1630; 1703–?	Indian raids, Parral mining	Mexicans, Tarascans	Silver
San Andrés de la Sierra (San Hipólito, Las Vegas, Guapixuxe, San Xavier, San José de las Apomas, San Diego de Tesaes), Nueva Viscaya	1581–1602; 1581–1644; 1628–1702; 1777	Acaxee, Xiximes, Tepehuán rebellions	African slaves, central Mexicans	Silver
San Buenaventura (La Mohina), Nueva Vizcaya	1779	None given	Not mentioned	?
San Juan del Río (Avino, San Lucas, Coneto), Nueva Vizcaya	1558; 1560–1585; 1622; 1693–1703; 1777–1800	Tepehuán uprising, ores	"Indios advenedizos" (newcomers), probably skilled miners brought up from the south" (p.235)	Silver
Santa Bárbara, Nueva Vizcaya	1567–1604; 1685–1707; 1777	Poor ores	Mexicans, Tarascans, Tarahumaras and Yaquis, Africans and Spaniards	Silver, lead
Siánori, Nueva Vizcaya	1590–1640; 1680;1725; 1750; 1763; 1777	Poor ores, Parral mining, Acaxee rebellion	African slaves, Indian mine workers from central Mexico	Silver
Copala (Pánuco, Materoy, San Antonio, Charcas), Sinaloa	1570–1591; 1700	None given	Not mentioned	?
Culiacán (Los Otomíes, Trinidad, Espíritu Santo, San Francisco, Las Vírgenes, Cariantapa, San Ignacio, Santiago de los Caballeros), Sinaloa	1545–1569; early 17th century; 1759–1777	Bonanza finished, Tepehuán rebellion	Not mentioned	Silver
Maloya (San Marcial, Cacalotlan, Maloya, Las Plomosas), Sinaloa	1587–1621; 1745; 1790 on	Indian uprising, Tepehuán rebellion	Spanish miners	Silver, gold
Rosario (Nuestra Señora del Rosario), Sinaloa	1655–1686(?)	None	Not mentioned	Silver, gold
Sinaloa (Los Frailes, Los Alamos, Nuestra Señora de la Concepción, Sivirijoa, Bacubiritio), Sinaloa	1683 on	None	Mexicans, Tarascans, African slaves, "mixed-race floating population"	Silver, gold
Ostimuri (Real de los Gentiles, San Ignacio de Ostimuri, San Ildefonso Huistimicori, Piedras Verdes, Baroyeca, San Nicolás, Rio Chico, El Potrero, Batmenaco, Guadalupe, Trinidad de la Peña Blanca), Sonora	1666–1697; 1739–1804	Pima rebellions, Yaqui and Apache uprisings/raids	Not mentioned	Silver
Sonora (Sinoquipe, Sanitago Tuape, San Francisco Xavier Nacatóbori; San Pedro de los Reyes, San Juan Bautista, Nacozari; San Miguel Arcángel, Bacanuchi, Motepori, San Antonio de la Huerta, Cieneguilla, Arizonac), Sonora	1640s–1768	Seri and Apache warfare	Indian mine workers, Yaquis	Silver, gold, placer gold

Table 4.2. Colonial Period Mines in the Los Cerrillos area, New Mexico

Mines	Period of Exploitation	Reason for Abandonment	Labor	Resource
Sierras of San Marcos	1581–1583	Brief prospecting	Spanish prospectors	Silver
San Marcos, El Tuerto	1600–1610(?)	"Officially" deemed unprofitable	Zaldivar and his servants, Tlaxcaltecans(?)	Silver
Roque Madrid's Mine	ca. 1680s	Pueblo Revolt	Unknown	Lead
Los Cerrillos	1693–1696	Pueblo uprising	Unknown	Silver
Santa Rosa	1697–1714(?)	Unknown	Unknown	Silver
Galisteo (?)	1749–1752	Placer deposit exhausted	Unknown	Gold

Zacatecas and Parral. Gerhard lists Yaqui and Tarahumara laborers at Santa Bárbara in its later periods of exploitation, with Mexican and Tarascan laborers participating as well, which was similar to the larger mining centers. The incorporation of Yaquis and Tarahumaras probably followed a trend for the region, where the Indians first served as coerced labor and were later hired as skilled, free wage laborers (West 1949:51). Spicer (1962) suggests that the Indians may have hired on as miners to escape the confines of the mission system.

Like many of the mines in Northern New Spain, those in the Cerrillos area had a brief period of exploitation in the late sixteenth century followed by more substantial use in the first decade of the seventeenth century (Table 4.2; Milford and Swick 1995). The official assessment of the mines deemed them unprofitable, but they continued to be worked, at least in part to extract lead. Spanish mining was terminated by the Pueblo Revolt of 1680 but resumed with the re-establishment of the colony in 1693. The second period focused on silver extraction; those efforts were again truncated by a Pueblo rebellion in 1696. Mining for silver and, possibly, lead occurred sporadically through the first few decades of the eighteenth century, with an interest in gold placer deposits developing in the mid-eighteenth century. In 1766 the official assessment of the area stated that the mines were "of no great value" and that they were not being worked (Milford and Swick 1995:52). Official assessments were tied to the financial interests of the Crown, however, leaving open the possibility that there may have been small-scale mining by individuals.

REFERENCING VALUE: A COMPARISON OF ASSAYS

From the initial entrada into New Mexico, mineral resources were given value based not only on precious metal content, but on the intersection of social and environmental resources necessary for the development of those resources. During the early sixteenth century, Spanish colonial elites mapped on to already established labor networks and craft production, leaving the extraction of metal largely in the hands of indigenous West Mexican smiths. But by the late sixteenth and early seventeenth centuries, when the New Mexico colony was established, mineral values were assessed through assay weights and productivity was evaluated on the basis of extraction technologies such as smelting, cupellation, and mercury amalgamation.

In a way, New Mexico's Pueblo communities were assayed as well, in terms of their acceptance of Spanish rule and Catholicism, but also in terms of productivity. Pueblos such as San Marcos, La Cienega, and Paa-ko may have acted as small-scale *haciendas de minas*. Spanish miners took advantage of a resident work force that could also supply agricultural products and knowledge of resources on the local landscape. Situating the initial industry within the Pueblos is striking in that, unlike the communities of West and Central Mexico, the Puebloans of New Mexico had no prior experience with extractive metallurgy. In addition to providing the Puebloans with knowledge of metal production, the mining industry exposed the communities to the various castas of New Spain society. Among those in the frontier mining industry were West and Central Mexican Indians, African and African descendent slaves, Indian slaves from other areas of Northern New Spain, and miners from communities in Europe, Northern New Spain, and other areas of the Spanish colonial system. The multiethnic nature of mining communities posed advantages and disadvantages to the maintenance of political and social autonomy in Pueblo communities. This social dynamic is reflected to a certain degree in the technology evident at Paa-ko, the implications of which are discussed in the chapters that follow.

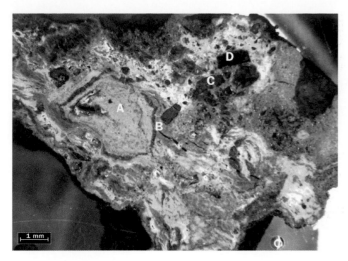

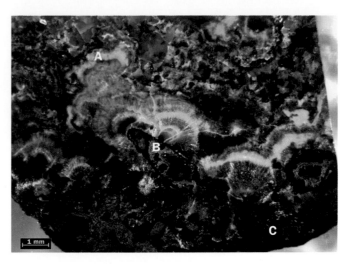

Plate 1. Copper ore: Sample LA162-211, in reflected, plain polarized light (PPL). A = malachite, B = chrysocolla, C = quartz, and D = weathered clay mineral. Photo by the author.

Plate 2. Copper ore: Sample LA162-338, in reflected, plain polarized light (PPL). A = malachite; B = XRF peaks Fe, Zn; C = XRF peaks Fe, Zn, Pb, Au. Photo by the author.

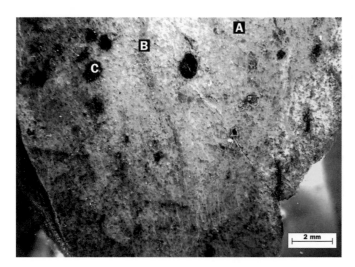

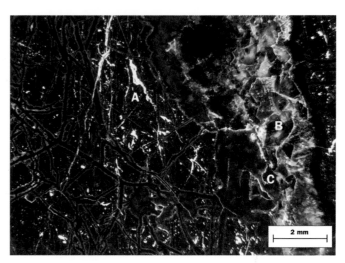

Plate 3. Copper ore: Sample LA162-206, in reflected, plain polarized light (PPL). A = chrysocolla; B = malachite, C = covellite. Photo by the author.

Plate 4. Copper ore: Sample LA162-214, in reflected, cross polarized light (XPL). A = chalcopyrite; B = malachite; C = iron hydroxides. Photo by the author.

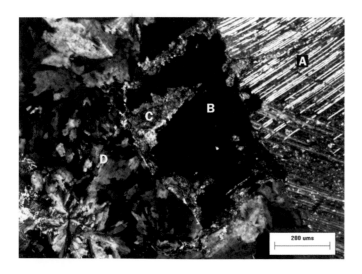

Plate 5. Galena in calcite gangue: Sample LA162-212, in transmitted, cross polarized light (XPL). A = calcite; B = galena; C = cerrusite; D = anglesite. Photo by the author.

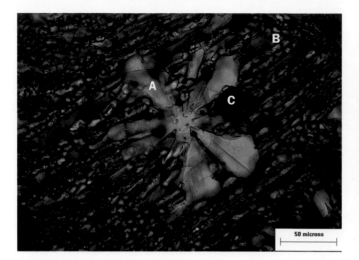

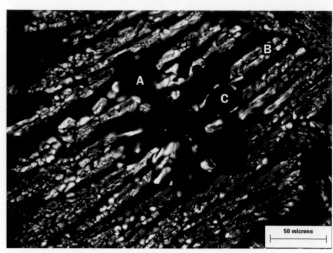

Plate 6. Slag: Sample LA162-72 in transmitted, plain polarized light (PPL). A = tridymite; B = fayalite; C = copper. Photo by the author.

Plate 7. Slag: Sample LA 162-72 in transmitted, cross polarized light (XPL). A = tridymite; B = fayalite; C = copper. Photo by the author.

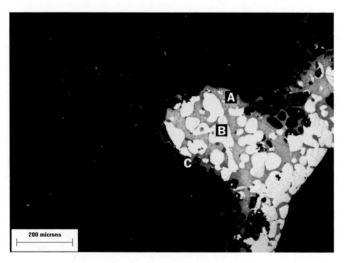

Plate 8. Fayalitic copper slag: Sample LA162-16, in reflected, plain polarized light (PPL). A = copper; B = iron; C = Cu or Fe sulfide. Photo by the author.

Plate 9. Fayalitic copper slag: Sample LA162-85, in transmitted, cross polarized light (XPL). A = magnetite; B = fayalite. Photo by the author.

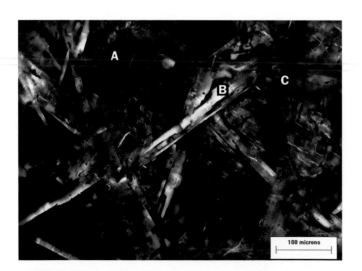

Plate 10. Melilite-fayalite copper slag: Sample LA162-105, in transmitted, plain polarized light (PPL). A = glass; B = akermanite; C = copper. Photo by the author.

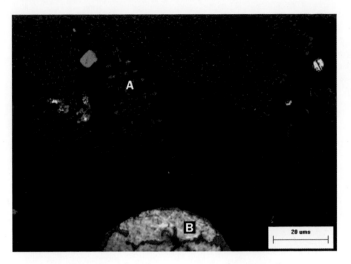

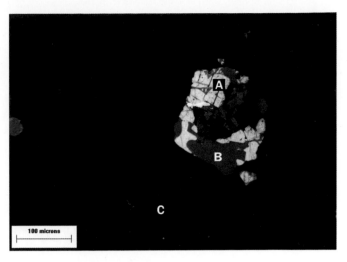

Plate 11. Magnetite-delafossite copper slag: Sample LA162-109, in reflected, plain polarized light (PPL). A = cuprite; B = copper. Photo by the author.

Plate 12. Lead slag: Sample LA162-55, in reflected, plain polarized light. A = galena; B = lead; C = lead glass. Photo by the author.

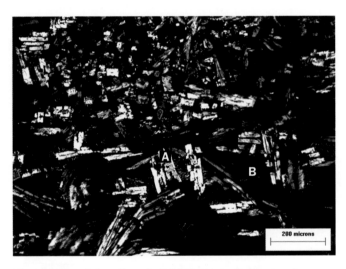

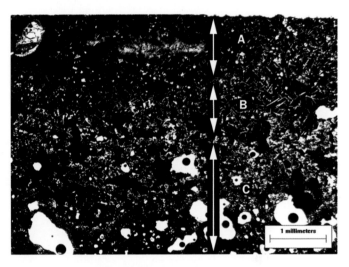

Plate 13. Lead slag: Sample LA162-74, in transmitted, cross polarized light (XPL). A = melilite; B = glass with XRF peaks for Ca, Zn, Si. Photo by the author.

Plate 14. Litharge and glass: Sample LA162-15, in reflected, plain polarized light (PPL). A = zone of glass; B = zone of litharge (PbO); C = ceramic. Photo by the author.

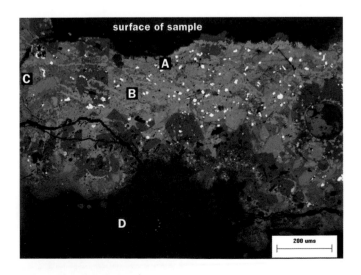

Plate 15. Litharge: Sample LA162-17, in reflected, plain polarized light. A = copper; B = litharge; C = lead glass; D = ceramic. Photo by the author.

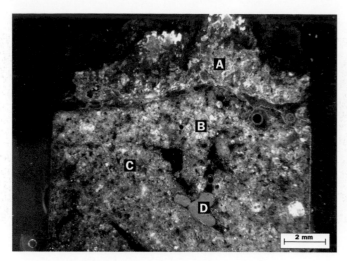

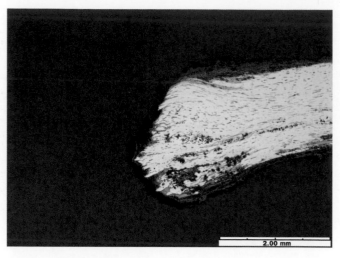

Plate 16. Adobe sample recovered from furnace Feature 90E/-168N/F1, in reflected, plain polarized light. A = mineralized surface layer with XRF peaks of Zn, Pb, Si, and Ca; B = highly vitrified adobe; C = adobe; D = lead; E = voids left by organic material. Photo by the author.

Plate 17. Cold-worked sheet copper recovered from the facility. Linear and compressed grains indicate that this piece was cold worked after it was last annealed. Photo by the author.

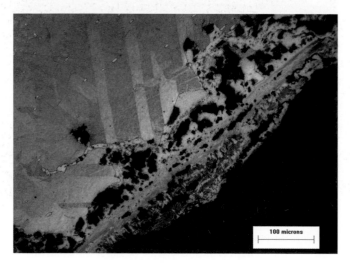

Plate 18. Annealing twins in sheet copper recovered from the facility. Photo by the author.

Plate 19. Sulfur recovered from the interior of the Western Terrace. Photo by the author.

CHAPTER FIVE

History of Excavations at Paa-ko

Paa-ko is located adjacent to the floodplain of the Arroyo San Pedro and contains two major spatial divisions. The South Division, or San Pedro Viejo I, consists of at least 10 adobe or masonry and adobe room blocks arranged in four plaza groups. The North Division (San Pedro Viejo II) has a similar structure, but exhibits a more complex occupational sequence. The two divisions are separated by a low-lying drainage. Both divisions were occupied between the late thirteenth and early fifteenth centuries, based on ceramic cross dating (Lambert 1954; Lycett 1997). The pueblo appears to have been abandoned during the mid-fifteenth century followed by a restricted reoccupation of the North Division that may have begun as early as the late sixteenth century and continued into the seventeenth century. The historical metallurgical facility, which dates to the seventeenth century, was constructed on the southeast slope of midden deposits adjoining the North Division (Figure 5.1).

EARLY RESEARCH

Paa-ko has a long history of research and archaeological excavation. The pueblo was first investigated by Adolph Bandelier in the late nineteenth century, when he visited and described the northern room block and plaza group. Bandelier recognized the presence of corrals in the historical plaza. The corrals, coupled with the pueblo's location and ethnographic information obtained from Santo Domingo Pueblo, led him to associate the site with the historical place names of San Pedro and Paa-ko (Bandelier 1892).

Nels Nelson's pioneering work in the Galisteo Basin included excavation at Paa-ko during 1914 and 1915. His work at the site was at the forefront of the development of

the direct historical approach to archaeological investigation that Kidder (1932) refined in his excavations at Pecos Pueblo. Nelson sought to characterize the occupational sequence at Paa-ko in terms of the known historical referents to the site and recent ethnographic data, working back stratigraphically from the historical to the prehistoric. This was, in fact, one of the primary reasons Nelson (1914:9) began work in the area, as he states:

> Here, it appeared, was an opportunity to prosecute a piece of research work in the most scientific manner, namely, by working back from the known to the unknown. There was at hand a very considerable amount of published ethnologic data on the Southwest, and investigations of the present Pueblos by Dr. Herbert J. Spinden of the Museum staff and others were in progress. It seemed possible in the light of these earlier findings and with the assistance of modern ethnologists to arrive at sound conclusions regarding the culture, character, and interrelations of the early historic Rio Grande villagers of the sixteenth and seventeenth centuries, and that much accomplished, the elucidation of the problems presented by the Pueblos of prehistoric times should be an easier task.

Nelson apparently planned to publish his work on the pueblo as part a larger monograph dealing with Tanoan pueblos but ended up pursuing other research interests. He may have thought that the Galisteo Basin pueblos offered a better case study, being more centrally located to Spanish colonial administrative and missionary power. The historical references to Paa-ko pale in comparison to the documentation available for the Galisteo pueblos in this

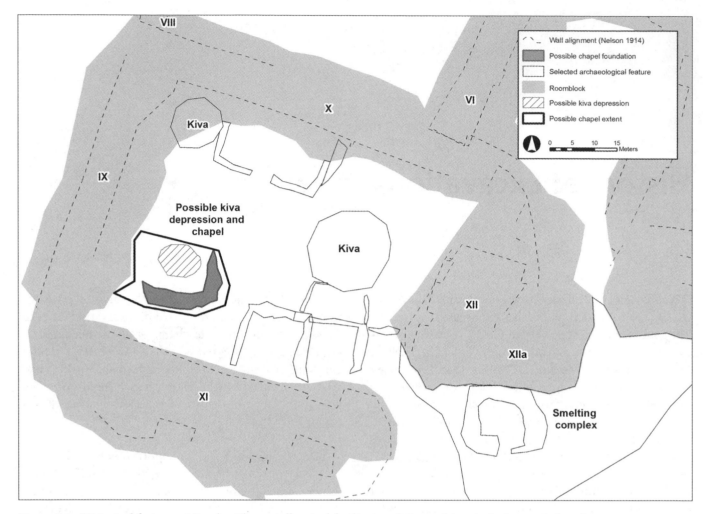

Figure 5.1. Historical features at Paa-ko: The metallurgical facility in relation to historical plaza and church. Map courtesy of Phillip Leckman.

regard. Although never published, his extensive field notes, map sketches, and collections from the site are housed at the American Museum of Natural History in New York.

From 1935 to 1937, the Works Progress Administration (WPA) funded a joint research project at the site. It was conducted by the School of American Research, the Museum of New Mexico, and the University of New Mexico. Marjorie Lambert used the WPA project records along with Nelson's notes, which were on file at the Laboratory of Anthropology in Santa Fe, to produce the primary monograph on the site (Lambert 1954). Additional excavation was conducted by University of New Mexico field schools in the summers of 1949 and 1950. The results of this work remain unpublished and are poorly documented.

Nelson and Lambert observed that there were two distinct occupations marked by a break in residence at the site, roughly dividing the occupation into prehistoric and historical periods (Nelson, cited in Lambert 1954). Nelson's work at Paa-ko precedes the Pecos Classification ceramic chronology established by Kidder (1932), so the break in occupational history at the site was observed primarily by the superimposition of architectural styles (with masonry construction overlying older adobe room blocks). Nelson did observe differences in the ceramic glaze styles, which he attributed to prehistoric and historic types. H. P. Mera (1933) included the site in his survey of Rio Grande Glaze Ware, and both his work and the work conducted by the School of American Research recognized an early component of the site represented by Glaze A types with a more limited historical occupation indicated by late Glaze types (Lycett 1997).

Following Bandelier's suggestion of a Tanoan affiliation for Paa-ko, Nelson claimed that the population was linked historically to the occupation of the Galisteo Basin pueblos, particularly San Cristobal and San Lazaro. Nelson and Lambert both suggested that the East Mountain region, and Paa-ko specifically, may have acted as a refuge for the population of these pueblos in times of stress, particularly in the aftermath of nomadic raiding during the first half of the sixteenth century. Both researchers also cite later seventeenth-century documents that suggest populations were moved from this area to the Galisteo Basin as part of a mission program of settlement and conversion during the early colonial period. The links among the populations of San Cristobal, San Lazaro, and Paa-ko suggested to Lambert a relationship between these historical communities and the modern comunities of Santo Domingo and the Tewa village at Hopi, which received migrants from the Galisteo Basin during the late seventeenth and early eighteenth centuries (Lambert 1954:6–7). The Tanoan affiliation of Paa-ko has been challenged by other researchers who cite historical links to Tiwa-speaking populations in the Albuquerque-Belen Basin (Hodge, Hammond, and Rey 1945). Both historical assessments may be valid. It would not be anomalous for a multiethnic pueblo to develop as a community used as a refuge in times of resource stress and social conflict.

The historical plaza, recognized initially by Bandelier through his observation of the similarity between the corral structures at Paa-ko and those at San Cristobal, was tested by Nelson and then more extensively excavated by the joint WPA excavations detailed by Lambert (1954:22–37). Until the University of Chicago project began, however, no complete map of the site existed, so the exact locations of each excavation area were uncertain. One of the prime objectives of the University of Chicago project was to correlate Nelson's sketch map of excavation areas and the record of excavation produced by the WPA excavations with observed topography to produce a comprehensive and accurate map detailing the history of excavations.

In 1914, Nelson excavated a series of rooms located adjacent to and north of the metallurgical facility. In addition to this room block, situated on the eastern side of the historical plaza, Nelson tested rooms in the north and west room blocks (Lambert 1954). He also partially excavated one of the historical plaza kivas and shovel-scraped a series of wall alignments in the plaza itself. Those wall alignments are now identified as the remains of a *visita* established at the site in the early seventeenth century (Lycett 2001).

The room block bordering the southern edge of the historical plaza was extensively excavated by the WPA joint research project (Lambert 1954); it was labeled the South House. Lambert reported a total of 125 rooms excavated

(including Nelson's work) that were associated with the historical occupation. The WPA excavations at Paa-ko were initially proposed by Edgar Lee Hewett to expose "how a Tanoan village of prehistoric and early historic times looked" in preparation for the site's inclusion into the Museum of New Mexico's State Monuments program (Lambert 1954:1). Excavation practices therefore focused on room construction techniques. The resulting monograph contains very little description of floor assemblages or spatial provenience data.

Nelson identified the outline of the north terrace retaining wall just south of his room block excavations, designating the metallurgical terraces as both a "house on heavy line" and a possible smelter, in his notes on a sketch map of the north division. Before the University of Chicago project, Nelson was the only researcher to identify the terraces as possible locations for metallurgical activity. Nelson's collections at the American Museum of Natural History include copper slag (catalogued as native copper) and sheet metal that were recovered from the rooms excavated adjacent to the facility (Lycett, personal communication). Lambert reports that copper and lead sheet metal and a heavier copper material, along with the remains of domesticated animals, were recovered from the South House and plaza kiva excavations. Lambert (1954:133, 160—162) noted that "many examples of malachite were found, particularly in the later portion of the ruin," but the WPA excavators made little reference to the dense concentration of ore and smelting debris found on the metallurgical terraces.

In summary, Nelson and Lambert thought that the significance of the site lay in its relationship to populations of the Galisteo Basin. Their primary concern was with the archaeology of the prehistoric period, and they made use of the direct historical approach because it indicated a primary relationship with existing Tano populations. Their focus thus tended to exclude the early colonial occupation and caused them to misidentify or under-pursue the identification of significant features on and adjacent to the historical plaza, such as the metallurgical facility and the *visita* structure. Their recognition of Paa-ko as a possible refuge for populations of the Galisteo Basin is interesting in that it recognizes a relationship between the fairly isolated nature of the pueblo and the potential for regional conflict, particularly in relation to Plains-Pueblo interactions of the protohistoric period. Paa-ko's relative isolation may also have allowed it to function as a refuge from the colonial oversight that was present in the more centrally located mission communities of the Galisteo Basin.

UNIVERSITY OF CHICAGO FIELD STUDIES PROJECT, 1996 TO 2005

Work at Paa-ko resumed in 1996, as the Northwestern University Summer Field Studies Program, under the direction of Mark Lycett (University of Chicago), with subsequent seasons conducted in a similar field school setting as the University of Chicago Summer Field Studies Program. In addition to documenting historical changes in the local environment and shifts in local land use and subsistence, the project sought to investigate the development of economic practices that were introduced during the early colonial period. To this end, the renewed excavations focused on extramural areas, which often functioned as work spaces, documenting changes in the use and maintenance of these areas from the precolonial through early historical periods (Lycett 1997).

Environmental data, including domesticated and wild plants, were recovered from test units excavated on the floodplain of the Arroyo San Pedro, from sediment cores of reservoir features, and from pollen samples taken from well-preserved surface contexts. These data reveal the effect of Pueblo habitation on the long-term ecology of the local environment. Distinct changes in the pollen record document the occupational history of the pueblo. Those changes correspond closely with Nelson's and subsequent researchers' understanding of the archaeological record of habitation. Evidence for the adoption of European plant domesticates was not present, however, suggesting a continuation of indigenous subsistence practices during the early colonial period (Morrison, Arendt, and Barger 2002).

Excavations in the historical plaza provided a wealth of data regarding changes in the use and conceptualization of extramural space through the early colonial period. The use and maintenance of the plaza as a work surface was extensive over this period, with more than seven resurfacing events documented in one test unit placed in the southwestern quarter of the plaza (Lycett 2004). Plaza excavations have also indicated a radical reorganization of space over time. Kivas were filled in; a small chapel (*visita*) was built over one kiva; and corrals were constructed. Structures along the south side of the plaza demonstrate a pattern of repeated burning, either as a form of maintenance of dung-filled corral structures, or as destructive events that affected the southernmost room block and the *visita* structure (Lycett 1999, 2004).

Spanish material culture and economic practices are indicated archaeologically by the presence of a limited amount of majolica, metal artifacts, and the remains of domestic animals throughout the deposits of the historical plaza. Late Rio Grande Glaze Ware ceramics made in colonial forms such as soup plates, candlesticks, and pitchers were also recovered in both plaza excavations and in the excavation of the metallurgical facility. Domestic animals present in the assemblage are dominated by sheep and goat remains but also included horse and bovine remains. The horses exhibit depositional patterning and cut-mark placement consistent with their use as food, suggesting a non-Hispanic food processing regime. Cut marks on the bones of domesticates and indigenous wild taxa were made by both metal and stone tools, indicating a synthesis of indigenous and introduced food-processing technologies (Sunseri and Gifford-Gonzalez 2002).

The most recent excavations of the historical component of Paa-ko suggest a continuation of indigenous subsistence practices alongside the partial adoption of elements of Spanish colonial material culture and subsistence. These adoptions were selectively incorporated into Puebloan practices, with an emphasis on the value of domesticated animals over European crops. The relative abundance of domesticated animals reported by Sunseri and Gifford-Gonzalez may indicate that the pueblo had a privileged position in relation to Spanish colonial distribution networks, although the majority of these remains could also have come from post-residential occupation contexts when the plaza was used as an extensive corral structure. A certain amount of distance from those networks is also apparent in that food taboos typical of Spanish colonial society, such as in the avoidance of horses as food, was ignored at Paa-ko (Sunseri and Gifford-Gonzalez 2002).

THE METALLURGICAL FACILITY

Excavation of the metallurgical facility was conducted through horizontal exposure in 1-m by 1-m grids with the goal of documenting contemporary or related depositional events. Full artifact recovery was practiced including the screening of all sediment removed from unit excavations utilizing a mesh size of 3.18 mm. In addition to typical archaeological artifact classes such as bone, pottery, and stone, metallurgical artifacts collected included metal, slag, refractory materials, ore, and mineral samples. Care was taken to recover all materials that may have been related to technological processes used at the site.

Sediments encountered in excavation were characterized by color, texture, structure, and consistency; this allowed for the observation of sequences of deposition and disturbance. Features were excavated separately from unit excavations and were documented in plan and profile views. General plan views of the facility were drawn after each contemporary work surface or large-scale depositional event was fully exposed. For a more detailed discussion of the methods structuring the excavation of the metallurgical facility at Paa-ko, the reader is referred to various reports by Mark Lycett (1997, 1999, 2000, 2001, 2004).

DATING THE WORKSHOP

The ceramic assemblage recovered from the workshop follows the distribution of ceramic types identified across the site by Nelson, Lambert, and the University of Chicago excavations. Of the diagnostic types present, late glaze, early glaze, and carbon-painted white ware comprise the assemblage. There is not a significant representation of other regional types (mineral painted white wares) or later material (eighteenth- or nineteenth-century types) associated with the workshop. This is consistent with Lambert's analysis and suggests that the workshop was constructed and used during the historical occupation of the Pueblo (Lycett, personal communication 2017).

For the most part, features and surfaces within the workshop contain types associated with both the prehistoric and historical occupation. This mixing is probably a result of prehistoric midden material being incorporated into the historical construction. Historical vessel forms and late glaze ceramics were recovered from metallurgical features, suggesting their use in feature operations. Basic wall and surface construction practices are consistent with those elements found within the historical component of the pueblo as a whole.

Twelve radiocarbon samples were submitted for analysis from material recovered from features and surfaces in the workshop (see Table 5.1). The samples consisted of 11 wood charcoal samples and one corn cob. Six samples were recovered from five separate contexts on the Eastern Terrace. Beta-115791 and Beta-115792 were samples of wood charcoal collected from a charcoal lens separating the upper and lower surfaces in 97E/-172N/F1; Beta-124325 consists of wood charcoal from a possible post hole; and Beta-124326 was a single corn cob from level 2 of 101E/-170N/F1, the linear furnace feature with associated iron artifacts and late glaze ceramic bowl fragments (Lycett 1998). Beta-146405 consisted of incompletely charred wood charcoal from the basal level of 101E/-168N/F2, adjacent to the northern

end of 101E/-170N/F1. Beta-146404 consisted of wood charcoal recovered from the base of 100E/-1168N/F1, a T-shaped masonry trench partially underlying the northern wall of the Eastern Terrace. When all six samples are considered in terms of their calibrated age range at two standard deviations, five of the six overlap significantly, suggesting a mid-seventeenth-century date. The calibrated range of Beta-115792 is significantly older than the known occupation of the pueblo and is clearly an outlier in the sample (Figure 5.2). Although Beta-146405 exhibits significant overlap with the majority of the samples, multiple calibrated age ranges, possibly due to root contamination, make it difficult to interpret.

Six samples from six distinct contexts were collected and analyzed from the Western Terrace. Beta-208450 consisted of a single piece of wood charcoal recovered from a charcoal lens adjacent to the upper terrace retaining wall in Feature 90E/-163N/F1, Level 2. Beta-208451 was a single piece of wood charcoal recovered from the base of Feature 89E/-170/F3, a pit feature adjacent to the furnace base, Feature 90E/-169N/F1. Beta-208452 was a bulk sample of wood charcoal recovered from an ashy surface associated with Feature 89E/-170N/F1 beneath collapsed adobe elements. Beta-208453 consisted of a single piece of wood charcoal recovered from the profile of 89E/-168N/F1, Level 1, a charcoal lens at the base of the north wall of the Western Terrace. Beta-208454 was a bulk wood charcoal sample recovered from 90E/-163N/F1, Level 3, a series of interdigitated silt loam and charcoal laminations at the base of the Northern Exterior Area. Beta-208455 was a bulk wood charcoal sample from Feature 88E/-170N/F3, Level 1, a D-shaped pit cut into Surface 7.

Three of the six samples are consistent with the date rage represented by the Eastern Terrace samples, Beta-208450, Beta-208453, and Beta-208454, all recovered from charcoal lens distributions. The two samples recovered from pits excavated into the interior of the workshop exhibit an earlier calibrated range (Beta-208451, Beta-208455). Beta-208452 overlaps both the seventeenth-century and earlier calibrated ranges.

Taken as a whole, 9 of the 12 samples correspond with a mid-seventeenth-century date range, consistent with the other archaeological indicators. Only one radiocarbon sample contained intercepts that post-dated the known occupation of the site; three samples exhibited intercepts that corresponded to the earlier occupation; and one outlier predated the known occupation significantly.

Table 5.1. Radiocarbon Samples from the Metallurgical Workshop

Sample Number	Material	Provenience	Date Range
Beta-115791	Wood charcoal	97E/--172N/F1, charcoal layer separating upper and lower surfaces of the Eastern Terrace	350 +/- 50 BP
Beta-115792	Wood charcoal	97E/--172N/F1, charcoal layer separating upper and lower surfaces of the Eastern Terrace	870 +/- 100 BP
Beta-124325	Wood charcoal	101E/-169N/F1, post hole, Eastern Terrace	310 +/- 50 BP
Beta-124326	Corn cob	101E/-170N/F1, linear metallurgical feature, Eastern Terrace	380 +/- 50 BP
Beta-146404	Wood charcoal	100E/-168N/F1, T-shaped metallurgical feature, Eastern Terrace	330 +/- 60 BP
Beta-146405	Charred wood	101E/-168N/F2, depression at northern end of 101E/-170N/F1, Eastern Terrace	260 +/-50 BP
Beta-208450	Wood charcoal	90E/-163N/F1, charcoal lens, Western Terrace	320 +/-40 BP
Beta-208451	Wood charcoal	89E/-170N/F3, pit adjacent to furnace base 90E/-169N/F1, Western Terrace	490 +/-40 BP
Beta-208452	Wood charcoal	89E/-170N/F1, ashy surface beneath adobe elements, Western Terrace	480 +/-60 BP
Beta-208453	Wood charcoal	89E/-168N/F1, charcoal lens at base of north wall, Western Terrace	320 +/-50 BP
Beta-208454	Wood charcoal	90E/-163N/F1, charcoal lens at base of Northern Exterior Area	400 +/- 50 BP
Beta-208455	Wood charcoal	88E/-170N/F3, D-shaped pit cut into surface 7, Western Terrace	520 +/- 50 BP

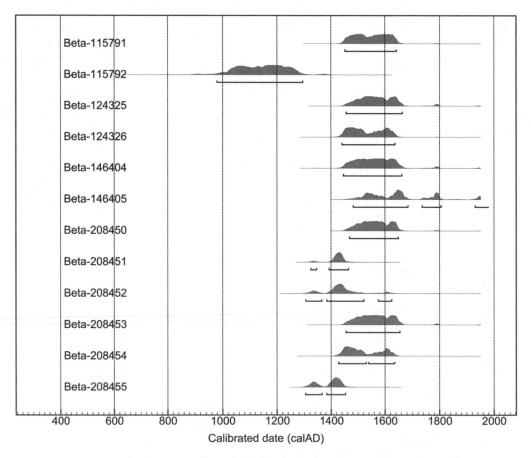

Figure 5.2. Calibrated date ranges for radiocarbon samples recovered from the workshop. OxCal plot generated from OxCal v4.3.2, developed by Bronk Ramsey (2017), accessed online November 1, 2017, using the r:5 IntCal13 atmospheric curve (Reimer et al. 2013).

CHAPTER SIX

Construction and Use History of the Metallurgical Facility: The Archaeological Evidence

The metallurgical facility was first encountered during the 1996 field season's surface collection and mapping program.[*] It was originally identified as a U-shaped masonry terrace located adjacent to the southeastern corner of the historical plaza. Two noticeable concentrations of slag and copper carbonate ore were on the southern edge of the eastern and western perimeters of the facility. Excavation of the facility began in 1997 and continued until 2005.

When the base of the deposits was identified, the facility was found to cover an area of approximately 165 square meters and consisted of two primary terraces, a southern one and a more restricted northern one. At some point in its history, the Southern Terrace was enclosed in a rectilinear masonry structure that defined interior and exterior areas of the workshop. Low masonry and adobe walls internally divided the terraces as well. Multiple construction and repair episodes were recognized in the superimposition of features related to the metallurgical technology and in dumping activities. Wall construction, the location of features, and the degree and method of refurbishing of work surfaces within the terraces is reminiscent of construction practices observed in the historical component of the pueblo. In particular, the maintenance of work surfaces is suggestive of the method of plaza resurfacing observed in the excavations of those features.

Repeated maintenance and reworking of the deposits associated with both terraces has created complex patterning across the facility as a whole. Post-depositional disturbance has also altered the coherence of the deposits. A major disturbance to the integrity of the deposits associated with the facility was due to a 6-m- to 7-m-wide, backfilled trench that was not associated with either Nelson's or the WPA excavations. The trench ran the length of the southern terrace and effectively bisects the deposits into western and eastern excavation areas (Figure 6.1). Re-excavation of the trench during the 1997 season revealed post-1940 material, which suggests a similar date for the original trench excavation. This undocumented excavation destroyed more than a quarter of the facility and made it impossible to establish a direct correspondence between Eastern and Western terrace segments.

Surface and wall construction, the intensity of use and re-use of the facility, and general artifact classes, were comparable among all excavation areas. The diversity of features found within the facility, the type and density of artifacts associated with metallurgy, and their patterning across the excavation area suggests that there were functional variations in the use of space within the Southern Terrace and between the Southern and Northern terraces. Within the Southern Terrace, features associated with metallurgy in the eastern and western excavation areas were found to be distinct, suggesting a functional differentiation between the two areas.

In addition to features directly related to the functioning of the metallurgical workshop, ancillary features were also found including water runoff and erosion control devices. As indicated by patterns of wall fall, evidence for repair and maintenance activities, and the depth of overburden washed down slope from room blocks north of the metallurgical facility, the terraces were subject to repeated runoff flooding during the facility's operation.

---

[*] This chapter summarizes the data generated during the 1996 through 2005 excavation seasons of the University of Chicago Field project. For a more detailed treatment of the depositional history and general artifact assemblage for the facility see Lycett 1997, 1998, 1999, 2000, 2001, 2002, 2003, 2004.

Figure 6.1. Southern Terrace, showing the Northern Exterior Area, the Western Terrace, Eastern Terrace, and the trench that bisects the facility. Prepared by author.

Wall construction patterns indicate that the facility as a whole underwent at least three major construction and use episodes. When first built, the facility was not contained by a masonry wall, but may have had a more ephemeral boundary. This is suggested by the presence of post holes around features encountered near the base of the facility in the western excavation area. The rectilinear plan of the facility was formalized in one construction episode well after most of the major features related to metallurgical processing were already established including furnaces in both excavation areas. Metallurgical activity in the Northern Exterior Area was also enclosed by masonry, with the construction of the northern retaining wall, an extension of the west wall of the terrace, and another north-south wall that abutted the northern terrace retaining wall and

extended to the north wall of the Southern Terrace (Figure 6.1). The Northern Exterior Area was repeatedly rebuilt. The east face of the west wall in this area appears to have collapsed on multiple occasions and the Northern Exterior Area's retaining wall exhibited multiple construction episodes and evidence of stress due to water flow from upslope areas.

The interior of the Western Terrace appears to have been used more intensively than the Eastern Terrace, resulting in seven distinct surface formation episodes. This may indicate a slightly longer period of use for the interior of the Western Terrace, or a more intensive practice that resulted in the deposition and preservation of surfacing episodes. Smelting activities appear to have been concentrated on this half of the facility and may account for the palimpsests

Figure 6.2. Eastern Terrace, lower surface and associated features. From Lycett 1999.

of burned surfaces that were found. The surfaces were most often defined by their degree of heat alteration or compaction.

EASTERN TERRACE EXCAVATIONS, FEATURES, AND SURFACES

Excavation of the metallurgical facility began on the eastern half of the southern terrace in 1997, initially as an exploration of the trench disturbance bisecting the terrace. Two 2-m by 2-m units were excavated along the long axis of the trench in the interior of the Eastern Terrace in the attempt to determine the depth of disturbance and to locate any intact deposits along the eastern edge of the trench. After the removal of disturbed sediment, excavators encountered a stone alignment associated with interdigitated matrices of burned silt and charcoal. Excavation expanded to the east and north, exposing the uppermost

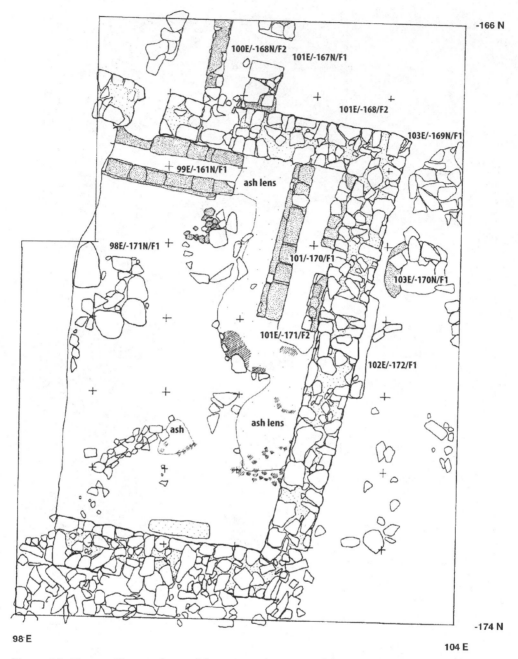

Figure 6.3. Eastern Terrace, base of deposits and associated features. From Lycett 1999.

deposits associated with metal working on this side of the terrace (Lycett 1999, 2000).

During the 1998 season, the uppermost courses of the east and south masonry walls of the Southern Terrace were exposed (Figure 6.2). The lower surface defined in 1997 was discontinuous to the east but appeared to be associated with a furnace (Feature 101E/-171N/F1). The lower surface adjacent to Feature 101E/-171N/F1 contained abundant charcoal flecking and ferrous inclusions. The overlapping of the lower and upper surface in the northeast corner of

the facility may have been a smaller furnace or a small combustion feature (97E/-172N/F1).

South of the combustion feature, a concentration of vitrified material and charcoal was found on the lower surface. The material was particularly dense in the south-eastern corner of the terrace, adjacent to the intersection of the east and south walls. The material was associated with a low mound of oxidized sediment. Little slag or crystalline material associated with metal was present in this accumulation. Rather, the material consisted of altered

Figure 6.4. Overview of Eastern Terrace: furnace features 97E/-172N/F1 and 101E/-170N/F1, base of excavations. Photo by the author.

adobe block or adobe surfacing material. Some of the vitrified material included a highly fluid glass, similar to lead glass that was observed elsewhere on the terrace. White accretions on the surface of some of this material tested positive for lead. Like the vitrified material recovered in combustion feature 97E/-172N/F1, this material was highly fractured. It probably was not formed in this location but was deposited there, perhaps for reuse in an additional smelting or refining process. In addition to this accumulation, an irregularly shaped shallow pit (101E/-172N/F1) was cut into the lower surface. It contained a high density of metal artifacts including iron and sheet copper.

The earliest metallurgical activity on the Eastern Terrace included a series of adobe and masonry structures (Figure 6.3). Though similar in form, these structures had different stratigraphies, degrees of heat alteration, and artifact assemblages, which suggests that they differed in function. Ventilation systems incorporated into the facility appear to have been more formally constructed in this earliest stage than the one associated with the combustion feature (97E/-172N/F1), which dates to the most recent period of use.

Combustion Feature and Associated Ventilation System: 97E/-172N/F1

The most recent period of use in the Eastern Terrace deposits was focused on a combustion feature (97E/-172N/F1) that had a ventilation system built into the uppermost course of the terrace's north wall (Figure 6.4). The system used a kiva-style deflector and ventilator shaft to provide draft for a combustion area that consisted of a low mound of interdigitated layers of burned earth and charcoal. The feature extended 6 meters in length, north to south, and was 2.2 meters wide (Figure 6.5). The southern edge of the feature was defined by a single-course masonry alignment with a small, sloped opening, presumably to facilitate ventilation from the south. The western edge of the feature had slumped into the trench; it consisted of a single course of unmodified sandstone pieces. To the east, no formal containment existed; the edge of the feature was defined by the termination of the mounded area and associated stratigraphy.

Figure 6.6 shows a cross section of the feature along the -171N unit row, at the southern end of the mound. Two burned surfaces, each capped by a stratum of nearly

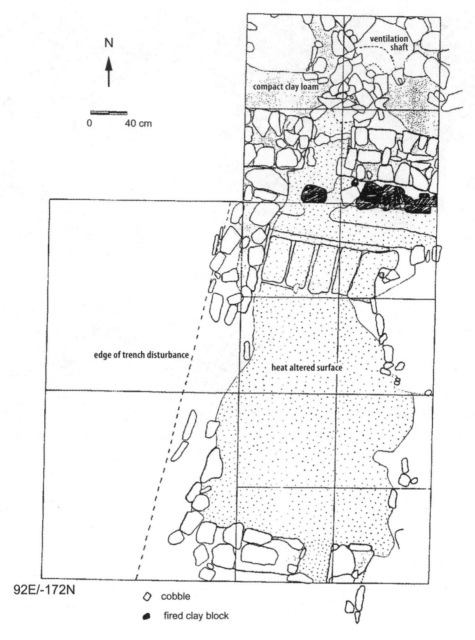

Figure 6.5. Feature 97E/-172N/F1: combustion feature and associated ventilation system. From Lycett 1998.

pure charcoal, can be seen in the profile. The uppermost surface was in turn capped by a burned, silty loam. This combustion feature is similar to charcoal accumulation features excavated in the Western Terrace and the Northern Exterior Area, although those features lacked ventilation systems. Ventilation systems were, however, defined in other features in the Eastern Terrace.

Vitrified material, slag, copper metal, and late glaze ware ceramics were recovered in moderate to high densities from Feature 97E/-172N/F1. The slag associated with the combustion feature contains minerals and glassy matrices that were probably produced through lead smelting and refining, although the predominant metal recovered consisted of worked sheet copper. A large accumulation of litharge (PbO), was recovered from this feature as well, suggesting an attempt at silver recovery using cupellation.

The vitrified material occurred in Feature 97E/-172N/F1 and on the upper and lower surfaces associated with it. This

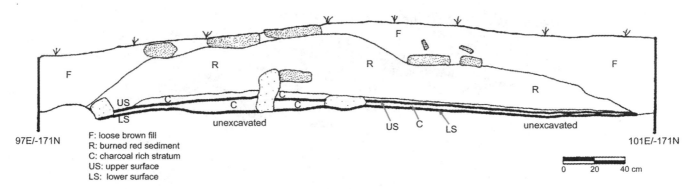

Figure 6.6. Profile of combustion Feature 97E/-172N/F1. From Lycett 1998.

F: loose brown fill
R: burned red sediment
C: charcoal rich stratum
US: upper surface
LS: lower surface

97E/-171N

101E/-171N

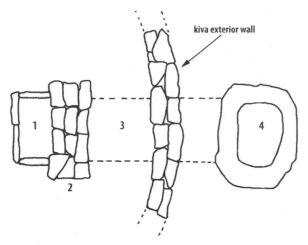

Figure 6.7. Kiva II ventilation system: (1) fire box, (2) free-standing masonry deflector, (3) ventilation trench, and (4) ventilation shaft. From Lambert 1954:35.

material is primarily an altered ceramic, possibly adobe block or a surfacing material. It is highly fractured and appears to have been redeposited from elsewhere. Small amounts of a gossan ore, consisting of copper carbonates, quartz, and iron hydroxides, were recovered from the feature but not in any great frequency compared to other areas of the facility.

The ventilation structure associated with Feature 97E/-172N/F1 is similar to a kiva ventilation system excavated by Lambert (1954:34–37) that is located in the northwest corner of the historical plaza (Figure 6.7). The area surrounding this ventilation system was highly heat altered, exhibiting heavy compaction and a highly oxidized appearance. This ventilation system appears to be an adaptation of local pyrotechnical knowledge applied to an introduced technological activity.

Furnace with Associated Ventilation System: Feature 101E/-170N/F1

Feature 101E/-170N/F1, a furnace, was a free-standing bin made up of two parallel adobe walls that were one to two bricks wide (Figure 6.8). The walls were 2.0 m long and were separated by a 0.40-m gap. It was built onto the substrate. The adobe walls were composed of bricks that were not standardized in size, indicating that they were not made in molds (Lycett 1999). The western adobe wall was two bricks wide and highly heat altered. The array of colors associated with temperature and atmospheric conditions of the furnace was preserved. The eastern wall was one brick wide and built in three courses on a foundation of large stone slabs. Stone elements capped the eastern wall of the feature across its northern half. The wall abutted the west face of the east wall.

Two superimposed ventilation openings (Features 102E/-170N/F1 and 103E/-170N/F1) were built through the east wall of the terrace opening into the interior of the furnace (Figure 6.9). The lower ventilation opening was capped by a stone lintel that was vitrified along its west face, the interior of the furnace. The feature was constructed before the north terrace wall was built and at some point its northern terminus was filled in to form a foundation for the north terrace wall. The feature's southern end was not enclosed and opened into a semicircular depression (Feature 101E/-172N/F2) that contained the same stratigraphy as the furnace including an abundance of copper sheet metal in its upper levels (Lycett 1999, 2000).

The fill within the feature consisted of two distinct strata. The upper level of the furnace was a loose brown organic fill that contained a high concentration of clay nodules, most likely from the decomposition of the adobe walls. In addition to moderate densities of slag, vitrified material, and ore, numerous metallic artifacts

Figure 6.8. Feature 101E/-170N/F1 with late glaze ware ceramics (indicated by black arrow). Photo by the author.

were present at this level including perforated and incised copper discs, sheet metal, and iron artifacts. The upper level of this feature contained the highest concentration of iron artifacts reported from any excavation conducted at Paa-ko. Included in this assemblage were the remains of iron chain, a lance point, and the fragments of what appear to be a sword. The ceramic assemblage in the upper layer also included several fragments of a Glaze F soup plate and nearly half of a Glaze F bichrome bowl, which dates the fill in the feature to the seventeenth-century occupation (Figure 6.8; Lycett 2000).

At the base of the upper stratum was a layer of completely oxidized, thin sandstone slabs, which disintegrated upon excavation. Immediately below the sandstone, alternating thin layers of ash, charcoal, and silt loam were encountered, although the majority of this stratum was found to be pure ash. The number of metallurgical artifacts declined in this stratum, but the numbers of other artifacts remained high.

Copper sheeting was not recovered from this level. A single radiocarbon assay was conducted on a corn cob with cupules that was recovered from this strata (Beta-124326). It yielded a seventeenth-century date (Figure 5.2; Lycett 2000).

Associated with the lower layer of Feature 101E/-170N/F1 was a thin ash lens that extended west from the furnace's southern terminus to the eastern terminus of a second adobe and masonry bin structure (Feature 99E/-161N/F1). This lens was 2 cm to 4 cm thick, having a greater depth and density adjacent to the southern opening of the furnace. It became progressively thinner to the west and north. Patches of a similar matrix were encountered to the south and southwest as well. Similar to matrices encountered in the lower levels of the Western Terrace, these accumulations appear to be directly related to work surfaces associated with furnaces. The ash matrix established a connection between the two bin features found on the interior of the Eastern Terrace, suggesting a functional

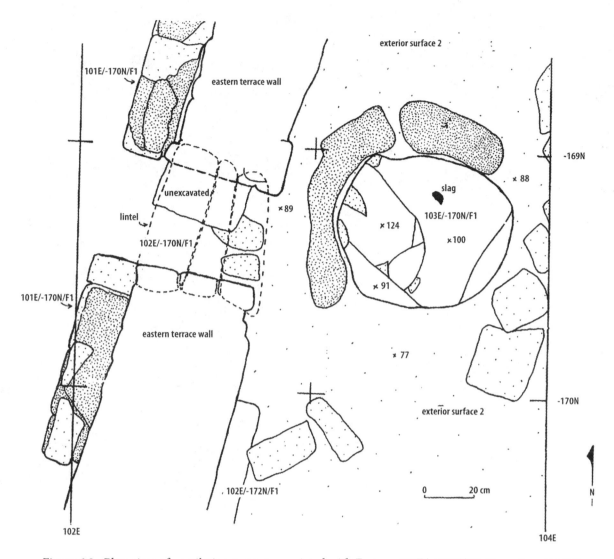

Figure 6.9. Plan view of ventilation system associated with Feature 101E/-170N/F1. From Lycett 1999.

link despite the fact that they appear to have had very different use histories.

Ventilation Shafts: Features 102E/-170N/F1 and 103E/-170N/F1

Two superimposed ventilation systems are associated with Feature 101E/-170N/F1 (Figure 6.9). Built into the east terrace wall and sharing the same inlet tunnel into the feature, the upper ventilation shaft was defined by a gap in the east terrace wall that was capped by four large sandstone slab lintels. The lintels were integral to the East Terrace wall construction. The lintel adjacent to the interior of the furnace exhibited complete vitrification on its western face. The outlet for the upper ventilation shaft was cut into the uppermost exterior surface on the east side of the east wall

of the terrace. The lower ventilation shaft was excavated as a tunnel extending from the interior of the furnace to a circular, adobe and stone-lined outlet, 60 cm to 70 cm in diameter, that was approximately 1.5 m east of the interior of the furnace. This construction is highly reminiscent of kiva ventilation shafts (Figures 6.7 and 6.9).

The two ventilation systems were not contemporary, as their exterior outlets were associated with two superimposed surfaces. The lower ventilation shaft was cut into an exterior surface extending throughout the northern and eastern exterior areas of the terrace. This surface was highly heat altered, appearing red-orange through oxidation, and was the surface upon which the eastern and northern walls of the masonry terrace were constructed. This lower exterior surface was capped by an additional

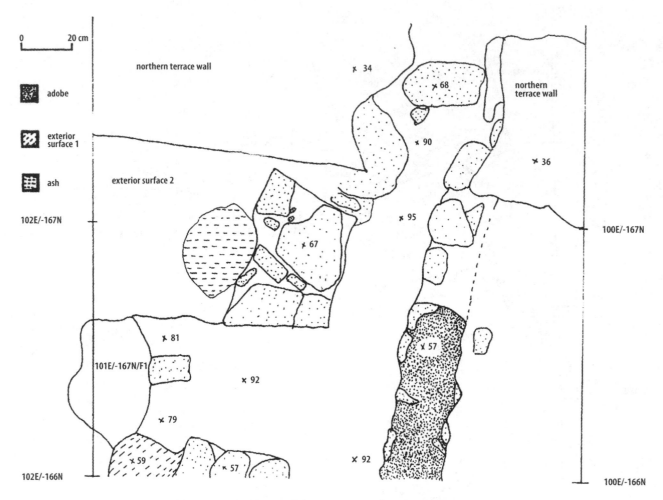

Figure 6.10. Feature 100E/-168N/F2 and associated features. From Lycett 2001.

heat-altered matrix associated with the outlet of the upper ventilation shaft of furnace Feature 101E/-170N/F1.

Masonry Bin: Feature 99E/-169N/F1

No ventilation system was associated with this masonry bin (Feature 99E/-169N/F1), and the feature did not have the same evidence for heat alteration as furnace Feature 101E/-170N/F1. Feature 99E/-169N/F1 consisted of a 1.65-m by 0.22-m bin that was oriented east-west. It was made of parallel stone walls that were heavily mortared with adobe and capped by highly burned adobe blocks. Based on its association with the ash lens extending from the furnace and its location at the base of the metallurgical facility's deposits, the stone-walled bin is thought to have been contemporary with furnace Feature 101E/-170N/F1.

Three stratigraphic layers were associated with the fill and function of the feature. The uppermost layer represented the capping of the feature by the construction and use of the lower surface associated with combustion Feature 97E/-172N/F1. The bin appears to have been intentionally filled with a loose silty loam and chunks of crumbled adobe. This capped a discontinuous layer of organic sediment. Very little metallurgical material was associated with the bin. Feature 99E/-169N/F1 was probably a storage facility associated with the furnace, although it contained no evidence for the storage of charcoal, ore, slag, iron, or copper. The feature may have been used to store an organic material such as wood that was used for some metallurgical processes.

T-shaped Masonry Furnace: Feature 100E/-168N/F2

This furnace (Figure 6.10) was most similar to Feature 101E/-170N/F1, although it was primarily of masonry and adobe mortar construction, similar to the bin Feature 99E/-169N/F1. It was situated in a comparable stratigraphic position to the furnace and masonry bin, although it was located outside of the masonry-defined space of the terrace interior. Feature 100E/-168N/F2 predated the construction of the masonry terrace walls. Running north-south, the feature measured 1.45 m by 0.30 m in size. It was probably slightly longer; the northern terminus of the feature extended beyond the area excavated. The furnace's western wall was a single-element-wide stone wall that was three to four courses in height, with abundant adobe mortar separating the stone elements. Its eastern wall was 50 cm away from the western wall. The eastern wall was of two-element-wide stone construction. Within the gap in the eastern wall of the feature was a shallow, subrectangular, charcoal-filled pit (Feature 101E/-167N/F1); it may have functioned as part of a ventilation system.

Feature 100E/-168N/F2 was partially filled with construction debris to create the exterior surface associated with the combustion Feature 97E/-172N/F1. Below the fill layer, Feature 100E/-168N/F2 contained layers of ash, charcoal, and a sandy loam matrix that were probably associated with the function of the feature. Metallurgical material recovered from these layers included copper carbonate, copper sulfide ore, and vitrified material. This feature was not as highly burned as Feature 101E/-170N/F1, but it was the only feature on this side of the southern terrace that was closely associated with copper-bearing ore.

Base of Eastern Terrace Deposits

At the base of the Eastern Terrace deposits was a compact, undulating, red-brown, silty loam matrix that contained charcoal flecking. It sloped to the south and southwest, following the slope of the natural substrate upon which the facility was built. This surface did not appear to be prepared, although large stone alignments were encountered that followed the general slope. These were not associated with metallurgical activity. The basal matrix differed from that encountered at the base of excavations associated with the Western Terrace in that the latter deposits contained a much higher density of metallurgical remains and was directly above the natural substrate of the hill upon which the terraces were constructed.

WESTERN TERRACE EXCAVATIONS AND FEATURES

Excavation of the Western Terrace took place between 1999 and 2005. In 1999, seven contiguous 1-m by 1-m units were opened at the southern end of the terrace in order to determine if intact deposits existed on that side of the facility. Intact deposits were encountered. In addition, the north face of the south wall and the east face of the west wall were found to be well preserved. Deposits encountered were comparable to the upper surface exposure of the Eastern Terrace, although a higher density and more diverse assemblage of ore was recovered from this area.

The 2000 season proceeded from this exposure in an attempt to define the horizontal extent of the facility. The excavation area exposed the upper courses of the north terrace retaining wall and deposits. It allowed us to observe variability in wall construction across the Western Terrace area, as well as variability in deposition between interior and exterior areas of the terrace. The interior of the terrace was excavated to expose an eroded adobe surface, possibly the last use surface of the facility (Figure 6.11). At that level the interior of the smelting facility extended from the southern masonry wall to the Northern Terrace retaining wall. Although an extensive area, metallurgical material was recovered in fairly light densities at this exposure, in contrast with the high density of materials encountered in surfaces 2 through 7, which are described below.

Masonry Construction of the Terrace

Construction of the masonry boundary of the terrace exhibits at least two construction episodes. Masonry walls were constructed of sandstone blocks, two to three elements wide, with adobe mortar incorporated in some walls. The preserved wall height varies from five to seven courses across the terrace. A later, less formal construction episode was apparent for all of the terrace retaining walls. On the Western Terrace, the north wall did not exhibit this latter construction phase. Instead, the west wall had a constructed gap that was more than 2 m wide. The gap was located 2 meters north of its intersection with the south wall of the terrace. This gap was partially infilled with adobe as part of the last phase of wall construction on the terrace. North of the intersection of the west wall and the north wall, the west wall widened to a meter in width, becoming an apparent core and veneer structure extending to the north and abutting the North Terrace retaining wall. This core and veneer wall was enigmatic but appears to have been a late construction that was only two courses high. It may have been a retaining feature built to help mitigate against the slumping of the west wall into the Northern Exterior area. Similar structures were built on the northern terrace to prevent soil flow into the terrace interior.

The walls defining the Northern Exterior Area, including the north wall, the west wall north of the gap, the Northern Terrace retaining wall and the east wall of the

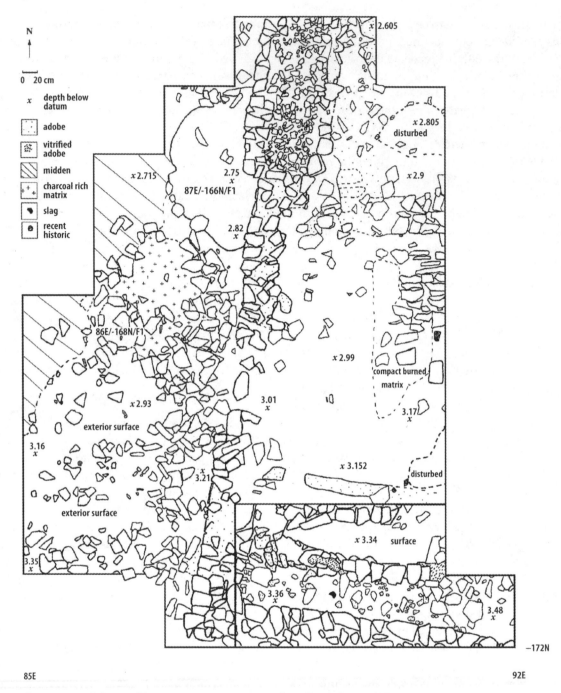

N

0 20 cm

x depth below datum

adobe

vitrified adobe

midden

charcoal rich matrix

slag

recent historic

x 2.605

x 2.805 disturbed

x 2.715

2.75 *x*
87E/-166N/F1

x 2.9

2.82 *x*

86E/-168N/F1

x 2.99

compact burned matrix

x 2.93

exterior surface

3.01 *x*

3.17 *x*

3.16 *x*

x 3.21

x 3.152

disturbed

exterior surface

x 3.34 surface

3.35 *x*

3.36 *x*

3.48 *x*

−172N

85E   92E

Figure 6.11. Western Terrace interior, upper surface. From Lycett 2001.

Northern Exterior area, were built on the natural substrate of the hill. This substrate also formed part of the foundation for the eastern room block of the historical plaza. The substrate appears to have been partially excavated or prepared to provide a level surface for wall construction. The interior of the terrace south of the north wall also appears to have been partially excavated to create a level working surface. The north terrace retaining wall and the east face of the west wall in the Northern Exterior Area contained evidence for multiple construction episodes, possibly repairs needed due to damage caused by slope wash. The Northern Terrace retaining wall may also have been part of an earlier construction episode that predated the metallurgical facility.

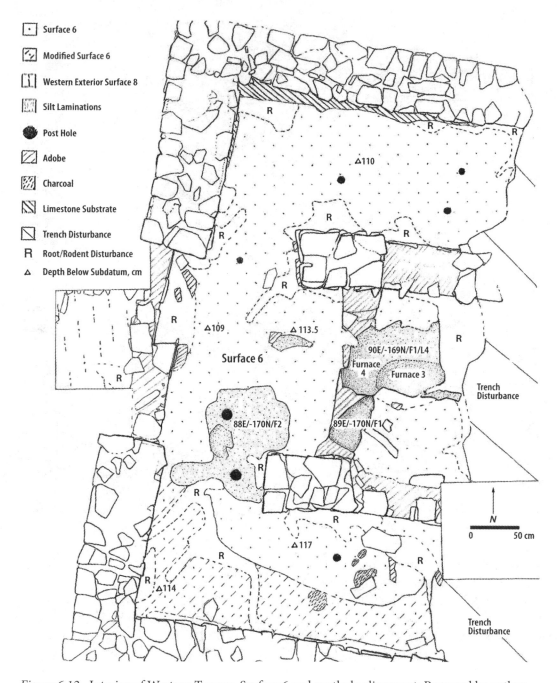

Figure 6.12. Interior of Western Terrace, Surface 6 and posthole alignment. Prepared by author.

The stone wall in the southern half of the Western Terrace appears to have been built on the plan of an earlier construction, which was indicated by a pattern of postholes in interior Surfaces 6 and 7. These may represent the construction of wind breaks or a shade structure (Figure 6.12). Stone element accumulations on the northwest edge of interior Surface 6 capped the postholes that encircled the intensive use area associated with furnace Feature 90E/-169N/F1, suggesting that this delimitation of space was, to some extent, formally construed.

Interior Surfacing Episodes

The interior of the Western Terrace contained a series of surface building and maintenance episodes capped by multiple surfaces formed through the use of pyrotechnical features. The deposits were reworked many times over the

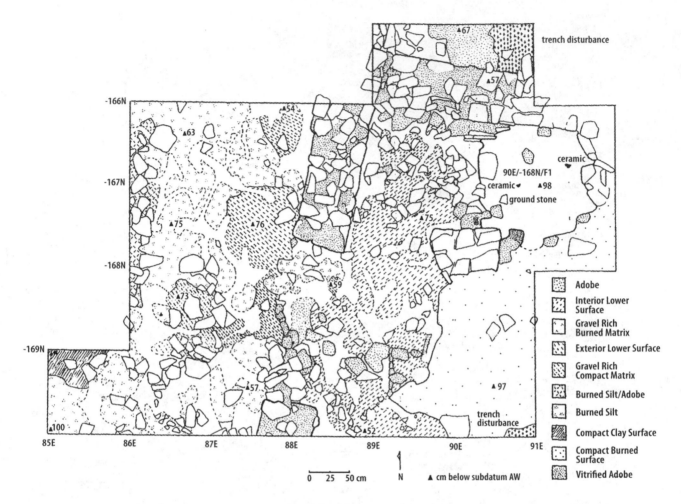

Figure 6.13. Western Terrace, interior Surface 3 and furnace Feature 90E/-168N/F1. From Lycett 2004.

use history of the facility. Wall collapse rubble and material from feature dismantling overlaid and partially disrupted earlier deposits. Rodent disturbance was extensive, particularly in the upper levels.

Seven surfacing episodes were documented in the interior of the Western Terrace. Surface 1 was encountered directly below the overburden that capped the metallurgical deposits on the terrace. It extended across the interior from the south masonry wall of the terrace to the north terrace retaining wall. Interior Surfaces 2 and 3 were restricted to the interior of the terrace between the north and south walls and were associated with the functioning of furnace Feature 90E/-166N/F1 (Figure 6.13). Interior Surfaces 4 and 5 were encountered directly below interior Surface 3 and were associated with the intensive use of furnace Feature 90E/-168N/F1 (Figure 6.14).

Interior Surface 6 was encountered at the base of the foundation walls supporting the construction of the first configuration of furnace Feature 90E/-168N/F1. A posthole pattern in this surface suggests that a wooden perimeter delimited the work space associated with the interior of the terrace during the initial use of the furnace.

Interior Surface 7 was associated with the first development of the terrace and the possible furnace Feature 88E/-170N/F3. It was restricted to the southern half of the interior of the terrace, from the south wall of the terrace to the stub wall located south of the north wall (Figure 6.15). This surface contained a different set of posthole placements from those encountered on interior Surface 6.

Furnace Feature 90E/-168N/F1 and Interior Surfaces 2 and 3

Interior Surfaces 2 and 3 (Figure 6.13) were highly disturbed by rodent activity along the western half the facility. Relatively intact deposits were associated with the use of furnace Feature 90E/-168N/F1. These surfaces and the use

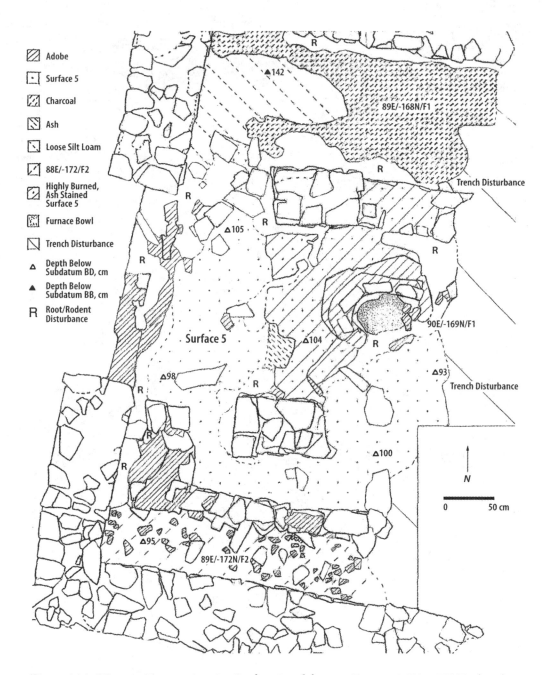

Adobe

Surface 5

Charcoal

Ash

Loose Silt Loam

88E/-172/F2

Highly Burned, Ash Stained Surface 5

Furnace Bowl

Trench Disturbance

△ **Depth Below Subdatum BD, cm**

▲ **Depth Below Subdatum BB, cm**

R **Root/Rodent Disturbance**

Figure 6.14. Western Terrace, interior Surface 5 and furnace Feature 90E/-169N/F1, bowl 2. Prepared by author.

of this feature contain the most complete evidence for the processing of galena-bearing ores and subsequent lead metal production found at the site. Galena processing in Feature 90E/-168N/F1 may have been the source of the glassy, lead-rich material recovered from the lower surface of the Eastern Terrace.

Furnace Feature 90E/-168N/F1 was a 1.69-m by 1.24-m subrectangular depression situated next to the south face

of the north terrace wall. The feature was associated with a highly oxidized matrix, vitrified adobe, and a well-preserved section of fallen stone wall. The elements of the wall segment were positioned vertically and were at least 10 elements long, filling the entire depression of the feature. Excavation revealed that the North Terrace wall was present along the -166N unit row, yet this section of wall fall appears to have originated from a free-standing wall

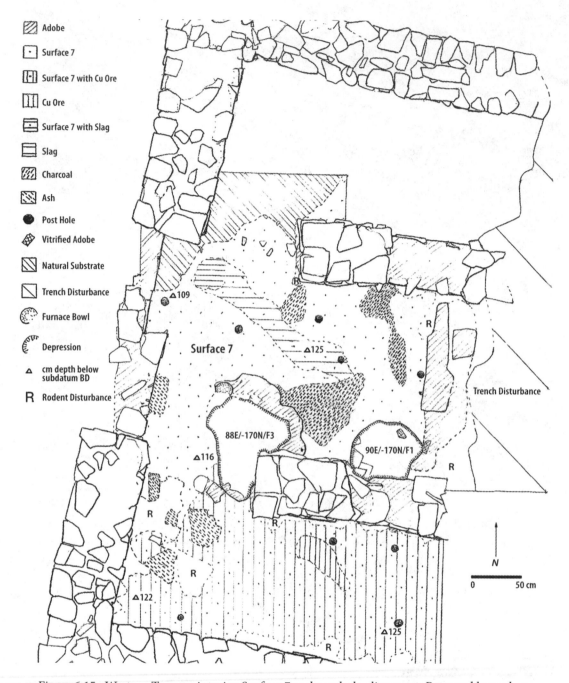

Adobe
Surface 7
Surface 7 with Cu Ore
Cu Ore
Surface 7 with Slag
Slag
Charcoal
Ash
Post Hole
Vitrified Adobe
Natural Substrate
Trench Disturbance
Furnace Bowl
Depression
cm depth below subdatum BD
R Rodent Disturbance

Figure 6.15. Western Terrace, interior Surface 7 and posthole alignment. Prepared by author.

stub associated with the south end of Feature 90E/-168N/ F1 (Figure 6.13).

This wall stub or masonry column was matched by a similar construction to the south, adjacent to furnaces associated with earlier use phases of the facility. These columns probably supported construction related to the functioning of furnaces as a heat shield or bellows foundation, or as a further support for the adobe refractory material used

in the construction of furnace shafts. Two heat-altered adobe elements were found in association with this wall stub. Along the footing's north face was a partially reduced adobe block fragment. A highly vitrified adobe block was found at the level of the lower interior surface adjacent to the east face of the footing. Both blocks exhibited a high degree of heat alteration along their eastern faces and exhibited vitrification on their interior walls. All of this is evidence of a high-temperature reducing process and a lower temperature-oxidizing process that would result in the deposition of a lead oxide crust (see Chapter 7 for a more detailed analysis of the material found in the furnace).

Feature 90E/-168N/F1 was nearly square, bounded on the south by the wall stub and a ring of compact matrix that extended around the features southeastern edge. The feature's western edge consisted of large stone elements incorporated within an adobe matrix. To the east, a similar boundary apparently existed, although this part of the feature was damaged by the trench that bisected the terrace. The feature was bounded on the north by the north terrace wall, three to four courses of which were exposed within the feature. The feature extended 32 cm below interior Surface 3.

The fill in Feature 90E/-168N/F1 consisted of wall fall elements above a surface of a friable, heat-altered, silty clay loam matrix with incorporated charcoal. This surface exhibited a higher degree of heat alteration adjacent to the north wall associated with two highly burned, gray-black, adobe blocks. These were found directly north of the vitrified adobe block on the southern exterior of the feature. This suggests that the feature was an area where intense, higher heat was focused. A similar pattern of heat alteration was seen in the furnace Feature 101E/-170N/F1 in association with the air intake from a ventilator shaft. No such opening was found in the north wall of Feature 90E/-168N/F1. Charcoal was associated with the feature in its southeastern corner.

The feature contained 1.6 kg of a lead-bearing ore that contained galena. Most of the ore was recovered from its southwestern quadrant, within the matrix associated with the wall fall. Slag densities were light, and no metallic lead was recovered from the feature, suggesting that the concentration of ore may have been a cache of some sort. Lead isotope analysis conducted on the galena from this feature is discussed in detail in Chapter 7.

Below the silty clay loam surface in Feature 90E/-168N/F1 was a more compact, more highly burned surface. The surface was gray-brown, like the heat-altered adobe blocks found on and above it. This surface articulated with the north wall and sloped up to the south to articulate with the wall stub foundation and the vitrified adobe along the southeast edge of the feature.

Wall-fall slabs still embedded within the sides of the feature were removed in this level. Slabs located in the southwest quadrant of the feature were burned on the edges that had been in contact with the lower surface of the feature. In this same area, surfaces of burned adobe

contained a semi-vitreous granular material. Fragments of this material that were analyzed optically through spot testing and by SEM-EDX suggest that it was primarily a lead mineral, probably a lead oxide. Two unusual conglomerates of charcoal fragments, cuprite, and metallic copper were found in the base of the feature. These samples were also submitted for lead isotope analysis (see Chapter 7).

Feature 90E/-168N/F1 did not bear close resemblance to other metallurgical features on the terrace. Though rectilinear in shape like the features in the Eastern Terrace, its degree of heat alteration, predominant use of stone masonry elements instead of adobe, and its association with lead-bearing ore, smelted copper, and unusual heat-altered materials suggests a different function from the Eastern Terrace features. Feature 90E/-168N/F1 may have been contemporary with the combustion Feature 97E/-172N/F1 on the Eastern Terrace and may represent one of the last furnaces constructed at the facility.

Interior Surfaces 4, 5, and 6 and Associated Features

The highest intensity of use for the Western Terrace was associated with the deposition of Surfaces 5 and 6 (Figure 6.12 and 6.14). Surface 4 appears to have been a leveling event where features heavily associated with Surfaces 5 and 6 were capped by adobe surfacing material and tabular sandstone elements. Surfaces 5 and 6 were related to the functioning of furnace Feature 90E/-169N/F1 and other features were part of furnace operation. Surface 5 in particular exhibited intense use. It was an accumulation of overlapping layers of heat-altered sediment and ash associated with furnace Feature 90E/-169N/F1.

Furnace Feature 90E/-169N/F1

Feature 90E/-169N/F1 consisted of a series of superimposed, oval furnace bases or bowls associated with interior Surfaces 5 and 6 (Figure 6.16). It was initially defined as a conical, flat-topped adobe collar rising 24 cm from interior Surface 5 that surrounded and encased a J-shaped, three-course-high alignment of sandstone elements. Surface 4 capped the feature. The sandstone and adobe collar was lined with a 5-cm-thick coating of a compact, heat-altered, reddish-brown adobe. Feature 90E/-169N/F1 appeared to have been positioned centrally in relation to the wall stubs on the interior of the terrace and was associated with a concentration of heat-altered adobe deposited on Surface 5 (Feature 89E/-170N/F1).

Four furnace bowl construction episodes were documented. Furnace bowls 1 and 2 were most likely associated

Figure 6.16. Western Terrace, Feature 90E/-169N/F1, Surface 5. Photo by the author.

with the use of interior Surface 5. Furnace bowls 3 and 4 were associated with interior Surface 6. Figure 6.17 is a profile showing the stratigraphy related to furnace bowl and collar construction. Table 6.1 describes the strata. The profile documents six strata (1–6), with stratum 4 being a disturbed matrix. Strata 2 and 3 both contained a high density of calcium carbonate nodules. This was true of the construction of the furnace collar as well, identified in profile as Stratum 5. The inclusion (or omission) of calcium carbonate nodules in particular strata within the lining of the furnace most likely indicates a technological practice. Certain materials appear to have been added to adobe used in the smelting terrace as evidenced by the analyses of the thermal properties of adobes recovered from excavation (see Chapter 7).

Level 1 in furnace Feature 90E/-169N/F1 consisted of a burned red-brown silt loam with gravel inclusions that lay on top of the first furnace bowl. The bowl was defined by an ashy, highly burned, charcoal-rich compact silt-clay loam that was light gray to gray in color. It was elliptical in shape, with its long axis oriented to the east northeast. The Level 1 matrix most likely represented either the infilling of the furnace in the construction of interior Surfaces 3 and

4 or an eroded furnace bowl. The ashy matrix defined as the surface of the furnace bowl appeared similar to the fine clay material of a ceramic slip and was found to slope down from the top of the second course of sandstone elements of the furnace collar. Furnace bowl 1 was partially disturbed along the circumference of the bowl interior to the collar. The bowl itself was 41 cm long (southwest-northeast) by 38 cm wide along a southeast to northwest axis. It had an 11-degree slope.

Excavation Level 2 removed furnace bowl 1 to expose a better preserved surface of the same construction, an ashy, highly burned compact silt-clay loam, with a slightly lighter color than furnace bowl 1. This second furnace bowl measured 40 cm by 45 cm, with a similar orientation to furnace bowl 1, but it contained a more dramatic slope of 18 degrees to the south and southeast.

The sandstone and adobe collar associated with furnace bowls 1 and 2 was well preserved along the north and northwest perimeter of the structure. Material similar to the collar construction including adobe material of the same consistency and heat alteration and a tabular sandstone slab was present at a lower stratigraphic level, 20 cm to the east of the furnace. This apparently was a slumped

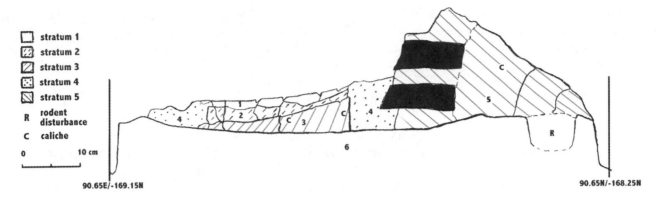

Figure 6.17. Profile of furnace Feature 90E/-169N/F1. Prepared by the author.

Table 6.1. Strata Description of Figure 6.17, Feature 90E/-169N/F1

Strata	Munsell Color	Texture, Structure	Consistency	Inclusions	Boundary
1	5YR 7/2 pinkish gray	Silty loam, platy	Compact	None	Clear
2	2.5YR 5/6 red	Silty loam, platy	Compact	Caliche	Clear
3	2.5YR 5/4, reddish brown	Silty loam, blocky	Compact	Caliche	Clear
4	5YR 5/4, reddish brown	Silty loam, granular	Friable	Gravel	Clear
5	2.5YR 5/6, red	Silty clay, blocky	Compact	Caliche	Clear
6	2.5YR 7/2, pale red	Silty loam, platy	Compact	None	Clear

or partially dismantled section of the collar; it capped a fragment of an amorphous copper nodule (Sample LA162-156). The collar was U-shaped and oriented with the open side to the south-southeast. This open side conformed with the direction of the slopes of furnace bowls 1 and 2. It may have been sealed by adobe at some point, as there were remnants of adobe material in the same alignment as the collar in this area.

Feature 90E/-169N/F1 was cross-sectioned to expose the construction of the furnace as it was defined in surface 5. The profile produced documents the deposition of furnace bowl 2 and the construction of the adobe and stone collar. At the exposure of furnace bowls 3 and 4, excavation proceeded horizontally, exposing the definition of this earlier construction phase associated with surface 6.

Furnace bowls 3 and 4 were excavated in levels 5 and 6 respectively and were most likely associated with interior surface 6. Furnace bowl 3 consisted of a thin resurfacing (1 to 2 cm thick) on top of furnace bowl 4, apparently in order to change the slope of the bowl when the interior diameter of the bowl was reduced. This resurfacing appears to have included the construction of the furnace collar on

surface 5, which reduced the diameter of furnace bowl 4 by half, from 90–100 cm to 45–50 cm. Furnace bowl 4 was also found to contain a much shallower slope than the subsequent bowls, approximately 3 to 5 degrees, and did not have a strong directionality. The remains of an earlier collar construction corresponding to the diameter of furnace bowl 4 was encountered in the excavation of level 4. This was preserved as a slight depression and color variation suggesting that stone or adobe elements were at one point placed in an orientation corresponding to a larger collar arrangement.

All of the furnace-bowl linings appear to have been made from the same material, a very consistent silt loam matrix with no inclusions. Furnace bowls 1 and 2 appear to have been placed on top of two highly fired adobe matrices with calcium-carbonate inclusions deposited to create bowl shapes, orientations, and slopes that were different from bowl 4—the initial furnace construction. The matrices were deposited within a boundary created by the silt clay matrix of the adobe collar built on furnace base 4. This collar reduced the diameter of the original furnace structure by half. The collar for furnace bases 1 through 3 may have been built in stages, as indicated by the vertical layering of adobe matrix from the northern exterior of the profile to the interior of the furnace. Four layers were discernable based on drying cracks in this matrix; the exterior two layers were 5 cm thick and the internal two layers were 10 cm thick. The layer adjacent to the interior of the furnace contained the tabular sandstone elements of the collar.

Although highly heat altered, color comparisons to experimentally refired adobes (see Chapter 7) indicate that none of the in situ remains associated with 90E/-169N/F1 were heated to temperatures above 900°C. This suggests that the furnace operated with lower temperatures than would have been needed to produce the copper products and byproducts of copper metallurgy recovered from the site, as these contain evidence of applied temperatures in excess of 1200°C. Although Feature 90E/-169N/F1 may have had different functions through time, it was most likely used for lower-temperature processes such as lead metal production. Other indications of lead production were present on surface 5 including lead slag, lead ores containing galena, and fragments of lead oxide or lead silicate material associated with heat-altered adobe.

Furnace or Fore Hearth: Feature 89E/-170N/F3

Feature 89E/-170N/F3 was clearly related to the function of furnace Feature 90E/-169N/F1. It consisted of a triangular basin that was 60 cm in length and 32 cm at its widest point. The feature was filled with ash and burned adobe, material that was probably deposited during its use life. The feature was orientated southwest to northeast. Its northernmost extent abuts the southwestern terminus of the adobe and stone collar of Feature 90E/-169N/F1. Excavated in two levels, level 1 exposed an extension of the ashy, burned furnace bowl lining from furnace bowl 2 into the northeastern end of Feature 89E/-170N/F3, suggesting a relationship between these two features. A large adobe brick was exposed along the southern edge of the feature. It was embedded in a dense concentration of ash encountered just below the debris associated with the capping of Surface 5.

Level 2 of Feature 89E/-170N/F3 consisted of an ash concentration that was 10 to 11 cm deep along the west wall of the basin. The ash constituted the majority of material in the feature. Toward the base of the feature, the ash concentration was interspersed with a silty clay loam that contained charcoal inclusions. The adobe brick along the southern edge of the feature capped the clay-rich matrix. The basin itself was excavated into a highly fired adobe and stone wall built on Surface 6 at 90E/-169N/F1. The basin's southern edge was made of stone facing from the southern

wall stub. The rim of the feature consisted of laminations of the highly fired, ash-stained surfaces encountered at the base of the adobe concentration that capped Surface 5. The basin was an unusual shape, nearly triangular, and consisted of a well-defined, compact matrix, that was highly burned and ash stained. The feature was 11 to 15 cm deep. The south and west walls of the basin were well defined, but the east wall appeared to have been dismantled or destroyed by rodent activity and pieces of wall fall from the southern wall stub. The bowl of the basin clearly sloped up along its eastern edge, suggesting that at some point it had a more substantial east wall. Small globular fragments of vitrified material were embedded in the west wall and base of the feature.

Feature 89E/-170N/F3 had at least two use or construction episodes based upon the buildup of the rim along the western edge. The first use or construction phase corresponded with a heat-altered silt and ash accumulation below interior Surface 5. This was capped by the second episode of rim building or surface use that may have been represented by the more extensive burned surface of interior Surface 5.

Feature 89E/-170N/F3 probably functioned in relation to furnace Feature 90E/-169N/F1. Its location adjacent to and below the southern edge of Feature 90E/-169N/F1 suggests that it was used to collect material coming from furnace bowls 1 and 2, acting as a fore hearth. Historical sixteenth- and seventeenth-century European furnaces used basins that were down slope from furnace bowls for the collection of metals and slag (Hoover and Hoover 1950:387). The ash accumulation could have been the remnants of spent fuel from the furnace, suggesting that Feature 89E/-170N/F3 was close to the tap hole of the furnace. The furnace lining that extended from furnace bowl 2 toward the basin may have been a remnant of the tap hole associated with this furnace bowl. Alternatively, the ash concentration may have been part of a different technological practice, perhaps related to cupellation.

Accumulation of Heat-Altered Adobe: 89E/-170N/F1

This feature consisted of a concentration of heat-altered adobe on a highly burned surface that emanated from the boundaries of Feature 90E/-169N/F1 to the 89E unit line, between the north and south stub walls. Initially identified after the removal of interior Surface 3, which was associated with the subrectangular furnace of Feature 90E/-166N/F1, the adobe accumulation appears to have been the remains of an adobe superstructure for furnace Feature 90E/-169N/F1. Feature 89E/-170N/F1 was excavated in two levels. The first level consisted of more than 50 kg of adobe. The adobe pieces exhibited little or no surface vitrification but had a consistency and hue of brick fired in a reduced environment. Artifact densities were low in this level, with some slag (100 g), one piece of a cuprous metal fragment, and 50 g of galena. The artifacts appeared to come from the decomposed adobe matrix, not the adobe brick. They may have been inclusions from within the material used in the construction of interior Surface 4. The adobe brick contained inclusions of calcium carbonate nodules and fibrous plant material as inclusions similar to the intact lining in furnace Feature 90E/-169N/F1. The concentration was immediately above a highly burned ash- and charcoal-rich surface that extended between the stub walls and terminated at 45° angles between the east and southwest edges of the collar of furnace Feature 90E/-169N/F1. This surface was an ash-impregnated, highly burned modification of Surface 5. Within the area covered by the burned surface, the presence of more concentrated ash and charcoal deposits associated with alignments of burnt adobe-like sediments suggest multiple depositional events on this surface including the alternating deposition of an ashy matrix with a highly burned platy silt loam. A portion of this latter matrix was associated with the triangular furnace or fore hearth Feature 89E/-170N/F3, further indicating a functional link between the two furnaces.

Charcoal Accumulation: Feature 89E/-168N/F1

Feature 89E/-168N/F1 consisted of a dense concentration of charcoal that extended for 3 meters along the base of the south face of the north wall of the Western Terrace. Its highest density of concentration was located in between the north face of the northern wall stub and the south face of the north wall in units 90E/-168N, 90E/-167N, 91E/-168N and 91E/-167N. Sectioned along the -167N line and excavated in one level, Feature 89E/-168N/F1 contained a capping matrix of burned earth that rested on a highly burned surface. Over 1.6 kg of charcoal were collected in the excavation of level 1. Other artifact densities were moderate to high as well, particularly ceramics (450g), slag (200g), and ore (300g). Flotation samples were collected and analyzed by Kathleen Morrison at the University of Chicago to determine wood species. The charcoal accumulation appears to have been deposited during the time when Surfaces 5 and 6 were in use.

Feature 89E/-168N/F1 is similar in its physical extent and density of charcoal to the charcoal accumulation feature 90E/163N/F1, which was found at the base of the Northern Exterior Area (described later). The profile along

the -167N line did not, however, demonstrate the same degree of layering of burned earth and charcoal evident in Feature 90E/-163N/F1. Feature 89E/-168N/F1 contained a fairly high density of galena; 300g were recovered. The lack of repeated deposition of surface-building materials in this area during the deposition of interior Surface 5 may have been due to the use of this feature as a staging area for materials that were to be used in furnace Feature 90E/-169N/F1.

Heat-Altered Adobe Accumulation, Ore Roasting Feature: 88E/-172N/F2

This feature consisted of a concentration of heat-altered adobe and tabular stone slabs that filled the area between the arced wall Feature 88E/-171N/F1 and the south wall of the terrace, extending through units 88E to 90E/-172N. Feature 88E/-172N/F2 contained more than 80 kg of adobe, which lay on top of a reduced, heat-altered surface that contained bonded and melted adobe brick fragments. This surface most likely corresponded with Surface 5, but was more highly heat-altered than the surface immediately to the north of the arced partition wall. The heat-altered surface was compact, bluish gray in color, and contained heavy charcoal and gravel inclusions. Level 2 consisted of the removal of this matrix to expose Surface 6.

Feature 88E/-172N/F2 appears to have been an area where reduced adobe brick was deposited as well as a combustion area that involved a low oxygen environment. This feature and subsequent levels in this area contained the highest concentration of sulfur found in the entire smelting terrace. Ore recovered from the feature included sulfide ores such as galena and chalcopyrite. This partitioned section of the facility may have functioned as an area dedicated to sulfide ore roasting as suggested by the presence of the ore and its possible byproduct, mineralized sulfur. Alternatively, a metallurgical process involving sulfur as an additive may have taken place there. See Chapter 7 for a more complete discussion.

Features Associated with Interior Surface 7

Interior Surface 7 (Figure 6.15) was the first surface deposited during the use of the terrace for metallurgical activity. Restricted to the southern half of the interior of the Western Terrace, the surface was impregnated with ash, charcoal, and pea-sized fragments of a copper carbonate ore contained malachite and azurite. The density of this ore was particularly high adjacent to the north face of the south wall and south of the possible furnace Feature 88E/-170N/F3 (described next). The posthole pattern seen in this surface suggest a use and conceptualization of the internal work-space of the facility that differed from the subsequent metallurgical activity focused on furnace Feature 90E/-169N/F1 and Surfaces 5 and 6.

Pit and Furnace Collar: Feature 88E/-170N/F3

This feature consisted of a D-shaped pit cut into interior Surface 7. The pit was shallow, 7 to 24 cm in depth, and was surrounded by a highly heat-altered adobe matrix that may have been a remnant of a furnace collar. The matrix was 10 to 30 cm wide along the northeastern edge of the pit, which appeared to be more highly heat altered than other parts of the feature. Cut into the western edge of this collar was a small, oval, ash-stained basin. It was 10 cm by 15 cm in diameter and was adjacent to the northern extent of the pit feature. Additional heat-altered adobe block remnants were encountered at the southern terminus of the pit feature in unit 88E/-171N. Although heavily disturbed by roots, the pit itself was burned at its base and was associated with materials from all stages of copper metallurgical processing including copper carbonate ore, smelted copper, sheet copper, and slag. The pit was apparently filled and capped with adobe to the level of Surface 6.

Feature 88E/-170N/F3 may have been the base of a furnace associated with copper metallurgy. Ash, charcoal, slag, and ore distributions centered around this feature and embedded in Surface 7 are suggestive of similar distributions observed for furnace Feature 90E/-169N/F1, particularly the offsetting of ash-stained and charcoal-stained matrices in relation to these features. Such offsetting may indicate the orientation of the furnaces, with ash staining representing proximity to the tap hole and charcoal concentrations the remains of furnace charging activity, which was typically placed to the rear of the furnace.

Pit Feature, 90E/-170N/F1

This feature consisted of a circular depression cut into Surface 7 that was located adjacent to the north face of the southern stub wall. Feature 90E/-170N/F1 was 65 cm in diameter and 27 cm deep. Excavated in one level, the matrix encountered in the interior of the pit consisted of a loose silt-clay with vitrified adobe fragments and small charcoal inclusions. The pit was excavated into the natural substrate of the hill underlying the terrace. The base of the pit and its eastern rim also contained vitrified adobe elements. These appear to have been displaced and had no discernable structural significance, but their association with a feature on Surface 7 suggests that there was a high-temperature furnace operation on that surface.

WESTERN EXTERIOR AREA

This area was excavated to try to define the west face of the west terrace wall and to define any surfaces or features associated with the area directly adjacent to the wall, such as ventilation shafts or trench features similar to those found on the Eastern Terrace. It soon became apparent that the density of large to mid-sized stone elements was much greater in this area than within the supposed west terrace wall alignment. The concentration extended 2 meters to the west from the gap in the west terrace wall and was present throughout the exterior of our exposure. No definite alignments were present in this concentration, though stone elements appeared to have been stacked in some parts. Concentrations of stones in units 87E/-168N and 87E/-169N were angled in such a way as to suggest a curvilinear arrangement. The stone element concentration was associated with three distinct matrices. Associated with the curvilinear stone element arrangement was a loose, unconsolidated matrix that contained charcoal. The charcoal fragments were fairly large (approx. 1 cm in diameter). Overall artifact densities were moderate, although there was one concentration of metallurgical debris. Capping the stone element concentration on the northwestern and southwestern edges of the excavation area was a more compact, mottled, charcoal-rich, heat-altered matrix. Adjacent to the exposure of the west terrace wall in units 88E/-168N and 87E/-170N there was a different heat-altered, compact matrix that appeared to have been associated with the lower level of the stone element concentration.

To the north of and articulated with the stone element concentration was a dense accumulation of metallurgical debris. The debris included more than 75 kg of slag and more than 1 kg of metal. This was designated as Feature 87E/-166N/F1. Two cross sections of the feature demonstrated that the slag concentration interdigitated with a loose, unconsolidated matrix. These two layers overlaid a compact, heat-altered matrix and were capped by an additional heat-altered matrix. This stratigraphy corresponded fairly well with the matrices observed in the area of the stone element concentration. The slag and stone element concentrations appeared to have been contemporaneous. Materials recovered from the slag accumulation feature were predominantly copper slags formed in a high-temperature, highly reduced environment (see Chapter 7 for a more thorough discussion of this material). Within the accumulation, a dense concentration of unprocessed metal was found, suggesting that it represented discard from a failed smelting event.

Additional slag accumulations were encountered at lower levels on the Western Exterior Area, predating the large slag accumulation Feature 87E/-166N/F1. This area appears to have been used consistently for the deposition of slag. The petrography of samples recovered in this area suggest that material was deposited from multiple smelting episodes. Almost all of this slag represents copper smelting activity, with very little lead slag or metal-refining debris such as litharge or lead silicate material present. This area may have served as a processing area for slag as well. All of the slag in this area is highly fragmented, suggesting an attempt to either obtain the metal trapped in the slag, or to fragment the slag for further use in other smelting charges.

NORTHERN EXTERIOR AREA

With the exposure of interior Surfaces 2 and 3, the north wall of the terrace was exposed, revealing a proscribed space between the north wall and the northern terrace retaining wall. Five surfacing events were found in this Northern Exterior Area; they were probably contemporary with interior Surfaces 2 through 6. Materials associated with these surfaces indicate a difference in functional use of the space compared to other areas of the facility and include concentrations of charcoal, smelted metal, malachite, and lead- or silver-refining debris.

Under the adobe melt found along the north face of the north terrace wall was a compact, heat-altered matrix in units 89E/-166N, level 5, 90E/-166N level 4, and 91E/-166N level 2. These levels formed a contiguous surface marked by a high density of charcoal. This surface was designated as Northern Exterior Surface 1. It occurred throughout the Northern Exterior Area below a capping of adobe melt along the -166N and -165N unit rows and below a concentration of wall fall and loose unconsolidated fill with charcoal and red silt mottling in unit rows -164N and -163N, adjacent to the south face of the north terrace retaining wall. At the interface between Northern Exterior Area Surface 1 and the overlying matrices, eroded adobe brick fragments were encountered in units 91E/-165N level 2 and 90E/-165N levels 3 and 4. Two fragments of a late glaze soup plate were also recovered from this interface in 90E/-164N level 4 and 90E/-165N level 3. The surface also contained a moderate density of metallurgical material, primarily smelted copper, and light densities of slag. One large fragment of litharge, associated with silver production, was recovered from 90E/-165N level 4. The surface was discontinuous in the -164N unit row because of rodent disturbance and wall fall from erosion of the upper terrace wall. Northern Exterior

Area Surface 1 articulated with the fourth and fifth exposed course of the north terrace retaining wall.

A second surface, found below Northern Exterior Area Surface 1, was designated as Northern Exterior Surface 2. This surface was better preserved than surface 1 and had a higher artifact density. Charcoal and ash concentrations were present along the north face of the north terrace wall. Stone element concentrations were also found, especially along the -164N unit row. Eroded adobe bricks occurred in the -165N unit row and adjacent to the upper terrace retaining wall in units 92E/-164N and 91E/-164N. The bricks appeared to be within or on the northern exterior surface 2. This surface articulated with the fifth and sixth courses in the northern terrace retaining wall and the second course preserved in the north face of the north terrace wall.

The high density of charcoal and ash present along the north wall appeared at first to be a discrete accumulation. But it soon became apparent that the charcoal lens was extensive and was associated with a highly burned and compact matrix below Northern Exterior Area Surface 2. The charcoal lens was associated with a high density of metallurgical material including small fragments of malachite, a concentration of smelted cuprous metal, and a fragment of a litharge cake. This concentration was associated with Northern Exterior Area Surface 3.

Northern Exterior Area Surface 3 was well preserved and associated with a fairly high concentration of metallurgical material along the north face of the north terrace wall and adjacent units in the -165N and -164N unit rows. Along the north wall, surface 3 was found to slope down to the west at the intersection of the north and west terrace walls. Following the charcoal concentration to the north, densities of metallurgical material continued to be high in unit 91E/-165N level 4 including copper and lead ores and smelted cuprous metal. A Catholic religious medallion cast from a copper alloy was recovered from level 4. Eroded, heat-altered adobe brick was also encountered in this area.

Charcoal concentrations on the surface tapered off to the north and then increased in density in the northwest corner of the Northern Exterior Area adjacent to the intersection of the upper terrace retaining wall and the massive stone-filled west wall. This concentration was also associated with pockets of a clay-rich matrix that was incorporated into the upper-terrace retaining wall construction at this level. Surface 3 articulated with the base of the seventh course preserved in the upper-terrace retaining wall in unit 90E/-163N level 8. Concentrations of heat-altered adobe were also found on Surface 3 in this unit. Northern Exterior Area Surface 3 was missing along the west terrace wall because the wall itself had collapsed along its east face, leaving a pile of stone elements where the surface would have been. Northern Exterior Area Surface 2 was built on top of the collapsed wall.

Below Northern Exterior Area Surface 3 were dense concentrations of heat-altered, undifferentiated adobe adjacent to the north wall. No formal features were identified in this concentration and it may have been related to surface preparation episodes in the interior of the Western Terrace. North of this accumulation was a highly oxidized red sandy loam that partially capped a dense concentration of silt and charcoal laminations (90E/-163N/F1). The oxidized loam extended primarily along the southern face of the north terrace retaining wall. Patches of this material were also found in the southwest corner of the Northern Exterior Area, partially capping the adobe conglomeration along the north wall. Adobe brick and concentrations of ash and burned limestone were found below Surface 3 along the east face of the west wall.

Interdigitating with the burned limestone and ashy matrices encountered in this area and below the adobe concentration along the north face of the north wall was a highly burned, compact, variegated, undulating silt clay. This was designated Northern Exterior Area Surface 4. This surface extended across the eastern half of the area, terminating to the east at a southern continuation of the eastern exterior wall (93E/-164N/F1) along the 93E unit line. To the west, Surface 4 partially overlapped a limestone-rich, ashy matrix. The limestone and ash matrix appears to have been the heat-altered natural substrate of the hill upon which the smelting terrace deposits were laid. The west face of the western exterior wall (88E/-166N/F1) and the north wall of the terrace were built into and on the substrate.

Northern Exterior Area Surface 4 was at the base of the terrace walls. The eastern exterior wall, though heavily damaged by trench disturbance in upper levels, was intact at its contact with Surface 4 and was found to extend from its abutment with the northern terrace retaining wall in unit 93E/-163N to the southeast quadrant of unit 92E/-166N. The eastern exterior wall did not articulate with the north wall of the Western Terrace in this area, possibly a result of trench disturbance or some displacement of wall elements in antiquity, creating a gap of 40 cm between the southern termination of the eastern exterior wall and the eastern extent of the north terrace wall.

Along the west face of the eastern exterior wall in units 91E and 92E/-164N and 92E/-165N were five groups of stacked tabular sandstone elements. The stacks, which sat on exterior Surface 4, were three to five elements in height

and arranged at equal intervals from each other adjacent to the west face of the eastern exterior wall on a slightly mounded portion of exterior Surface 4. Concentrations of charcoal and burned silt, similar to matrices encountered in the excavation of combustion Feature 90E/-163N/F1 (described next) were incorporated within the structure of each stack. These stone accumulations may have been part of the activity associated with the combustion feature.

Combustion Feature: 90E/-163N/F1

Combustion Feature 90E/-163N/F1 consisted of a dense concentration of charcoal along the south face of the north terrace wall. It extended throughout the units along the -163N line adjacent to the north wall and into the northern half of units 89E–92E/-164N. The feature contained 17 interdigitated layers of silt and charcoal and was 12 cm thick. At least four use episodes were represented in those layers. The first resulted in the deposition of charcoal and burned silt loam on the natural substrate and exterior surface four. The second use consisted of excavation into that laminate to create pits (noted in units 90E/-163N and 92E/-163N). The third use was a capping of the pit features with more layers of charcoal and silt. Finally, the entire feature was capped with a burned silt loam.

The charcoal and silt accumulation apparently extended across the Northern Exterior Area at some point, but was partially removed prior to the formation of exterior Surface 3. Artifact densities were light within this feature but included galena and some cuprous metallic fragments. Wood charcoal was the dominant material—2.1 kg were recovered for macrobotanical analysis. Three flotation samples and one sample for radiocarbon assay were collected as well.

Feature 90E/-163N/F1 was similar to combustion Feature 97E/-172N/F1 in the eastern smelting area (Lycett 1998). Feature 90E/-163N/F1 differs from this feature in its multiple laminations of burned silt and charcoal that appear to correspond to a single prepared surface (exterior Surface 4). Feature 90E/-163N/F1 also appears similar to the charcoal concentration (Feature 89E/-168N/F1) located in the interior of the Western Terrace below interior Surface 4. The two features may have been contemporary.

NORTHERN TERRACE EXCAVATIONS

The Northern Terrace was a 12-square-meter area north of the western terrace excavations, in between the north terrace retaining wall and an adobe room block identified as Nelson's room block XIIa (Lycett 2001). The Northern

Terrace was at a higher elevation than the Southern Terrace, and the surfaces associated with metallurgical activity on the terrace capped multiple layers of adobe melt from the decomposition of the room block to the north. No features directly related to metallurgy were found, but metallurgical artifacts such as smelted and sheet copper, iron, slag, ore, and litharge were recovered from the two heat-altered surfaces identified in this area. The south face of the Northern Terrace retaining wall revealed a history of reconstruction due to water damage from upslope run off. The northern terrace excavations exposed a small check dam of small to medium stone and midden material containing seventeenth-century artifacts built adjacent to the area of greatest damage to the retaining wall. The dam was probably built as an attempt to mitigate slope runoff during the operation of the facility. Similar features were encountered in the western exterior area.

COMPARISON OF METALLURGICAL FEATURES

As indicated by the construction history of the facility and its associated features, the metallurgy at Paa-ko was both intensive and extensive. Diverse features related to metal processing were found at the site and it is apparent that metalworking took place over many years, as indicated by multiple resurfacing and wall construction episodes. From the earliest evidence of metallurgical activity on the terrace, the facility was constructed as a formally defined space. The first structure, found on Surface 7 in the Western Terrace interior (Figure 6.15), was indicated by the posthole remnants of a ramada-like structure. It was eventually replaced by masonry construction.

The features related to metallurgy were diverse. Although some similarities existed, such as the charcoal accumulations features or the linear trench features of the eastern terrace, on closer examination, all of the features were distinct in their construction and use history. This diversity reflects two primary aspects of the metallurgical technology used at Paa-ko. First, operations included roasting ore, smelting copper and lead ores, and refining metals or assaying ores through cupellation and a method involving indirect heat. These activities produced a suite of similar features. Second, the processes involved with these operations were subject to experimentation that created variations among features of similar form.

Furnaces

Furnaces encountered on the terrace were of two general types, the bowl furnaces of the Western Terrace, and the linear trench furnaces of the Eastern Terrace. Bowl furnaces were more typically associated with smelting regimes (more highly reducing atmospheres), and the higher density of ore and slag recovered from the Western Terrace in relation to the Eastern Terrace suggests that smelting was concentrated on this side of the facility. Feature 90E/-169N/F1, the only bowl furnace with a series of intact bases, did not appear to have been heated to the degree necessary for the production of the copper slag recovered from the facility, although furnace base temperatures may have been considerably lower than those produced higher up in the furnace. In fact, the only evidence for temperatures over 1200°C found at the site was the vitrified lintel encountered at the ventilation inlet for the linear furnace, Feature 101E/-170N/F1. This area was not associated with high temperature slag, although glassy, vitrified material containing lead was recovered in the vicinity of this structure. It is possible that bowl furnace bases used in the production of the high temperature copper slag did not survive the production process and would have been removed after each smelting event.

Two of the bowl furnaces were associated with ancillary, ash-stained depressions. Feature 90E/-169N/F1 was most likely connected to the triangular ash-filled Feature 89E/-170N/F3, which may have functioned as a secondary furnace or as a fore hearth. The concentration of ash found in this feature suggests that it had a secondary function as an oxidizing furnace, perhaps as an initial step of metal refinement after the smelting regime. The D-shaped depression of Feature 88E/-170N/F3 probably represents the excavated remains of a furnace base as well, and is similarly situated adjacent to an ash-filled depression.

The linear trench furnaces do not fully correspond to historical depictions of furnace types, but they are somewhat similar to the wind furnaces used for crucible operations described in the sixteenth- and seventeenth-century metallurgical treatises of Agricola and Ekert, or the roughly contemporary linear muffle furnaces described by Barba (1923; Hoover and Hoover 1950; Sisco and Smith 1951). The evidence for the refining of metals was greater on the Eastern Terrace, suggesting that the linear furnaces that exhibited heat alteration may have functioned as cupellation furnaces. The linear design of the furnace, with air inlets perpendicular to the furnace chamber, suggests the attempt at creating a chamber that provided a range of temperatures in a predominantly oxidizing atmosphere, similar to a muffle furnace. Materials could have been manipulated at various temperatures and oxidizing conditions by placing them relative to the blast coming into the center of the furnace. If a less oxidizing environment or a lower temperature was required, the material could have been shifted to either side of the inlet. The structure of these features would have allowed workers to position themselves in relation to the blast in order to manipulate materials. They would have been shielded from heat by the back wall of the furnace. The ability to easily modify temperature and atmosphere conditions was essential for working with materials of unknown composition.

Charcoal Preparation and Ore-Roasting Features

Charcoal accumulation features were also a formal type of technology evident at the facility. Charcoal accumulations were present in the early and late phases of the facility. They were found at the base of deposits in the interior of the Western Terrace and the Northern Exterior Area, and in the most recent deposits found in the interior of the Eastern Terrace (Feature 97E/-172N/F1). These features were broadly similar in construction, made up of linear mounds of earth and charcoal, but closer inspection revealed distinct differences. At the base of deposits on the Northern Exterior Area, Feature 90E/-163N/F1 consisted of stratified, alternating layers of charcoal and a fine silt loam, while the most recent accumulation, Feature 97E/-172N/F1, had a more limited layering of earth and charcoal. Feature 89E/-167N/F1, in the interior of the Western Terrace, did not appear to be extensively stratified. This feature contained a fairly high density of galena, whereas no galena was found in the Eastern Terrace feature, and a more limited occurrence of galena was found in the Northern Exterior feature.

The charcoal accumulations may have had multiple functions. On the one hand, they may have been small-scale charcoal preparation sites, as the capping of charcoal beds with earth is consistent with the technology of charcoal processing. On the other hand, the charcoal accumulation along the south face of the north terrace wall in the Western Terrace interior may have been the remnant of a larger accumulation stored for use in bowl furnace Feature 90E/-169N/F1. The presence of galena within the charcoal matrices of features 89E/-167N/F1 and 90E/-163N/F1 may indicate that they also functioned as locations for the roasting of ore as a pretreatment for smelting. The charcoal bed of Feature 90E/-163N/F1 was associated with a series of sandstone element pedestals, indicating that the bed was used as a location for the ambient heating of materials, a practice often used during assay (Barba 1923; Holmyard 1957; Hoover and Hoover 1950).

Feature 88E/-172N/F2 was more closely associated with the roasting of sulfide minerals. Chalcopyrite and galena ores were concentrated in this area and sulfur was found embedded in the matrices at its base. The concentration of adobe brick in this feature may represent the storage of adobe for use in firing events or as a component of the roasting technology. Barba (1923:187) noted the use of adobe structures in the roasting of finely ground ores during the seventeenth century.

SUMMARY

The archaeological evidence for the metallurgy at Paa-ko suggests that practitioners used a variety of techniques and modified them over time. For example, furnace Feature 90E/-169N/F1, with its multiple bowl bases, suggests a reconfiguration of the basic smelting technology involved with the feature, perhaps in an attempt at reducing furnace volumes in order to better control atmospheric conditions. Some features probably had multiple functions. Furnace Feature 90E/-166N/F1, although associated primarily with lead ore and the byproducts of lead smelting, also contained evidence for the low temperature reduction of a copper carbonate ore. Similarly, Feature 101E/-170N/F1 was probably originally designed as a furnace involved with cupellation, but may have functioned as a forge towards the end of the occupation of the facility, as indicated by its associated cache of iron and copper artifacts.

CHAPTER SEVEN

Metal Smelting, Refining, and Copper Working at Paa-ko: Materials Analysis

The metal, slag, refractory material, and ores recovered from the Paa-ko smelting facility were selectively sampled and analyzed in order to better understand the spatial distribution of materials and their association with defined features or contexts of deposition. These analyses helped define the technologies used at Paa-ko.

The analyses included petrographic and metallographic observations, as well as qualitative and semi-quantitative elemental characterizations using SEM-EDS and XRF. Lead isotope analysis was conducted to provide geological sourcing data for select ore and metal samples. Temperature ranges for recovered refractory material were obtained through re-firing experiments. In addition, copper sheet produced at the site was documented photographically.

In all, 340 samples were analyzed; 24 are described here. They were selected because they provide typical examples of particular classes of materials that were identified in the full sample. Table 7.1 provides a summary of the analyses of the 24 samples.

ANALYSIS METHODS

The materials selected for analysis were digitally photographed and given sample numbers (LA162-1 through LA162-34). Slag and mineral samples were prepared in one of two ways: (1) as polished thin sections to be observed using optical microscopy in transmitted and reflective light or (2) as thick epoxy mounts polished on the upper surface for use in reflective light and scanning electron microscopy with energy dispersive spectroscopy (SEM-EDS). Metal samples and selective samples of refractory material were also prepared as polished epoxy mounts. Polished thin sections were prepared by commercial laboratories, while polished epoxy mounts were prepared by the author. The polished mounts of slag, metal, and ore minerals were studied in reflected plane- and cross-polarized light and with Nomarski interference contrast. The thin sections were studied in both transmitted and reflected plane- and cross-polarized light using petrographic and metallographic microscopes. Observations were documented using digital microphotographs.

Chemical characterization of samples was done using SEM-EDS analysis and micro-XRF analysis of polished thick sections made from the same samples analyzed under optical petrography. SEM and EDS data were obtained using a Hitachi Model S-2460N variable pressure SEM located in the Material Sciences and Engineering Department at the University of Arizona. Samples were observed under both variable and high vacuum modes after coating with a thin layer of sputtered carbon. The XRF analysis was conducted using an EDAX Eagle III μ-Probe with a spot size of 20μm. The probe was in the Geosciences Department at the University of Arizona.

The micro-XRF and SEM-EDS analyses provided qualitative chemical analysis. The focused XRF analysis was also used to provide semi-quantitative data on slag and ore samples. There are advantages and disadvantages to each analytical method. The advantages of the focused XRF analysis include time saved in carbon-coating and better detection limits because background emission levels are minimal (due to the absence of *bremsstrahlung* radiation produced by electron beam/sample interactions in SEM-EDS analysis). This has allowed for semi-quantitative data to be generated that reflects phase composition for copper concentrations as low as 10 ppm (as opposed to a typical 1000 ppm detection limit for EDS set at 30 kV

Table 7.1. Characteristics of Samples Discussed in the Text: Provenance, Optical, and Elemental Analysis

Sample Number	Provenance	Phases Identified Optically	Elemental Analysis	Major Elements and Oxides Identified	Material
LA162-15	100E/-171N/F1/L2	Glassy, lead prills, litharge, silicate laths	SEM	Lead, silicon, calcium, potassium, aluminum	Litharge/ lead
LA162-16	97E/-172N/L1	Fayalite, tridymite, glass, copper, iron, sulfur	SEM	Iron, silicon, calcium	Copper slag
LA162-17	102E/-172N/L3	Glass, magnetite, litharge, silicate laths, lead , copper	SEM	Lead, copper, iron, calcium, silicon	Litharge with copper/iron
LA162-18	Feature sweep	Glass, melilite, magnetite	SEM	Iron, calcium, silicon, potassium, aluminum	Calcium-rich slag with iron
LA162-21	99E/-170N/F1/L2	Glass, melilite, lead, copper	SEM	Lead, silicon, calcium, potassium, aluminum; prill lead, copper	Calcium-rich lead slag
LA162-23	90E/-168N/F1/L1	Calcite, galena, carbonate	SEM	Lead, calcium, zinc	Lead/zinc ore
LA162-24	87E/-168N/L5	Glass, fayalite, tridymite, copper, iron, sulfur	SEM	Iron, silicon, calcium, copper	Copper slag
LA162-54	90E/-162N/L5	Glass, delafossite, magnetite, copper	None	None	Copper slag
LA162-55	91E/-162N/L5	Glass, litharge, melilite, cerrusite ore remnant, lead	None	None	Lead slag
LA162-72	88E/-168N/L3	Glass, tridymite, sulfides, fayalite, melilite, copper, iron	XRF	Iron oxide, silicon dioxide, calcium oxide	Copper slag
LA162-74	90E/-168N/F1/L2	Silicates, feldspar, unknown rhomboid	XRF	Calcium oxide, silicon dioxide, zinc oxide, iron oxide, lead, sulfur	Lead slag
LA162-85	88E/-169N/L8	Glass, fayalite, tridymite, sulfides, copper, iron	XRF	Iron oxide, silicon dioxide, calcium dioxide, iron, copper	Copper slag
LA162-102	90E/-169N/L5	Glass, fayalite, tridymite, sulfides, copper	None	None	Copper slag
LA162-105	89E/-166N/7	Glass, melilite (akermanite)	XRF	Iron oxide, silicon dioxide, calcium oxide, iron, copper	Copper slag
LA162-109	88E/-170N/7	Glass, cuprite, copper	XRF	Iron oxide, silicon dioxide, copper oxide, copper, iron, lead	Copper slag
LA162-206	100E/-168N/F2/L4	Malachite, chalcopyrite, covellite	XRF	Copper, sulfur, silicon dioxide, copper oxide	Copper ore
LA162-209	91E/-163N/L2	Galena, calcite	XRF	Lead, sulfur, zinc oxide; mixed phase: zince, iron, calcium, copper, silicon oxide, manganese, lead	Lead/zinc ore
LA162-211	87E/-169N/L7	Malachite, iron hydroxides	XRF	Copper oxide, silicon dioxide; copper, gold	Copper ore
LA162-212	92E/-166N/L3	Galena, calcite	XRF	Calcium oxide, silicon oxide, lead dioxide; lead sulfur	Lead ore
LA162-214	90E/-172N/L7	Chalcopyrite	XRF	Copper, iron sulfur, vanadium, gold; copper oxide	Copper ore

Table 7.1. (continued)

Sample Number	Provenance	Phases Identified Optically	Elemental Analysis	Major Elements and Oxides Identified	Material
LA162-337	100E/-171N/F1/L2	Glass, litharge, silicate laths, lead	XRF	Lead oxide; lead; ash: silicon dioxide, calciumoxide, potassium oxide	Litharge
LA162-338	101E/-172N/L3	Malachite, cuprite, quartz, iron hydroxides	XRF	Iron copper, silicon, lead, gold; copper oxide	Copper ore
LA162-339	100E/-172N/F1/L2	Glass, quartz inclusions, lead	XRF	Lead oxide; lead-silicon dioxide; ash: calcium, potassium; lead, barium, silver	Lead slag/ glass
LA162-340	90E/-168N/F1/L1	Refractory with lead inclusion, mineral crust	XRF	Zinc oxide, lead dioxide, silicon dioxide, calcium oxide (crust; lead silver copper	Adobe

Key: SEM = scanning electron microscopy
XRF = X-ray fluorescence

accelerating voltage). Advantages to SEM-EDS analysis include a smaller spot size (0.5–20μm) for EDS analysis and better quality imaging, which allows for more precise spot placement on compositionally distinct features within a sample. Micro-XRF analysis also has a greater penetration depth than SEM-EDS, sometimes making it difficult to correlate spot placement with phase composition if the phase is thinner than the depth of penetration.

Stable lead isotope analysis was conducted on 12 ore and 12 metal samples in order to infer the sources of the lead and copper ores and to determine if the metal recovered correlated with the ore signatures. The analyses were conducted by Alyson Thibodeau (University of Arizona, Geosciences Department) on the multicollector-ICPMS in the laboratory of Joaquin Ruiz in the Geosciences Department of the University of Arizona. Lead isotope ratios were compared to data generated by Thibodeau and her colleagues on galenas from Cerrillos and several major ore deposits on either side of the Rio Grande Rift and to data generated by investigations of southwestern and Mexican ore sources (Thibodeau and others 2013; Habicht-Mauche and others 2000; Hosler 1994; Huntley and others 2007).

Experimental refiring of refractory material was conducted to estimate the maximum temperatures reached by the archaeological samples through a comparison of color and texture variations produced in furnace conditions ranging from 800 to 1100 °C. These data, coupled with petrographic and chemical characterization studies of slag and refractory material, has allowed for the reconstruction of temperature and atmosphere conditions reached by the smelting technology engaged in at the facility.

Copper sheet samples were documented photographically with digital images and color slide film. Marks left on artifact surfaces in processing the copper to sheet metal were noted, and weights and dimensions were recorded for each sample analyzed. Metallographic analysis of polished mounts using optical metallography in reflected light was conducted to further define production sequences and composition.

ORE SAMPLES

Four kinds of primary ores—three copper and one lead— were recovered from the facility, as determined by metallic content and gangue minerals. The three copper ores are (1) gossan ores that are primarily malachite $[Cu_2CO_3(OH)_2]$ but also include iron hydroxides such as limonite $[FeO(OH)_nH_2O]$ produced by weathering of iron sulfide minerals; (2) ores that are primarily chrysocolla $[(Cu,Al)_2H_2Si_2O_5(OH)_4 \cdot nH_2O]$ with remnant copper sulfides such as chalcopyrite $(CuFeS_2)$ and covellite (CuS); and (3) sulfide ores, primarily chalcopyrite with some occurrence of covellite and malachite. The lead ores recovered from the facility contain primary minerals of galena (PbS), sphalerite (ZnS), and calcite $(CaCO_3)$, along with carbonates of lead and zinc such as cerrusite $(PbCO_3)$ and smithsonite $(ZnCO_3)$, and sulfates of lead such as anglesite $(PbSO_4)$. A zinc silicate is also associated with this ore and is most likely hemimorphite $[Zn_4Si_2O_7(OH)_2 \cdot H_2O]$, which commonly occurs with smithsonite (Nesse 2000). Both the lead and copper ores suggest that colonial miners at Paa-ko exploited the oxidized zones of the supergene alteration of primary deposits associated with iron, copper, zinc, and lead sulfides such as chalcopyrite, pyrite, sphalerite, and galena, with calcite and quartz as the primary gangue minerals.

Samples LA162-211 and LA162-338

Samples LA162-211 and LA162-338 are copper ores that consist primarily of malachite. LA162-211 (Plate 1) was recovered from Surface 7 of the Western Terrace interior. In reflected light, the sample contains malachite [$Cu_2CO_3(OH)_2$], cuprite (CuO), quartz, and iron sulfide minerals. The iron sulfides are highly oxidized and partially replaced by iron hydroxides suggesting that the ore comes from a gossan deposit. Clay minerals are also present in the sample.

The minerals identified optically in Sample LA162-211 were analyzed utilizing the Eagle II XRF with a 20μ spot size. The XRF analysis suggests that more than 86 Wt% of the copper-rich mineral is CuO, corroborating our optical identification of malachite (Plate 1:A). Other metal oxides identified that would influence smelted metal composition include Fe_2O_3 (0.76 Wt%), ZnO (0.62 Wt%), and Au_2O_3 (0.2 Wt%). Chrysocolla may also be present given the high silica content of some of the copper rich minerals (Plate 1:B). Quartz occurs throughout the sample (Plate 1:C). Carbonates, alumina (AL_2O_3), and iron oxide were identified in the sample as well, as a mix of altered country rock and oxidation. One grain in particular, probably a weathered clay mineral, has significant values of gold (3.56 Wt%)(Plate 1:D).

Sample LA162-338 (Plate 2), recovered from the lower surface of the Eastern Terrace, appears to be less weathered than LA162-211. It contains larger malachite crystals and remnant sulfide minerals. Like LA162-211, malachite, cuprite, quartz, and iron hydroxides were the primary minerals identified optically. XRF analysis indicated a higher concentration of iron, with iron rich minerals also contained a higher concentration of zinc and gold (Plate 2:B). Unlike LA162-211, this sample also contains lead in significant amounts. A partially oxidized chalcopyrite grain contained 1.39 Wt% gold, with lead at 1.4 Wt% (Plate 2:C).

Sample LA162-206

Sample LA162-206 (Plate 3) is a copper ore recovered from deposits within the T-shaped masonry furnace, Feature 100E/-168N/F2, that was found north of the north terrace wall on the Eastern Terrace. In section, under plain polarized light, the ore has a fine cryptocrystalline matrix with green and pink internal reflections. Within this matrix are inclusions of a dark gray to sky blue mineral. These exhibit bright orange internal reflections in cross polarized reflected light, diagnostic of covellite (CuS) (Plate 3:C). A vein of malachite, as a secondary enrichment product, runs through the sample as well (Plate 3:B).

XRF analysis suggests that the predominant cryptocrystalline mineral is a copper silicate, probably chrysocolla (Plate 3: A). Gold is present, not in the same concentrations as the previous samples, but in a significant amount (0.55 Wt%). Zinc is also present (0.27 Wt%). Copper sulfide minerals are present in Cu to S ratios similar to those reported for covellite (Goh, Buckley, and Lamb 2006), confirming the optical assessment.

Sample LA162-214

Copper sulfide minerals are rare in the assemblage recovered from the facility. In general, they appear to be concentrated on the west terrace, in association with deposits along the south terrace wall, an area that also contained concentrations of sulfur within excavated matrices. Sample LA162-214 was recovered from this area (90E/-172N/L7). In reflected plain polarized light, the sample exhibits a bright yellow color and is highly reflective, suggesting chalcopyrite. A small grain of a grayish-blue alteration, most likely covellite, of the predominant mineral occurs along one edge of the sample. A vein of malachite with quartz runs through the sample as well (Plate 4:B). Iron hydroxides are also present within this zone (Plate 4:C).

XRF analysis confirms the optical analysis, suggesting that the predominant mineralization within the sample is chalcopyrite (Plate 4:A). In addition to copper, iron, and sulfur, vanadium (3.34 Wt%) and gold (1.66 Wt%) are present in significant quantities as well. The association of gold with chalcopyrite may suggest an original provenance from within either the New or Old Placers mining districts (Milford and Swick 1995).

Samples LA162-23, LA162-209, and LA162-212

These three ore samples contain galena in a calcite gangue. Sample LA162-23 was recovered from the basin-shaped furnace (Feature 90E/-168N/F1) found on Surfaces 2 and 3 of the interior of the Western Terrace. This sample is from a cache of 1.6 kg of galena-bearing ore recovered from the feature. Samples LA162-209 and LA162-212 were recovered from the Northern Exterior Area of the Western Terrace. They may have been remnants of ore roasting in charcoal accumulation Feature 90E/-163N/F1.

Sample LA162-23 was prepared as a polished thin section and observed petrographically before being analyzed using SEM-EDS for a qualitative assessment of the optically identified phases' element composition. In transmitted, cross-polarized light, most of the sample consists of carbonates, with calcite as the predominant gangue mineral. Quartz is also present. Opaque minerals observed in transmitted light were identified in reflected light as galena. Spectra produced through SEM-EDS suggests the predominance of lead, calcium, and zinc, identifying the ore as a lead-zinc ore.

Samples LA162-209 and LA162-212 contain similar mineralogies. They were prepared as polished sections and analyzed using XRF. Minerals identified include calcite ($CaCO_3$) (Plate 5:A), galena (PbS) (Plate 5:B), cerrusite ($PbCO_3$) (Plate 5:C), anglesite ($PbSO_4$) (Plate 5:D), and sphalerite (ZnS). Both samples contain galena with significant contents of silver and gold. The galena in sample LA162-209 contains gold at 1.0 Wt% and silver at 0.58 Wt%, well within the economic margin of seventeenth-century Spanish technology. Similarly, galena in LA162-212 contains 0.43 Wt% gold and 0.35 Wt% silver, suggesting that both metals may have figured prominently in the precious metal recovery methods engaged in at the site.

SLAG

Slag is produced as a byproduct of smelting technology. It contains silicates, oxides, and metals that are produced through the interaction of the metallic contents of ores and their gangue, the fuels, and refractory materials during the smelting process. The identification of mineral and metallic phases within slag samples allowed for the reconstruction of the basic technology of the smelt that produced them. The mineral characteristics also enabled for the inference of the required temperature and atmosphere conditions necessary for the successful production of metal from various ores. The calcium and iron content of the slag is important for understanding the technology at Paa-ko, as the presence or absence of calcium has a major influence on the smelting technology.

Another structuring value is the application of reducing (CO) or oxidizing (CO_2) atmospheres at temperatures in excess of 1000° C. In addition to the composition of the smelt, the observation of the thermal transformation of quartz within samples is a proxy indicator of the temperatures reached in the furnace. The rapid transformation of α to β quartz at 573±5 °C in the furnace causes quartz grains to fracture. If quartz is heated beyond this range,

or if silica-rich liquids are held at high temperatures and cooled slowly, other forms (polymorphs) of silica are produced that have optically distinct crystal habits and properties. For example, tridymite is stable above 867 °C but converts to cristobalite at temperatures in excess of 1250 °C (Deer, Howie, and Zussman 1966) (Plates 6 and 7:A). These high-temperature polymorphs are preserved in slags because they solidify too rapidly for the reverse transformations to forms that are stable at lower temperatures.

The slag samples discussed here can be grouped according to the metals identified optically in section. Copper slag is the predominant slag recovered from the facility and exhibits a wide range of compositional and atmospheric indicators. Both oxidizing and reducing conditions are indicated by the copper slag analyzed. Lead slag is more rare, perhaps because of post-production recycling of material. The lead slag also indicates a technology using a high-temperature process.

Fayalitic Copper Slag: Samples LA162-16, LA162-24, and LA162-85

Copper slag is present throughout the facility and was incorporated into surfaces and deposition events across its use history. Sample LA162-16 was recovered from the linear combustion feature excavated on the upper surface of the Eastern Terrace in 1997, whereas samples LA162-24 and LA162-85 were recovered along the Western Exterior Area and the interior of the Western Terrace respectively. All three exhibit a predominant mineralization involving the production of iron silicates with high temperature silica polymorphs and a copper-iron alloy, often found encased in envelopes of sulfide mineralization (Plate 8). Magnetite is also present in some samples (Plate 9). These samples were prepared as polished thin sections and observed in transmitted plain and polarized light. LA162-16 and LA162-24 were subsequently analyzed using SEM-EDS whereas sample LA162-85 was analyzed utilizing XRF.

Sample LA162-16 (Plate 8) exhibits well-defined crystal formation in thin section, with prismatic and dendritic crystals forming between large, undigested rock fragments. Crystals exhibit strong pink to green pleochroism and have straight extinction with high second order birefringence. These characteristics suggest that they can be identified as fayalite (Fe_2SiO_4), although the observed pleochroism is unusual. SEM-EDS analysis suggests that the major elements present within these minerals are iron, silica, and some calcium, congruent with the optical identification.

Sample LA162-24 is predominantly composed of large light-gray laths, or skeletal crystal forms, in a light brown microcrystalline matrix. These skeletal crystal forms were unresponsive to stage rotation under cross-polarized light. Rosette crystal forms exhibiting low birefringence and undulating extinction are dispersed throughout the sample. These latter minerals are the high temperature silica polymorph of tridymite. Rounded drops of metal are finely dispersed throughout the section and exhibit iron dendrites within a copper matrix, with the whole drop often encased within blue-gray iron–copper sulfide envelopes. SEM-EDS analysis confirms the optical assessment of the rosette forms as being primarily silica, which suggests that the skeletal crystal forms are fayalite as well, as they gave similar spectra to the crystals analyzed in Sample LA162-16.

Sample LA162-85 (Plate 9) is similar in section to LA162-24, with skeletal crystal forms associated with high-temperature silica polymorphs and a copper-iron alloy. XRF analysis suggests that the skeletal crystal forms are approaching the composition of fayalite, with iron to silica ratios approximating that reported in the literature (Deer, Howie, and Zussman 1966). Calcium partially substitutes for iron in the fayalite, and iron ratios are somewhat higher perhaps due to the fine dispersal of copper-iron droplets throughout the matrix and the fact that the crystal laths are still skeletal and have not fully formed (Plate 9). Metal drop composition is primarily iron and copper, with silver and gold content similar to that observed in the copper silicate ore analyzed (Sample LA162-206).

Melilite-Fayalite Copper Slag: Samples LA162-72, and LA162-105

These samples come from similar contexts to the two fayalite-dominated samples just described. Sample LA162-72 was recovered from the Western Exterior Area of the Western Terrace and Sample LA162-105 came from the interior of the Western Terrace in deposits above surface 4. Both samples were prepared as polished thin sections and observed optically before mounts were prepared for XRF analysis.

Sample LA162-72 is similar to the fayalitic copper slag samples in that it came from a highly reduced atmosphere and contains high temperature silica crystals, both as rosette forms and as small remnant silica grains visible in section as a halo of more translucent material surrounding the quartz. High-temperature silica polymorphs are surrounded by dendrites of a mineral in the melilite solid-solution series ($(Ca, Na)_2(Al, Mg, Fe_2) + [(Al, Si)SiO_7]$), which are distinguished by their anomalous blue birefringence and peg structure. Numerous rounded copper grains, many with blue-gray sulfide envelopes and sulfide inclusions, are present. Some of these inclusions are covellite (CuS).

Sample LA162-105 contains a dark glass that is probably calcium and iron-rich; it has a mineral assemblage similar to Sample LA162-72. Rounded copper-iron grains are finely distributed throughout the matrix. Large fractured quartz grains are present and were attacked by the Ca/Fe rich glass, forming crystals of melilite (Plate 10). The XRF analysis of both samples suggests that fayalite still dominates the mineral assemblage of both LA162-72 and LA162-105. Melilite could not be positively identified, probably because the crystals are a smaller diameter than the minimum 20 µm spot of the Eagle II XRF. The XRF analysis suggests a similar overall composition to the fayalite-rich slag, with iron oxide and silicate weight percents matching these samples. The XRF indicates that calcium played a role in the formation of both sets of materials. Their compositional differences as indicated optically may be due to local variations in the composition of the melt within a single run of a furnace rather than between smelts.

Magnetite-Delafossite Copper Slag: Samples LA162-54, LA162-109

These samples represent a variation in copper-production technology that utilized a more oxidizing atmosphere at similar temperatures to copper produced under reducing atmospheres. Sample LA162-54 was recovered from the Northern Terrace adjacent to the north-terrace retaining wall. Sample LA162-109 was recovered from the interior of the Western Terrace at the exposure of surface 5. Both samples represent the production of copper without the reduction of iron, and the copper metal found within each sample is fairly pure.

Sample LA162-54 was studied only as a polished thin section; it is primarily glassy with a few molten rock fragments. A high density of copper prills are present but there is no metallic iron. The microstructure is not homogeneous, with variations in copper and iron across the sample producing zones rich in delafossite ($CuFeO_2$) or magnetite (Fe_3O_4) respectively. Some copper sulfides are present on copper drop boundaries and cuprite (CuO) as a corrosion product is visible in cracks in the sample.

Sample LA162-109 is completely opaque in thin section. In reflected light, many round copper grains are present throughout the section with no metallic iron visible, although iron is a part of their composition as indicated by XRF analysis. Under high magnification (100x), fine crystals of cuprite are visible through their red internal reflections. XRF data suggests that copper is the predominant element present within this fine phase, confirming the optical data (Plate 11). Both the mineralization and the formation of glass for these samples suggests that they represent an oxidizing smelt conducted under similar temperature ranges to the more reduced slag samples, although no high temperature silica polymorphs were observed.

Lead Slag: Samples LA162-55 and LA162-74

The presence of lead slag indicates that the smelting of lead ores was conducted in order to recover precious metals and not the lead itself. Lead can easily be produced from galena using a simple hearth and a wood fire under oxidizing conditions, producing little or no slag. The smelting of lead minerals under strongly reducing conditions is done to make sure that all of the silver-containing minerals within the ore are reduced so that the silver is absorbed by the lead (Craddock 1995). Silver is then recovered from the resulting lead metal by cupellation (preferential oxidation and removal of lead). Craddock (1995:221) reports that slags produced from this process in antiquity were primarily iron silicates formed by the high temperature, highly reducing conditions of the furnace. The composition of the lead slags from the facility at Paa-ko indicate a similar process.

Sample LA162-74 was recovered from the basin-shaped furnace (Feature 90E/-168N/F1) associated with a large cache of galena-bearing ore (see previous description of Sample LA162-23) and other evidence for the smelting of lead-bearing minerals. Sample LA162-55 is of a similar composition and was recovered from the Northern Terrace, adjacent to the Northern Terrace retaining wall. Both samples were observed petrographically as polished thin sections and were found to exhibit large crystal growths, primarily of melilite. Lead drops are present in both samples and appear to be surrounded by corrosion products such as litharge (PbO), minium (Pb_3O_4), or cerussite ($PbCO_3$). In Sample LA162-55 (Plate 12), both galena and cerrusite are present as remnant ore minerals within the slag. Sample LA162-74 (Plate 13) also contains lead or zinc-silicates, or both. XRF analysis conducted on LA162-74 confirms the presence of melilite with weight percentages for CaO, Al_2O_3, and SiO_2 approximating the values reported in the literature (Deer, Howie, and Zussman 1966). Zinc is also present in glassy phases in amounts ranging from 9.24 Wt% to 13.33Wt% (Plate 13:B). Galena is present as a remnant ore mineral in this sample as well.

The production of melilite as the predominant silicate with slag formation for these materials reflects the ore composition, with calcite as the primary gangue mineral. It is also suggestive of furnace conditions within which high

temperatures and reducing atmospheres were achieved. These conditions are similar to those achieved for copper smelting at the site, and the basic approach to the technology may have been the same for each smelting regime.

METAL REFINING

Although crucible remains were not recovered from the facility, evidence for the refining of metals by cupellation is present in the form of litharge cakes and associated lead glass. Lead metal is extremely rare at the site, with only a few drips recovered outside of its presence in slag and refining debris. It was probably too highly valued as a metal to become incorporated in the deposits. Much of the lead at the site may have been further processed to recover its precious metal content. This would have converted it from its metallic form to lead oxide, or litharge, which is present in moderate quantities at the facility.

Cupellation extracts an alloy of silver and gold from lead metal by placing the lead in a ceramic vessel or hearth lined with bone or wood ash and heating the metal to temperatures around 1000 °C in a strong current of air. The lead metal is converted to litharge (PbO), which absorbs other metal oxides and reacts with the ceramic or ash-lined vessel, leaving the gold and silver in their molten state. The button of precious metal that remains when all litharge has been absorbed may be further refined through the separation of gold from the silver using strong mineral acids (parting), by cementation with common salt to drive off silver as silver chloride vapor, or by converting silver to silver sulfide by exposing it to sulfur while it is molten, leaving the gold unreacted (Craddock 1995). This last technique may have been conducted at the facility.

Samples LA162-15, LA162-17, LA162-337, and LA162-339

These four samples, as well as most of the material similar in composition, were recovered from the interior of the Eastern Terrace in association with combustion Feature 97E/-172N/F1. The concentration of this material with surfaces associated with this feature suggests that it was a locus for cupellation. Samples LA162-15 and LA162-17 were prepared as thin sections for petrographic analysis and then analyzed using SEM-EDS. Samples LA162-337 and LA162-339 were prepared as polished mounts for reflected light microscopy and analyzed using XRF. Samples LA162-15 and LA162-337 are similar in their mineral and metal compositions and elemental data, as they come from the same context, although Sample LA162-337 contains an additional phase not found in the other two samples. This additional phase is similar in composition to Sample LA162-339. Sample LA162-17 is similar to Sample LA162-15, but also contains some interesting differences in composition.

Sample LA162-15 (Plate 14) exhibits dense mineralization stratified into layers of acicular crystals in a yellowish-red glass, overlying a layer composed of prismatic and highly birefringent minerals. At the base of the section is a partially digested ceramic, attacked by the yellowish-red glass (Plate 14). Larger rounded lead metal drops are present at the contact between the glass and the ceramic body. SEM-EDS analysis of the upper two strata indicates that they are dominated by lead, suggesting that the mineralization observed is a form of lead oxide and not a lead silicate. In the lower section of the sample this ratio changes with silica figuring more prominently, and additional elements such as potassium, calcium, and aluminum are strongly represented.

Sample LA162-337 exhibits a similar stratigraphy to Sample LA162-15 but with an additional phase of a black glass with quartz and perhaps K-feldspar inclusions capping the sequence. This material resembles Sample LA162-339. XRF analysis corroborates the optical and SEM-EDS data, suggesting that this material is primarily litharge with PbO present at its upper strata at 80.44 Wt%. A large metal drop within the sample was found to be 97.61 Wt% lead with the addition of cadmium (1.53 Wt%) and minor traces of manganese, copper, and silver. The lead glass capping the sequence in this sample is composed of lead oxide and silica with the addition of iron and zinc oxide. At the base of the sample, where the lead oxide interacts with the ceramic body, the elemental data suggests that this material is probably composed of wood ash as opposed to bone ash due to the higher ration of calcium and potassium in relation to phosphorous.

Sample LA162-17 (Plate 15) is broadly similar to these samples, exhibiting a layer-cake formation of crystallization composed of lead oxide, capping a partially digested ceramic base. It differs from samples LA162-15 and LA162-337 in that it contains a surface enrichment of small, finely dispersed, rounded copper droplets. SEM-EDS analysis suggests that copper, calcium, and iron oxides play a larger role in the composition of this sample more generally. This sample may represent the cupellation of a copper-rich lead.

In reflected light Sample LA162-339 appears to be composed of a black glass that has interacted with quartz and other mineral inclusions producing yellow and reddish phases. XRF analysis indicates that its composition is similar to samples LA162-15, LA162-17, and LA162337 with lead oxide dominating the glassy phase, but with the additional inclusion of Fe_2O_3 up to 4.52 Wt%. Calcium and potassium are present as well. Metallic lead droplets are present within the black glassy phase and contain some barium and silver.

REFRACTORY MATERIALS

Heat-altered and partially vitrified adobe formed a significant portion of the assemblage recovered from the facility. It was found in association with ore, slag, and metal concentrations. This spatial patterning suggests that refractory materials accumulated in proximity to locations where smelting and metal-processing activities occurred. Three such accumulations and four adobe brick fragments were refired to determine the temperature ranges that altered the adobe. Samples of adobe material include three partially vitrified adobe brick and one heat-altered adobe brick. Adobe exhibiting high-heat alteration and partial vitrification was sampled from the adobe accumulation adjacent to the south wall of the terrace (88E/-172N/F2) and from the basin-shaped furnace (Feature 90E/-168N/F1). An additional adobe sample, recovered from the Western Exterior of the Western Terrace, exhibited a low-fired appearance.

Sections of the bricks were observed with Leica and Olympus stereo microscopes equipped with magnification ranges from 7.5x to 70x. Observations were made of the fabric, consistency, and porosity of the adobe. For the three vitrified bricks, the sections clearly revealed the color banding associated with different temperature and atmosphere gradients (Figure 7.1). Characterizations of each color variation were made using a Munsell color chart. Few published examples of refiring experiments on furnace refractory material exist, so a sampling strategy was devised following the suggestion of Pamela Vandiver (University of Arizona, MSE), and the protocols established for the replication and analysis of Medieval brick (Wolf 2002). Each color and consistency gradient was sampled as rough quarter-inch sections; four sections of each gradient were produced for each experimental temperature regime. The experimental temperature regimes began at 800°C and increased at 100°C intervals for a maximum temperature of 1100°C. Soak times were set at 30 minutes. The quarter-inch sections were arranged on fire brick palettes to be able to observe the effects of each temperature regime on each gradient. As each temperature regime was completed, sets of samples were removed to document changes in color and consistency.

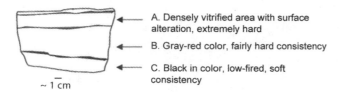

A. Densely vitrified area with surface alteration, extremely hard

B. Gray-red color, fairly hard consistency

C. Black in color, low-fired, soft consistency

~ 1 cm

Figure 7.1. Color and consistency gradients of refractory material. Prepared by the author.

Samples were fired in a Lindberg electric furnace, Model # 51848, with a temperature limit of 1100°C. The furnace reached each temperature gradient of successive 100°C intervals in 10 minutes, giving it a heating rate of 10°C per minute. Firing was conducted in an oxidizing atmosphere, which may have contrasted with the original firing conditions of the archaeological samples. This discrepancy may have influenced the results of the experiment in two ways. First, associations between sample color and temperature regime may have been skewed depending on the degree of non-oxidized iron present in the original samples. Second, temperatures at which changes in consistency and glass formation occur in an oxidizing atmosphere may have been about 50°C higher than similar changes in a reducing atmosphere (Maniatis and Tite 1981), although this may not be the case for clays containing less than 5 percent calcite (Mirti and Davit 2004). Discrepancies of 50°C are at a finer resolution than the refiring regime employed in the experiment and may not be as critical in assessing the range of temperature involved in metallurgical activity represented by the adobe refractory material.

Color characterizations of the refired samples were made using the Munsell color chart. The refired samples were again analyzed optically using the low-power microscopes to document changes to the fabric, consistency, and porosity due to refiring. Five polished sections were made of samples exhibiting various ranges of vitrification. These samples included both unaltered and refired sections and were analyzed optically with an Olympus petrographic microscope with magnification ranges of 25x to 200x.

The optical characterization of all four samples suggest that they have similar compositions. The adobe was found to contain a high sand content, on the order of more than 60 percent by visual estimation. Sand grains were well-rounded. A few larger rock fragments of sandstone and quartz were present. Charcoal flecking was not observed, nor were other inclusions normally associated with the use of midden material as the raw material for production, as is historically and archaeologically documented for

contemporary examples of Pueblo adobe production (White 1996). The only suggestion of organic material observed were long, linear voids apparently left by the decomposition or combustion of grass or straw (Plate 16:E). The use of grass or straw as a temper was most likely an introduced Spanish practice. Straw temper has been documented from later mission contexts and is noted in eighteenth-century Spanish colonial documents as being necessary for increasing the strength of adobe block (White 1996:349). Victor Mindeleff's (1886) nineteenth-century characterization of Pueblo architecture also noted a difference between the straw-tempered adobe in the mission buildings at Zuni as opposed to the nontempered adobe in domestic structures.

The refiring experiment indicates that the adobe bricks sampled contain evidence for the use of a range in temperature and atmosphere conditions within the smelting facility at Paa-ko. Adobe recovered from Feature 88E/-172N/F1 exhibits the highest temperature ranges out of the sampled adobes. Its lowest fired section appears to have been brought to a temperature of 1000°C and its mid- and high-fired sections were fired in excess of 1100°C. Its depth of vitrification of up to 2 centimeters suggests that the brick was exposed to such temperatures for a long period of time (Kingery and Gourdin 1976). The adobe brick recovered from the Western Exterior Area appears to be the lowest fired sample, with a change in consistency occurring between 800°C and 900°C.

The adobe samples recovered from furnace Feature 90E/-168N/F1 went through a range of temperatures, from a low of 900°C at their lowest fired sections, to 1000°C at their mid-fired sections, to temperatures in excess of 1100°C for their vitrified sections. Both bricks also contained mineralization on the exterior surface of their vitrified sections that had a vitrification point well below that indicated by the highest heat alteration of the adobe itself. Glass was produced in the experiment from a layer of mineralization observed at the surface of each block in temperature ranges between 800 °C and 1000°C. This suggests the presence of lead in similar concentrations as that found in lead glaze (De Benedetto and others 2004; Tite and others 1998). The presence of lead was also indicated by the formation of small droplets of lead metal at the interface of the glassy surface alteration and the vitrified adobe layer.

The formation of a lead glass from the interaction of the mineralized layer and the vitrified adobe suggest the possible composition of the mineralized layer as a sublimate from the smelting process of lead ores. XRF analysis was conducted on a polished sample from this section of the adobe that was not processed in the refiring experiment.

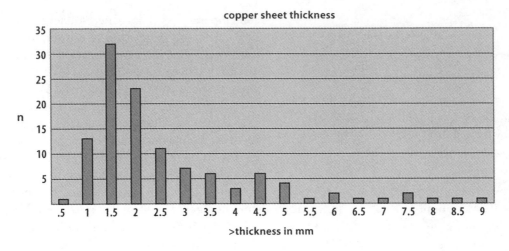

Figure 7.2. Sheet copper thicknesses. Prepared by the author.

Results indicate that this material is a combination of zinc, lead, silica, and calcium oxide (Plate 16:A). This composition would be consistent with the volitization and subsequent redeposition of these elements on refractory material involved in a smelting regime using lead ores like those in the analyzed samples.

The XRF analysis also identified a large prill of metallic lead embedded within the semi-vitrified section of this sample. Coupled with the discrepancy between the temperatures of vitrification evident in the interior of the adobe and the melting point of the mineralized layer on its surface, this suggests that the adobe may have been reused. It could have been scavenged from another furnace that obtained higher temperatures and therefore produced the observed vitrification; or the adobe reflected multiple uses of the furnace through various temperature regimes in different smelting operations. The presence of lead within the vitrified layer may be due to similar refirings in antiquity that reduced a former mineralized layer and produced lead metal that became incorporated within the matrix of the adobe. Alternatively, lead metal or a lead mineral may have been incorporated into the adobe fabric in the process of furnace manufacture and was subsequently reduced or remelted during furnace operation.

COPPER WORKING

Evidence for copper-working technology at Paa-ko is limited to the analysis of copper sheet discarded as cut offs in the production process. Copper sheet was produced from fairly pure copper metal (≥99 Wt%). A comparison with smelted copper from the site, much of which contains a high iron content, suggests that a refining operation may have been conducted before the metal could be worked into sheet. This may have been a simple operation consisting of the remelting the metal in an open container, thereby oxidizing the iron, which would float to the surface where it could be skimmed off and discarded. Or a process was used by which clean quartz sand was added to form a fayalitic slag that could be poured off (Craddock 1995:203). Sulfide inclusions are present in most of the pieces observed, suggesting that the sulfide inclusions were retained through the refining process and into the composition of the sheet copper. These inclusions can be observed as stringers that exhibit deformation due to repeated hammering in one direction (Plate 17). A comparison of 109 sheet copper fragments suggest that sheet was consistently hammered to thicknesses between 1 and 2 mm (Figure 7.2).

Alternatively, the copper sheet may have been produced through a different smelting regime than that represented by the iron-rich nodules predominant in the assemblage. Copper-isotope analysis conducted by Alyson Thibodeau suggests that the copper sheet was produced from ore material with similar lead-isotopic signatures as local ore bodies, but with different copper isotope signatures from the smelted iron-rich nodules (see discussion below). The difference between the two cuprous metals reflects the differences between ores used in the smelting process, with the iron-rich nodules being produced from an ore similar to the analyzed ore samples LA162-211 and LA162-338, and the copper sheet being produced from ores more similar to sample LA162-214.

Copper sheet was both cold- and hot-worked. Some pieces demonstrate evidence for a final stage of annealing as indicated by twinned grains with little evidence of deformation stress (Plate 18). Deformation stresses and compressed grains are common though, showing that many were left in the cold-worked state. Many examples contain large perforations that retain splayed metal on their exiting edge. Smaller sheet fragments were removed from larger pieces by being split along strain lines using a hammer and chisel, utilizing the increase in brittleness produced in copper after repeated working in order to break off forms. Some of these forms appear to be blanks, or consistent cut-off patterns in trapezoidal shapes (Figure 7.3). Since the majority of pieces are scrap, evidence for the final stages of production are largely absent.

Only two "finished" copper sheet artifacts were recovered from the facility. Both appear to be ornaments; one is a perforated and stamped disk (Figure 7.4), the other a foot-shaped, incised pendant (Figure 7.5). A similar foot-shaped pendant was recovered during the WPA excavations in the 1930s (Lambert 1954). The perforated and stamped disk evidently was polished or abraded to remove manufacturing marks. The design of small circles stamped around its central perforation appears to have been made with a tool similar to a leather punch. The foot-shaped pendant appears much less finished and retains the chisel marks used to separate it from a larger piece. Its design is similarly rough and is incised along one face using a sharp implement.

The repeated hammering and annealing evident in the metal-working technology at Paa-ko may have been an extension of colonial period metal-working traditions introduced from West Mexico. The copper-producing villages of Michoacán were known for the manufacture of copper vessels such as kettles, chocolate pots, and *comales* that were highly valued in the colony. Traditions of copper work are still practiced in this region today, with the village of Santa Clara del Cobre producing vessels for the tourist and art markets, continuing a copper-working technology that originated in precolonial indigenous metal working (Maldonado 2006). Large vessels are typically produced through the manufacture and joining of copper sheet including the raising of copper through a hammer and anvil technique, with repeated annealing. A similar approach to the technology appears to have been implemented at Paa-ko.

LEAD- AND COPPER-ISOTOPE ANALYSIS

Lead and copper isotope analysis was conducted by Alyson Thibodeau (Department of Geosciences, University of Arizona) on 10 galena samples, 2 malachite samples, 4 smelted copper nodules, and 8 metallic copper artifacts from the

Figure 7.3. Blank exhibiting chisel marks and perforation. Photo by the author.

Figure 7.4. Perforated and stamped disk. Photo by the author.

Figure 7.5 Foot-shaped pendant. Photo by the author

facility. Samples were analyzed using a multicollector inductively coupled plasma mass spectrometer (MC-ICP-MS) located at the University of Arizona. Lead-isotope ratios for the analyzed pieces strongly correlate with each other, suggesting that the base material came from the same geologic area (Figure 7.6). The lead-isotope ratios in the Paa-ko materials fall within the range of galena and

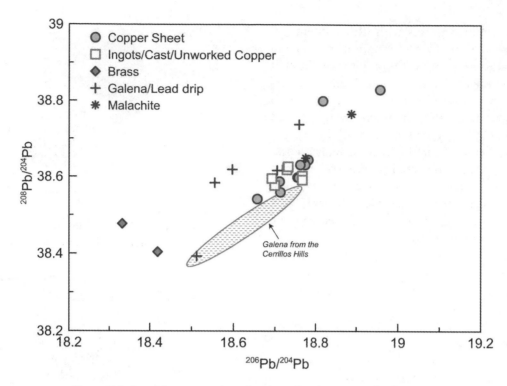

Figure 7.6. Lead-isotope ratios of various Paa-ko materials. Courtesy Alyson Thibodeau.

turquoise from the region, suggesting that they came from local geological sources such as the Cerrillos Hills, the San Pedro Mountains, and Tijeras Canyon.

Excluding four brass samples, all analyzed materials have similar lead isotope ratios, suggesting that they were produced from a restricted geological source. In comparison to lead isotope ratios for galena and turquoise obtained from the Cerrillos Hills sources, the materials from the workshop demonstrate enough similarity to suggest a local origin, but fall outside of the strong trend line exhibited by the Cerrillos data, suggesting that they originated from a different geological source.

Similarly, the correspondence between the galena and malachite samples suggest that both ores were obtained from a geologically related source whose lead isotope ratios are not yet measured. Note here that no isotopic measurements are yet available for the New Placers Mining District, which is the closest mining district to Paa'ko. The strong correlation between smelted metal and copper sheet suggests that the copper sheet found in the archaeological assemblage was produced at the facility as opposed to being recycled from copper artifacts produced in West Mexico or other areas of the Spanish colonial world. Recycling did

occur at the site, however, as evidenced by the inclusion of brass with distinct isotope ratios within the assemblage. Although local ores contain both copper and zinc, smelting them would not produce brass, as the zinc will volatilize into the atmosphere. Brass was produced by the cementation process—heating molten copper, zinc oxide, and charcoal in a tightly sealed crucible. There is no evidence that brass was ever produced in in New Mexico during the Spanish colonial period.

The copper-isotope analysis suggests a differentiation in the production process for copper (Figure 7.7). The smelted copper nodules and the worked copper sheet form two analytically distinct clusters. This suggests that they were produced from different source materials. Copper ores from hydrothermal deposits and ores associated with weathered deposits (such as malachite and azurite) are more highly fractionated, producing more positive copper isotope ratios. Copper ores produced from primary sulfide (hypogene) deposits generally have copper isotope ratios closer to zero or in the negative range. The smelted copper nodules analyzed appear to contain copper isotope ratios consistent with weathered ore sources, whereas the worked copper sheet appears to contain isotope ratios associated

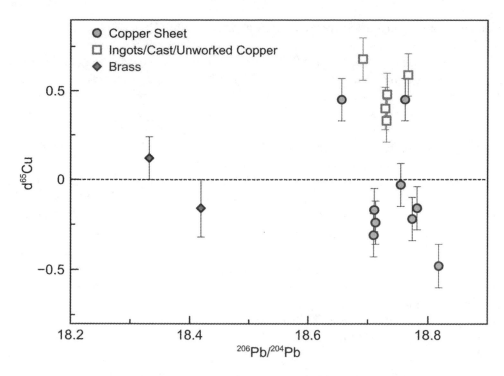

Figure 7.7. Copper-isotope ratios in relation to lead-isotope ratios, showing clustering that suggests different source materials for copper sheet, unworked copper, and brass. Courtesy Alyson Thibodeau.

with primary sulfide (hypogene) ores such as chalcopyrite (Thomas and Thibodeau 2010).

The copper-isotopic ratios suggest that the sheet copper was produced from ores not well represented by the assemblage at Paa-ko. The majority of ore recovered from the excavations of the workshop were associated with weathered, gossan deposits. The sheet copper could have been produced off site, from an ore body with lead isotope ratios similar to local sources. Chalcopyrite nodules were recovered in the excavation of the workshop, although in much smaller quantities than the weathered gossan. Similarly, the abundance of galena in association with primary minerals such as sphalerite and calcite in the assemblage suggests that less-weathered ore bodies were being exploited as well. Alternatively, the distinction between the finished metal objects and the copper nodules may be the result of technological practice conducted at the workshop. If the primary function of the workshop was concerned with the individual assay of different ore bodies rather than large-scale extraction of metal, then distinct copper isotope ratios may be carried through the reduction, refining, and smithing processes, reflecting different assays.

DISCUSSION

Based on these analyses, metal production at Paa-ko involved high-temperature smelting of both copper and lead ores. Copper-smelting technology appears to have been quite variable, as there is evidence in the various slags of both oxidizing and reducing atmospheres. Lead ores were smelted, most likely to recover gold and silver. Smelted metal was treated by cupellation, through which precious metals were concentrated and refined. This process is indicated by the presence and composition of litharge and lead glass. A final step involved the working of copper to produce sheet copper ornaments.

Copper and lead ores used in the process are consistent with ore bodies found in the Cerrillos Hills and the San Pedro Mountains. The mineral associations and characterization of the samples based on the petrographic data outlined here reveal mineralogical characteristics that are found in both localities. Lead-zinc ore is the primary ore of the Santa Rosa Mine in the Cerrillos Hills, which is known to have been exploited during the Colonial and Territorial periods (Milford and Swick 1995), although similar mineral associations are reported for the New Placers district in the San Pedro Mountains as well. The gold content of the copper ores and their association with gossan deposits suggest that their original provenance was within the New Placers district. These ore characteristics and the proximity of the district to Paa-ko makes New Placers the most logical source for the ores smelted at the facility. The district became a major site of placer gold mining in the mid-nineteenth century and the area's San Pedro mine became a significant producer of copper in the late nineteenth and early twentieth centuries (Finlay 1922; Northrop 1996).

It is problematic to assess ore value from the spot identification method of the XRF analysis used here because it is not a bulk analysis per se. But precious metal values from the analyzed galena and copper ore confirm at least the possibility that Escalante's assay of 1581 was accurate. The analyses support the claims by colonists in 1601 that Zaldívar had discovered rich ores in the vicinity of El Tuerto. An evaluation of these claims based on the personal history of Oñate and Zaldívar as miners have been detailed by Milford and Swick (1995). As evidence of early seventeenth-century mining practices, the ore from the facility suggests that fairly rich ores were available and procured by miners of this period.

The ore composition also adds a twist to the account of the apparent falsified assay of 1600, long cited as either evidence for the lack of profitable deposits in colonial New Mexico or as an elite conspiracy to discredit the value of the colony (Milford and Swick 1995). In 1599 Oñate sent silver ores to the viceroy of New Spain. The ores were assayed publicly but produced only copper. If there was an emphasis on copper ores in early seventeenth-century New Mexican mining, the discrepancy could have been caused by the assay technology applied and not the copper ores themselves. All three of the archaeologically documented early colonial smelting localities (Paa-ko [LA 162], San Marcos Pueblo [LA 98], and San Francisco del Tuerto [LA 240]) were associated with copper ore or copper smelting slag (Vaughan 2006; Warren and Weber 1979).

The materials analyses indicate that the technology used at Paa-ko was organized around the production of precious metal through the smelting and refining of copper and lead. Copper ores exhibit the greatest diversity in the assemblage, suggesting their importance in the technology, and copper metal and metallurgy dominates the facility. The precious metal values indicated by XRF analysis suggest the reason for this. It is tempting to assess the technology at Paa-ko from the perspective of mining interests, as organized around the recovery of both gold and silver. The occurrence of copper ores in association with the earliest known furnaces may be viewed not as an anomaly in Spanish practice, but rather as a strategy of wealth acquisition that is congruent with seventeenth-century concepts of the association of copper as "the origin and foundation of all silver mines" (Barba 1923:72). Such associations may have significantly influenced the approach taken to ore reduction at the facility at Paa-ko.

How was knowledge of copper mining and smelting held by the miners of colonial New Spain? Operations at the Paa-ko facility may be viewed through two cultural and technological lenses—West Mexican and Spanish. Sixteenth- and seventeenth-century colonial copper production was consistently linked with the indigenous communities of the former Tarascan state in Michoacán, a population base that provided much of the labor and skilled knowledge for the mines in the north (Bakewell 1971; Barrett 1987). It has been assumed that their knowledge was transferred to the processing of the silver oxide and silver sulfide ores found in the northern mines. The use of copper sulfate (*magistral*) in the patio process meant that the ability to exploit copper ores was essential (Bakewell 1971:147). Copper mines in West Mexico were owned by indigenous communities up until the first decade of the seventeenth century and copper metallurgy continued to play an important part in West Mexican colonial economies (Barrett 1987). If community ties were maintained, as is suggested by the persistence of tribal identity in seventeenth-century Zacatecas barrios, then knowledge and interest in copper production may have been maintained as well. Copper production at Paa-ko may have been influenced by mineralogical knowledge, technical expertise, and value frameworks rooted in the traditions of native West Mexican smiths.

Spanish colonial metallurgy was an outgrowth of technologies developed in Europe and the Americas. One distinctive method, developed in Mexico in the 1540s, was the patio process that used mercury amalgamation. It became the primary ore-reduction strategy used in Zacatecas and Parral, and was also used during the early colonial period in New Mexico (Probert 1969). The historical roots of this technology lie in the theory-laden practice of Islamic and Christian monastic alchemy of the late medieval period. The contemporary description of both the theory and process of mercury amalgamation in the volume *El arte de los metales*, by Alvaro Alonso Barba, the curate of the Parish of San Bernardo, Potosí, Bolivia, first published in 1640, is particularly informative about the seventeenth-century theoretical basis for the technology. Although Barba was probably one of the premier practical metallurgists of the period, his practice was rooted in alchemy (Barba 1923; Holmyard 1957). He argued that the success of mercury amalgamation was due to the manipulation of the basic properties of matter as described in the "sulfur-mercury theory" originally proposed by Jabir ibn Hayyan, the eighth-century Islamic alchemist. Although considered unscientific today, this theory provided the structural framework for the very successful technology of the patio process, as well as Barba's own "hot method" of mercury amalgamation (Platt 2000; Salazar-Soler 1997).

The sulfur-mercury theory of the formation of metals held that all metallic substances were produced by the interaction of two idealized substances that held similar characteristics to those of actual sulfur and mercury. The sulfurous substance was considered hot and dry, whereas the mercurial substance was considered cool and wet. The combination of the two in various proportions created the assorted metals (Barba 1923:43-51). Gold and silver were unique because of their "perfect mixture." This property was, in turn, indicated by color: "Gold is yellow or red, the color being due to the heating effect of the purified Sulfur on its Mercury or humidity" (Barba 1923:53).

In order to manipulate minerals and obtain certain metals, it was necessary to influence the various qualities inherent within mineral substances through the balancing of hot and cool or dry and wet properties (Holmyard 1957:75-76). This was conducted through a series of operations, sometimes using metallurgical techniques (through manipulation of heat, fuel, minerals, and atmospheres within various furnaces) and at other times using the techniques of the chemist or apothecary (through the preparation of elixirs). Mercury was often paired antagonistically with substances such as vitriol, or copper sulfate, thought to represent its opposite. Vitriol was considered detrimental to the effects of mercury, but at the highest level of transformation the two were linked (Barba 1923:101). It is interesting in this regard that the key to the patio process was thought to be the addition of copper sulfate in the mercury amalgam process (Probert 1969).

The operations used to affect changes on or within substances were extremely varied but generally were organized as a series of stages or cycles of processing that were identified by the color and textural transformations of materials (Gage 1999). Color indicated process, with degrees of transformation indicated by various stages: white for the calcination of a material, black for its reduction, red for its ultimate transformation, and so on. Color designations varied by historical period and individual experience. Their use as a direct indicator of transformational change made color a "language of movement" (Gage 1999:152). In other words, color was an external indication of internal processes of transformational change.

In the mining industry of New Spain, metal extraction technologies were organized based on the characterization of the ore body as either "red" ores (*colorados*) or "black" ores (*negrillos*), where external color indicated internal properties. Both *colorados* and *negrillos* could be rich in silver or other metals, but the processing technologies required of each were quite distinct. Red ores were considered to be dry and thus amenable to mercury amalgam processing. Red coloring is repeatedly used as a reference for silver deposits in landscape descriptions of the period. This projection of value contributed to the naming of the Little Colorado drainage by the Farfan expedition. In color associations of the sixteenth and seventeenth century, green copper ores could be indicative of red ore internal qualities, perhaps through their association with gossan deposits (Barba 1923:97). Alternatively, copper was held as "the origin or foundation of all silver mines," in that copper "gives the color to the silver ore known as *negrillos*" (Barba 1923:72-73). Black ores (typically sulfide ores) required additional processes, such as roasting or calcination, and were more amenable to smelting technologies. Interestingly, Barba's terminology (produced in early seventeenth-century Peru) included the intermediate color designation of *mulatos* for ores that combined the qualities of red and black ore, suggesting a similitude with contemporary social categories (Barba 1923:97).

At Paa-ko, the distinction between red and black ores may have been a strong structuring framework for ore acquisition and the organization of the technology itself. The copper carbonate ores may have fallen both under the auspices of *colorado* designations through their association with gossan deposits, and with *negrillos*, because of their copper content and potential for containing silver. The predominance of copper carbonates at Paa-ko may reflect their semiotic connection to the rich silver ores of Zacatecas that were processed by mercury amalgamation. Evidence for amalgamation technologies are lacking at Paa-ko, although one malachite sample and a fragment of copper sheet submitted for lead isotope analysis contained unusual levels of mercury contamination (Thibodeau, personal communication, 2006), which suggests that mercury was a component of the technology at some level. Some of the malachite ore was smelted under a different technological regime than other ores, using oxidizing conditions that produced slag containing cuprite, delafossite, and magnetite (e.g., samples LA162-54 and LA162-109), perhaps indicating that the perception of their internal qualities was more aligned with *colorados* designations. Alternatively, the high temperatures reached during their production may indicate an application of technology more amenable to *negrillos*.

Ores containing lead and copper sulfides were clearly processed as *negrillos*. Galena-bearing ores and copper sulfide minerals were both roasted in beds of charcoal and earth and smelted under high-temperature, highly reducing conditions. The formation of iron and calcium silicates within the slag from the processing suggests that the furnaces were operated at a minimum temperature range between 1125 °C and 1225 °C, based on phase diagrams for the calcium silicate-iron silicate system. The transformation of silica to high-temperature crystal forms and the refiring data on adobe refractory support this observation. Similarly, the production of copper-iron alloys within the iron silicate slags also demonstrates the application of a highly reducing smelting technology operated within these temperature parameters. Temperatures within these ranges could only be achieved through the application of a forced draft system.

After smelting, lead and copper must have undergone further processes for the recovery of precious metal. Litharge and lead glass remains from the Paa-ko facility are evidence that the metallurgists attempted to recover silver from the lead produced by ore reduction. A question remains as to how precious metals could have been recovered from the copper produced at the site. Historical and technical literature on the recovery of gold and silver from copper is less extensive than that describing either cupellation or mercury amalgamation. The liquation of copper cakes, where the silver content of copper was removed through its admixture with lead, was a major industrial development of early Renaissance Northern Europe (Sisco and Smith 1951). Liquation seems unlikely at Paa-ko, as typical byproducts of the process (such as spongy copper masses, copper scale, and liquation thorns composed of lead oxide and copper sulfide) have not been recovered (Sisco and Smith 1951:224–226).

Agricola's treatise of 1558 suggests some possible practices that do have material correlates at the facility:

> From time to time small pieces of sulfur, enveloped in or mixed with wax, are dropped into six *librae* of the molten copper, and consumed. . . . Then one and a half *sicilici* of powdered saltpeter [potassium nitrate] are dropped into the same copper and likewise consumed;

then again half an *uncia* and a *sicilicus* of sulfur enveloped in wax; afterward on and a half *sicilici* of lead-ash enveloped in wax, or of *minium* made from red-lead. Then immediately the copper is taken out, and to the gold button, which is now mixed with only a little copper, they add *stibium* [antimony sulfide] to double the amount of the button; these are heated together until the stibium is driven off; then the button together with the lead of half the weight of the button, are heated in a cupel. Finally, the gold is taken out of this and quenched [Hoover and Hoover 1950:463–464].*

This method relies on the addition of sulfur to a gold-rich copper as a means for refining gold through the production of copper sulfide. As Hoover and Hoover (1950:462–463) note, these methods "are based fundamentally upon the sulfur introduced in each case, whereby the copper is converted into sulfides and separated off as a matte. . . . In a general way the auriferous button is gradually impoverished in copper until it is fit for cupellation with lead." Ercker's 1580 treatise on assay technology describes a similar method for parting gold from silver through the addition of sulfur, copper, and lead. In this method, silver is granulated and then combined with sulfur in a sealed glazed pot and heated "in a ring of slow fire" in order to produce a sintered mass. This was then added to granulated copper in a crucible and placed in a wind furnace where lead was repeatedly added to form a *regulus*. Gold was recovered through the use of parting acid (Sisco and Smith 1951:172).

Some variant of the technology described by Agricola and Ercker may have been practiced at Paa-ko. The nature of copper (as articulated by Barba) would have suggested to seventeenth-century practitioners that it was amenable to processing by an addition of sulfur. Copper's red color was thought to be due to the abundance of sulfur in it, which would also lead it to be more refractory than other metals. By taking advantage of this internal "imperfection," the addition of sulfur would have increased its earthy nature, thereby separating it from the more perfect gold. Such a process would be self-evident based on contemporary understanding of material properties, as Barba states, "it will be easy for anyone who understands the Principles to find other ways. Sulfur, mixed with a little Lead, is all that is needed to alter the copper without detriment to the Gold" (Barba 1923:253). The same would have been true of silver

---

**Librae, *sicilci*, and *unica* are units of weight; the modern compound names are the author's addition.

and gold, for in the hierarchy of metals, silver was still not as perfect internally as gold (Barba 1923:53).

Sulfur was found in fairly high concentrations at Paa-ko, embedded in interior surfaces five through seven of the Western Terrace (Plate 19). It was also found concreted to ceramic bases recovered from the Western Exterior Area. This is probably due to its use in an attempted refining operation, perhaps a cementation process involving sulfur in addition to salt. The fact that copper sulfides found their way into the copper sheet artifacts produced at the site, despite the necessity for their refinement in earlier stages of the production process to remove metallic iron, may suggest that sulfur was reintroduced somewhere in the refinement process. The linear bin furnaces of the Eastern Terrace are also reminiscent of Ercker's "wind furnaces" for the parting of gold and silver using sulfur, and could have functioned similarly by providing a low fire in a primarily oxidizing atmosphere (Sisco and Smith 1951:179). The byproduct of such operations would have been a copper or silver sulfide matte, which would have been resmelted to recover the metal, and then melted with lead and cupelled. Sample LA162-17 may represent a final stage in this process as it appears to be the product of the attempted cupellation of a copper-rich lead. Sulfur may also have been produced on the site as an additional industrial byproduct of the roasting of sulfide ores, as sulfur was a valued product used in other Spanish colonial industries such as in the production of medicines and gunpowder.

Gold and silver were absent from the archaeological deposits at Paa-ko and lead was extremely rare because these materials were removed into other spheres of exchange within the Spanish colony. Copper, on the other hand, remained at the site. Copper was a byproduct in the precious metal production technology, but it became a primary product in the metal-working technology centered on copper sheet production and the manufacture of objects of adornment. Its further processing was under the auspices of the pueblo itself. As a material that had fallen out of immediate colonial spheres of exchange, it was given value in the local context of Puebloan production practices.

CHAPTER EIGHT

Material Value and Personal Value: Creating Wealth within Colonial Systems of Appropriation

Jim: We were both struck by the clarity of something your mom said. "Make yourself of value by wearing something of value." What were the circumstances when she said that—what were you doing and what did she see? What did she mean?

Milford: I think it was the jewelry that I was wearing, and it wasn't Zuni jewelry. It was the gold that I was wearing. On one arm I had about five bracelets on and she made a point, saying that I was just like this certain man who used to adorn himself a lot. I can't remember that man's name. I told her, "Well, they are valuable." She used that term, Do' kwa hol deh'uliu do' ddehyak'yanna, meaning when you wear something of value you will be valued. I guess by the ancestors. It is hard to translate it back but I think that's what the whole thing was about.

[Milford Nahohai to Jim Ostler in Ostler, Rodee, and Nahohai 1996:123]

It is difficult to define the metallurgical production regime at Paa-ko in terms of its ultimate goals or success. Clearly, the metallurgists were attempting to recover precious metals from lead ores and perhaps from copper ores as well. The ore mineralogy and elemental data suggest that precious metals were there to be recovered, although the amount actually recovered is unknown. The galena ore found at the site was fairly rich and had mineral associations to similar ores exploited in the mining districts of northern New Spain that would have been familiar to colonial metallurgists. This contradicts the historical record's negative assessment of the mineral resources of New Mexico and suggests other reasons (political or social) for their lack of development.

Despite the presence of precious metals in the ores found at the site, however, most of the metallurgical efforts at Paa-ko went into copper smelting. What is clear is that one of the final stages of the production cycles involving copper included the manufacture of copper sheet that was subsequently polished, incised, and pierced to make objects of adornment. This apparent culmination of the technology seems to be at odds with the intensive smelting regime represented by the iron and calcium silicate slag that formed the bulk of the assemblage.

Excavation of the Paa-ko metallurgical facility and subsequent analyses of the materials recovered have raised several questions. Did the technology used produce the results anticipated by the seventeenth-century Spanish colonial metallurgists of Paa-ko? Was the production of an unworkable copper-iron alloy evidence of inexperience in applying of a technology to a familiar material, or is it an example of the experienced application of a technology to a misidentified material? In general, what aspects of the technology are "expert" and what are "experimental?" Does the facility represent a failed industry, or a successful industry using a model that is different than that assumed in the historical record?

In order to address some of these questions it is necessary to take a step back from the technological analysis and frame the technology in its historical context through perspectives generated by various aspects of New Mexican colonialism. These include the context of the colonial mining industry, as well as the system of precolonial Puebloan mineral exchange. Seventeenth-century Paa-ko was a place where colonial regimes of value impinged upon the pueblo's traditional practices of production, exchange, and value construction. Because the facility was embedded within the spatial and economic fabric of a pueblo, colonial activities would have directly affected the pueblo's economy and social structure. The activities and pueblo-colony interactions changed over time and are best viewed in terms of the progression of colonial occupation from initial encounters to more structured appropriative contexts. By framing the technology at Paa-ko within the changing context of Spanish colonialism in New Mexico during the seventeenth century, it might be possible to gain a sense of the underlying social conditions that influenced the changing technological repertoire seen at the facility. Understanding colonial Spanish value systems are a key to understanding these changes.

EARLY COLONIAL NEGOTIATIONS OF VALUE

The mining industry was the premier creator of value in the seventeenth-century Spanish colonial world. The search for minerals (the search for wealth) intersected with Puebloan practices for the creation of value. As discussed previously, colored minerals were used extensively in ritual production during the Pueblo IV period, in the painting of katsina masks, prayer sticks, and ceramic vessels. Archaeologically, minerals were important components in Puebloan exchange systems, linking communities across broad regions to specific places, helping to create and recreate the memory of origins and migrations. Color designations of minerals referenced social distinctions, geographic associations, and spiritual connections.

In the interactions between Spanish colonial metallurgists and Puebloan pigment procurers, color played a significant role in establishing the values and potentials of landscapes, although the meanings of various colors were different for the two groups. Where Spanish colonists associated "red" and "black" ores found in newly encountered landscapes with their wealth-bearing potential, Puebloans associated colors with directionality, as cosmological reference points in a socialized landscape and universe (Whiteley 2012).

Colors and the internal properties that they represented were manipulated medicinally by both Spanish metallurgists and Puebloan ritual practitioners. For Spanish metallurgists, transformations of color indicated a transformation of character. Embedded within metallurgical color terminology was a discourse concerning the link between spiritual transformation and the transformation of matter. Alchemical and metallurgical processes were often conceptualized as healing processes; the internal properties of a substance were balanced in order to perfect it (Barba 1923; Holmyard 1957). There was a general blurring of distinctions between substances that were

"healing" in the transformation of metals and those that were deemed efficacious for the curing of ailments. Materials such as sulfur, alum, and verdigris that were used in metallurgical processes were listed as medicines in the Salazar inspection of the Oñate colony (Hammond and Rey 1953:220, 255). Litharge and greta (both lead oxides) were ingredients in many of the medicines available in the Spanish colonies during the sixteenth century (Simpson 1937). The conflation of metallurgical properties and medicinal practices has continued into the present in the folk remedies of northern Mexico, for example, in the treatment of *empacho*, a stomach ailment, by the dangerous practice of ingesting powdered litharge (Ackerman and Baer 1988). Litharge (lead oxide) was a pivotal material for the refining of silver, drawing parallels between techniques for the curing of the metallic body and the human body.

Within the healing practices of the Northern Tewa, color is an indicator of identity through its association with moiety divisions and seasonal qualities, rather than a "language of movement," or process of transformation, as was assumed in Spanish metallurgical practices. The use of specific colors in practice (such as in the use of colored corn at sodality initiations) is an indicator of identities related to village, moiety, and individual, based on membership in ritual sodalities (Ford 1992:226). Color is also one of a series of identity-establishing attributes for medicines used to heal ailments based on hot or cold imbalances (Ford 1992:132–134), although this aspect of Tewa practice may have been influenced by Spanish medicinal practices (Parsons 1966).

Historically, how were the similarities and differences in color associations negotiated within the framework of early colonial ore prospecting? What is apparent from the early historical encounters is the repeated offering and acceptance of copper carbonate and copper sulfide ores, despite the predominant focus of sixteenth- and seventeenth-century Spanish colonial metallurgy on silver oxide or lead sulfide-bearing silver ores. In 1581, Gallegos accepted "samples of a copperish steel-like metal," probably chalcopyrite, thought to be rich in silver. In 1582, Luján and Espejo were also shown copper deposits, which Espejo claimed to be silver rich (contrary to Luján's assessment). Farfan de Godos was brought to the same mines in 1598 and was impressed with the deep blue color of the ores, suggesting that they may have been smalt, a byproduct of cobalt-silver ore processing in Europe. The material, however, was almost certainly azurite (a copper carbonate), as there are no cobalt ores in the region.

The apparent focus on copper ores within the technology at the metallurgical facility at Paa-ko may have been a further extension of negotiations of value, focused on the dual meaning of Puebloan emphasis on the value of blue-green and Spanish ore values positioning copper as "giving the color" to silver ores (Barba 1923; Plog 2003). Although only three seventeenth-century smelting facilities have been excavated to date, all three reflect a technology within which copper ores play a significant part despite their being located adjacent to lead ores with a profitable silver content in the Cerrillos and New Placers Mining Districts (Vaughan 2001, 2006; Warren and Weber 1979). The three major mining communities identified in the historical record, La Cienega, San Marcos, and El Tuerto, were all occupied pueblos when the New Mexico colony was established (Barrett 2002; Milford and Swick 1995). It is significant that the facilities at San Marcos Pueblo (LA 98) and Paa-ko (which may have been El Tuerto of historical record) were built within pueblos that had a long history of occupation.

The incorporation of Spanish facilities within a Puebloan context suggests a setting in which indigenous labor, knowledge, and skill were viewed as vital to the success of mining practices. These were the initial contexts for the appropriation of labor and material resources, but they were also the contexts within which those potential sources of wealth were evaluated. A kind of double assay occurred in early colonial documents, where mineralogical assessments were coupled with evaluations of the docility and hard-working nature of indigenous peoples. The result of this process placed a perhaps not unwarranted emphasis on copper minerals, as well as an emphasis on the potential of incorporating the populations of the Galisteo Basin into the mining industry and the missionization scheme.

SHIFTING CONTEXTS OF PRODUCTION

The determination of material value during the early colonial period was negotiated within contexts where indigenous knowledge and labor played central roles. Such contexts were the roots of future appropriations under Spanish colonialism. For the mining industry, its development hinged on the continued attempt to exploit the same mineral resources that played a central part in precolonial exchange. The Spanish colonists used other precolonial materials in similar ways. The Plains-Pueblo bison-hide exchange and regional textile trade were goods in the precolonial system that figured prominently in efforts by colonial elites to obtain wealth (Pierce 2006; Webster 1997, 2000).

The production of these items under colonial tribute entailed a shift in the way traditional production activities were scheduled and organized within pueblos. Webster (2000:203) documents that by the mid-seventeenth century, tribute demands forced Puebloans not only to reschedule the seasonal production of cloth, but also affected traditional gendered divisions of labor. The primarily male production of cloth that took place within ritual space was moved to primarily female household- and workshop-production contexts (Webster 2000:203). New technologies were also introduced, with wool and knitting techniques becoming increasingly important towards the end of the seventeenth century. Bison-hide preparation and use followed a similar trajectory, such as hides being made into clothing or used as canvases for paintings (Pierce 2006).

In the decades following initial colonization, workshop production was instituted by various governors as a way to generate personal wealth through the production of a higher volume of tribute goods. Both hide painting and textile manufacture were conducted in such contexts under the governorship of Juan de Eulate (1618–1625) and Luis de Rosas (1637–1641). Workshop contexts were multiethnic and included Pueblo and Mexican Indian workers (Pierce 2006:139). Goods produced were traded in the mining centers of Northern New Spain, especially Parral. Perhaps because of the volume and profitability of this trade, cloth and hides became mediums of exchange, with individual pieces having monetary equivalents (Pierce 2006).

It may be useful to view the facility at Paa-ko as a workshop context that was formally delimited by the terraces of masonry construction. The facility represented a new social context of work that was unrelated to any household, kiva, or plaza workspace context. Metallurgical facilities, particularly those involved with time-dependent processes such as smelting and forging, are often highly structured in order to both limit and facilitate productive action within their spaces (Keller and Keller 1996). The highly structured space of the facility at Paa-ko would have entailed a similar restrictive structuring of action within it. The internal organization of the facility was related to activities such as wood gathering and charcoal preparation, mining, and ore sorting. As with textile production, these activities may have impacted traditional productive actions and social structures of action such as gendered divisions of labor or particularly for mining and the appropriation of minerals, with tasks that were under the direction of ritual sodalities.

WEST MEXICAN METALLURGISTS

Indigenous West Mexican miners and metal workers played a pivotal role in the establishment of new mining ventures throughout northern New Spain. The attempted establishment of the New Mexico mining industry probably involved individuals from these communities as well. Aspects of the technology at Paa-ko suggest this involvement, particularly the development of copper sheet-metal production. But perhaps more significantly, the role of West Mexican metallurgists as free laborers within the industry may have provided a different model of colonial interaction than that offered by either tribute *encomienda* relationships or the doctrinal and paternalistic production systems of the missions.

As a group of skilled laborers, West Mexican metallurgists held an ambiguous social position in the northern frontier in that the mobility made possible by wage labor allowed for a certain autonomy from colonial structures, which attempted to limit the economic opportunities of certain social classes or ethnic *castas*. The mobility of this skilled labor force was a cause for great concern to mine owners in Zacatecas after the founding of Parral in the 1640s, when many of the West and Central Mexican miners moved north to take advantage of better wages (Bakewell 1971; West 1949). In fact, one of the draws of New Mexico for colonial elites involved with mining may have been the potential that some of that labor could be replaced with *encomienda* and *repartimiento* rights, for which the mine owners of Zacatecas repeatedly petitioned the Spanish Crown (Bakewell 1971:122).

West (1949) notes that the role of West Mexican skilled labor in the mining industry of the late sixteenth and early seventeenth century was an evolving one, developing from roots that were more exploitive, when *repartimiento* was legal in the first half of the sixteenth century, to a state of semi-autonomy as wage laborers. Spicer (1962) also suggests that communities with long, generational engagement with the Spanish colonial mining industry were able to take advantage of both the insular and fairly protected community of mission life and the more liberal social and monetary opportunities of the mining frontier. West Mexican indigenous miners could potentially shift between the two contexts, depending on which was less oppressive at any given time.

The ability to shift between mission and wage labor contexts may have placed such individuals in a pivotal position between pueblo communities and colonial elites. Although inseparable from the conceptualization of the Spanish mining community in a larger sense, West Mexican metallurgists clearly had their own social and wealth-gaining strategies. The fluctuation between, and manipulation of, colonial contexts of production within their own frameworks of value is reflected in the relationship West Mexican metal producers had with the production of copper and its association with the establishment of a regional currency (Meek 1948). A copper-rich gold alloy, *tepuzque*, produced in Central and West Mexico, was an early form of currency on par with the silver peso in the sixteenth century. Its use had antecedents in the precolonial preference for gold-copper alloy compositions (Hosler 1994). *Tepuzque*, as well as debased gold bullion, was considered an unofficial money, often preferred within indigenous markets to the official silver currency in the early sixteenth century. The Crown attempted to put a stop to its use many times, finally outlawing it in 1591 in the attempt to stabilize the value of silver coinage. Its use continued into the seventeenth century, and other, local, copper-based currencies (*tlacos*) developed in later centuries (Meek 1948:67).

The use of unofficial copper and copper-gold alloy currencies in addition to officially sanctioned silver coinage affected indigenous economies in New Spain in conflicting ways. West Mexican copper-producing communities were able to take advantage of the need for small denomination currency by offering sheet copper coinage. Meek (1948:70) reports that in the 1540s this coinage was briefly sanctioned by the Crown, and copper planchets produced in Michoacán and stamped in Mexico City became acceptable forms of exchange. The use of copper as an exchange medium may have displaced Central Mexican indigenous small currencies, such as cacao, and copper metal currency was highly resisted by these populations.

Such alterations of monetary value were made possible by the power, through labor, of West Mexican smiths. As a kind of situated agency, the technological skill of these communities allowed for the imposition of alternate regimes of value. This agency operated within and bridged both the small-change economies of daily transactions and the increasingly global economic relationships afforded by New Spain's silver production. Don Juan de Oñate's first act as the royal inspector of mines in Spain in 1624 was to request to bring with him "six Indian metal smelters and refiners from the Indies." This reflects the position of such individuals within global spheres of exchange (Hammond and Rey 1953:1157).

WEALTH AND VALUE

The situated agency of West Mexican metallurgists, particularly in regard to the production of metallic worth, provides a useful framework for understanding the relationship between Puebloan producers and the value of the objects that they produced. West Mexican metallurgists were the primary labor force in the construction of Spanish colonial wealth, in that they mined, smelted, and refined the metals that were used ultimately for currency in local and global markets. Yet they also established alternate forms of wealth, through the establishment of alternative currencies that challenged and shaped the value of silver currency over time. Their situated agency ultimately allowed for a certain degree of mobility between mission and mining social contexts.

This reflects what de Certeau (1984) referred to as the difference between the tactics of those under the weight of a dominant culture versus the strategies of the dominant in the construction of culture (de Certeau 1984). In modeling individual agency as improvisational creative action rather than planned actions of direct opposition, de Certeau suggests that tactics manipulate such structural orders through a creative engagement with them:

> The actual order of things is precisely what "popular" tactics turn to their own ends, without any illusion that it will change any time soon. Though elsewhere it is exploited by a dominant power or simply denied by an ideological discourse, here order is *tricked* by an art. Into the institution to be served are thus insinuated styles of social exchange, technical invention, and moral resistance, that is, an economy of the "*gift*" (generosities for which one expects a return), an esthetics of "*tricks*" (artists' operations) and an ethics of *tenacity* (countless ways of refusing to accord the established order the status of a law, a meaning, or a fatality) [de Certeau 1984:26, emphasis in original].

The metallurgy of Paa-ko suggests tactical play with the way metal was ordered in terms of value. Copper became the foundation for a technology normally assigned to silver. Thus the technology usually assigned to the production of metallic worth through bullion became a technology that produced objects of adornment, making metal a symbol of self-worth.

This shift in emphasis suggests play between local and global economies. The split in the economic spheres of value for each metal is suggested in the Viceroy Mendoza's negative assessment of the New Mexican colony in 1602:

> When silver or copper, which they say abound, are discovered, we could introduce some form of coinage to circulate there. Some could be coined in that country and the value set low enough so as to leave a profit for the merchants who might bring and sell copper in bars. This seems impossible since the cost of transportation would be more than its worth. It also seems impossible to put it in circulations by ordering the copper coined here [*New Spain*]. It would circulate at a higher value, and the same would be true of the coin of that land circulating here. If the value here were not excessive or much greater than its value there and that it often commands in other kingdoms, not much profit could be made, although in such a case we might use an alloy if we found some thing from which to make it. Unless they send coin or goods to this country to obtain money or to exchange it for what they need, there would be no way of establishing commerce. Even when this matter of coinage finds a better solution, whatever is sent there will be extremely expensive, in view of the cost of transportation. . . .
>
> Even though it is not certain that there is silver, if means were found to establish copper coinage, this would encourage and facilitate trade and aid in the support of the Spaniards there, even if the profits were not large. They have nothing to sell from which they can obtain cash, and poverty is everywhere.
>
> [Hammond and Rey 1953:913–914; emphasis added]

Although this text was most likely produced in an effort to discredit the colony and the efforts of Oñate, as Trigg's (2005) analysis of household economic relationships in the early colony suggests, this assessment of poverty may not be far off the mark. The viceroy's comments also reveal the dichotomy between the small change economy of copper currency and the regional and global exchange facilitated by silver currency or bullion. It draws a distinction based on class, that copper facilitated exchange within the exchange practices of the poor, but silver could not be used in the same way. In a currency based on the weight of precious metal, the reduction of a peso to small denominations would reduce it in size to such an extent as to make it unusable for exchange. There is a peculiar equation between the value of metal and the types of exchange possible within certain social classes. The hierarchy of metals and the internal qualities of states of perfection that they represented mirrored the social hierarchy of economic transactions within which they played a part.

The selective changes in economy and subsistence at Paa-ko during the early colonial period may be evidence for the development of a tactic of wealth appropriation by the Pueblos that sought to capitalize on the local construction of value available within the colonial system, through metallic and livestock holdings separate from the dominant mission and colonial elite communities. Both forms of wealth were mobile, which may have made them increasingly valued in the context of intense social disruption and contraction of indigenous settlement throughout the seventeenth century (Lycett 2002). The recovery of sheet copper from the metal workshop, as opposed to the extraction of silver and gold, may be viewed as an appropriation of metallic value at the local level. The engagement with copper smithing technology at Paa-ko may represent the attempt to establish a local form of wealth that could take advantage of small-scale economic transactions among Puebloans or non-elite colonists. During the seventeenth century, few colonial *estancias* were able to produce goods beyond their subsistence needs, suggesting that local exchange practices predominated. These systems integrated Puebloan and Plains productive practices, often in complex ways (Trigg 2005).

The partability of wealth as metal may have been a major structuring factor for the actions of both Spanish colonial metallurgists and Puebloan smiths at Paa-ko and other colonized Pueblo communities. Copper sheet pendants, crosses, and cut off materials have been recovered from seventeenth-century archaeological contexts at contemporary Pueblos incorporated into the colonial system such as Gran Quivira and Pecos (Kidder 1932, Vivian 1964). From ceramic depictions on late glaze ceramics, we know that similar pendants were worn in culturally syncretic contexts (Mobley-Tanaka 2002). It seems likely that the copper produced at Paa-ko may have been incorporated into these communities. The recovery of copper sheet scrap at these sites also suggests that copper smithing practices were at least partially incorporated within Pueblo communities more broadly. For Spanish colonial metallurgists the recovery of precious metal allowed either for the obtainment of a wage or the creation of wealth as bullion, both means of social mobility. For the people of Paa-ko, and perhaps other colonized Pueblo communities, the production of sheet copper ornaments can be perceived as a transformation of material that began as a product of Spanish colonial wealth extraction into one that signified personal or familial worth as objects of adornment. Both forms of wealth referenced larger regimes of value within regional and local respective practices and both were mobile.

The creation of objects of adornment from copper metal may also have been another play on value based on artistic trickery, as de Certeau (1984) styles such actions. Production regimes established by Spanish metallurgists that involved minerals important in Pueblo ritual divorced such connections by creating bullion. Within the final stages of the production regime at Paa-ko, such value designations were turned around through the re-appropriation of metal as objects of adornment. Whereas copper minerals as pigments were used in the creation of inalienable goods such as katsina masks, giving value to the mask and to the individual sponsoring its production, the production of metal wealth as material goods under Spanish colonialism created wealth that was parallel to that of currency, valuable because of its transferability in exchange. As the conversation between Milford Nahohai and Jim Ostler cited at the beginning of this chapter suggests, the re-appropriation of this material as an object of adornment can be viewed as an act that re-establishes a certain quality of the inalienable, referencing notions of value attached to an individual or family, establishing the inalienability of a sense of self-worth.

The play between opposing regimes of value in the production sequences at Paa-ko may also relate to competing notions of labor in the early colonial workshop context. Returning to Kopytoff (1986:89), the biographies of objects and the construction of their value through their migrations in and out of extremes of comodification and singularization can be seen as analogous to the biographies of individuals and the social construction of the person. The production of bullion clearly references the production of specie, tied to an economy based on commodities and geared toward the establishment of monetary equivalencies in price. Labor involved in this pursuit, as tribute or wage labor, is alienated in the classic sense of the term. The use of copper metal, most likely a byproduct of precious metal production at the facility, for the production of objects of adornment suggests a reconnection of labor and the object of production. To use Kopytoff's terms, in turning a commodity into a singularity, indigenous metallurgists at Paa-ko suggest an oblique reference to a Pueblo economic model where value of objects and individuals is established in the context of social production.

Such referencing using metal objects of adornment became important in later centuries with the development of Pueblo and Navajo silver jewelry traditions. Silver jewelry became both a means for referencing a family's wealth and a means for financing ritual obligations through loan. Although silver jewelry did not become prominent until the mid-nineteenth century, this technology may have earlier roots in the use of copper (Adair 1944; Bird 1992). The technology at Paa-ko may have been an early recognition of the self-referencing quality of metal to denote personal value and worth as objects of adornment.

CONCLUSION

The metallurgical technology used at Paa-ko was the product of the interactions among various regimes of value. Rather than view the technology as a conflict between expert and novice applications of metallurgical knowledge, the resultant technology may best be viewed as part of intersecting social constructs that were at play as the colony was established. Although *encomienda* records are non-existent for Paa-ko during this period, the workshop was most likely an attempt by a colonial elite to structure Puebloan action and mineralogical procurement strategies towards material gain. Yet the very perception of what material gain entailed was in flux during this period and involved a complex interplay among the assessment of value based on congruent semiotic systems, local and regional economies, and social classes and their associated labor relationships.

As a site of cultural construction, the Paa-ko facility is significant as a material record of seventeenth-century metallurgical practices and their intersection with Puebloan productive practices. The technology and resulting production cycles identified at the site may also represent a situated discourse on the nature of wealth and the role of social power in the creation of value. Extractive metallurgy played a major economic and social role in the formation of the Spanish colonies, but it was dependent upon the labor and skill of indigenous peoples whose situated agency played with colonial notions of value through the insertion of local means of wealth acquisition and indigenous frameworks for value construction. At Paa-ko this is represented by a focus on copper metallurgy and the production of copper sheet metal used for objects of adornment.

This reversal of the alienation of value through the establishment of currency that specifically referenced self-identity or self-worth emphasizes the importance of the situated agency of Puebloan practitioners within colonial production regimes. Other early colonial industries and social structures within which Pueblo people participated have similar histories of appropriation and re-appropriation, such as the incorporation of domestic plants and animals into subsistence and ritual economies, the increased use of wool textiles over time, and the submersion of Spanish political offices within pueblo social orders (Lomawaima 1989). From a historical perspective, the importance of the Paa-ko metal workshop lies not solely in the record that it reveals about the development of early colonial metallurgy and the transference of technology to the pueblos, but also in the sets of social practices that it preconfigures. It was not only metal as a material and substance of value that was appropriated and incorporated within Pueblo economies during and after the early colonial period, but a contradictory sense of value itself. Although extractive metallurgy in the region did not become a viable industry until the early nineteenth century (and appears never to have been adopted by the pueblos), the kind of dual referencing of value regimes possible through the use of metal objects of adornment as symbols of personal worth and items of wealth persisted. For example, the reworking of American silver dollars in the late nineteenth and early twentieth century into dragonfly pendants, crosses, and *najahe* and their use as symbols of a family's worth, objects used to obtain pawn, objects of adornment, and high art, challenged dominant American notions of dollar value. The metallurgy at Paa-ko is an historical antecedent, similarly embodying and challenging notions of value and worth.

References Cited

Ackerman, A. B., and Roberta D. Baer
   1988   Toxic Mexican Folk Remedies for the Treatment of
           Empacho: The Case of Azarcon, Greta and Albay-
           alde. *Journal of Ethnopharmacology* 24:31–39.
Adair, John
   1944   *The Navajo and Pueblo Silversmiths.* Norman:
           University of Oklahoma Press.
Adams, E. Charles
   1991   *The Origin and Development of the Pueblo Kat-
           sina Cult.* Tucson: University of Arizona Press.
Alonso, Anna Maria
   2004   Conforming Disconformity: 'Mestizaje,' Hybrid-
           ity, and the Aesthetics of Mexican Nationalism.
           Cultural Anthropology 19(4):459–490.
Appadurai, Arjun
   1986   Introduction: Commodities and the Politics of
           Value. In *The Social Life of Things: Commod-
           ities in Cultural Perspective,* edited by Arjun
           Appadurai, pp. 3–63. Cambridge, England:
           Cambridge University Press.
Armstrong, Douglas V.
   1998   Cultural Transformation within Enslaved
           Laborer Communities in the Caribbean. In
           Studies in Culture Contact: Interaction, Culture
           Change, and Archaeology, edited by James G.
           Cusick, pp. 378–401. *Occasional Paper* No. 25.
           Carbondale Illinois: Center for Archaeological
           Investigations.
Bakewell, P. J.
   1971   Silver Mining and Society in Colonial Mex-
           ico: Zacatecas, 1546–1700. *Latin American
           Studies* 15. Cambridge, England: Cambridge
           University Press.

   1984   *Miners of the Red Mountain: Indian Labor in
           Potasi, 1545–1650.* Albuquerque: University of
           New Mexico Press.
Bandelier, Adolph F.
   1892   Final Report of Investigations Among the Indi-
           ans of the Southwestern United States. *Papers of
           the Archaeological Institute of America, American
           Series* No. 4, Part 2. Cambridge: Archaeological
           Institute of America.
Baragallo, Modesto
   1955   *La mineria y la metalurgia en la America
           Espanola durante la epoca colonial.* Buenos
           Aires: Fondo de Cultura Economica.
Barba, Alonso A.
   1923   *El arte de los metales.* Translated by Ross E.
           Douglass and Edward P. Mathewson. New York:
           John Wiley & Sons.
Barrett, Elinore M.
   1987   *The Mexican Colonial Copper Industry.* Albu-
           querque: University of New Mexico Press.
   2002   *Conquest and Catastrophe: Changing Rio Grande
           Pueblo Settlement Patterns in the Sixteenth and
           Seventeenth Centuries.* Albuquerque: University
           of New Mexico Press.
Beidelman, T. O.
   1989   Agonistic Exchange: Homeric Reciprocity and
           the Heritage of Simmel and Mauss. *Cultural
           Anthropology* 4(3):227–259.
Bice, Richard A., Phyllis S. Davis, and William M. Sundt
   2003   *Indian Mining of Lead for Use in Rio Grande
           Glaze Paint: Report of the AS-5 Bethsheba Project
           Near Cerrillos, New Mexico.* Albuquerque:
           Albuquerque Archaeological Society.

Bijker, Wiebe E.
1995 *Of Bicycles, Bakelites, and Bulbs: Toward a Theory of Sociotechnical Change.* Cambridge: MIT Press.

Bird, Allison
1992 *Heart of the Dragonfly: The Historical Development of the Cross Necklaces of the Pueblo and Navajo Peoples.* Albuquerque: Avanyu.

Blanchard, Ian
1989 *Russia's 'Age of Silver': Precious-metal Production and Economic Growth in the Eighteenth Century.* New York: Routledge.

Bolton, Herbert E., editor
1963 *Spanish Exploration in the Southwest.* New York: Barnes and Noble.

Borah, Woodrow W.
1992 Price Trends of Royal Tribute Commodities in Nueva Galicia, 1557–1598. *Ibero-Americana* 55. Berkeley: University of California Press.

Bourdieu, Pierre
1977 *Outline of a Theory of Practice.* Cambridge, England: Cambridge University Press.

Braatz, Timothy
2003 *Surviving Conquest: A History of the Yavapai Peoples.* Lincoln: University of Nebraska Press.

Bronk Ramsey, Christopher
2017 OxCal v4.3.2, accessed online at https://c14 .arch.ox.ac.uk, November 1, 2017.

Bunzel, Ruth L.
1932 *Zuni Katcinas: An Analytical Study.* Washington, D.C.: Bureau of American Ethnology, Smithsonian Institution.

Burkholder, Mark A., and Lyman L. Johnson
1990 *Colonial Latin America.* New York: Oxford University Press.

Capone, Patricia W.
2006 Rio Grande Glaze Ware Technology and Production: Historic Expediency. In *The Social Life of Pots: Glaze Wares and Cultural Dynamics in the Southwest AD 1250–1680,* edited by Judith A. Habicht-Mauche, Suzanne L. Eckert, and Deborah L. Huntley, pp. 216–231. Tucson: University of Arizona Press.

Capone, Patricia W., and Robert W. Preucel
2002 Ceramic Semiotics: Women, Pottery, and Social Meanings at Kotyiti Pueblo. In *Archaeologies of the Pueblo Revolt: Identity, Meaning, and Renewal in the Pueblo World,* edited by Robert W. Preucel, pp. 99–113. Albuquerque: University of New Mexico Press.

Couturier, Edith B.
2003 *The Silver King: The Remarkable Life of the Count of Regla in Colonial Mexico.* Albuquerque: University of New Mexico Press.

Craddock, Paul T.
1995 *Early Metal Mining and Production.* Edinburgh: Edinburgh University Press.

Crown, Patricia L.
1994 *Ceramics and Ideology: Salado Polychrome Pottery.* Albuquerque: University of New Mexico Press.

Cushing, Frank H.
1979 *Zuni: Selected Writings of Frank Hamilton Cushing.* Lincoln: University of Nebraska Press.

Cusick, James G.
1998 Historiography of Acculturation: An Evaluation of Concepts and Their Application in Archaeology. In Studies in Culture Contact: Interaction, Culture Change and Archaeology, edited by James G. Cusick, pp. 126–145. *Occasional Paper* No. 25. Carbondale, Illinois: Center for Archaeological Investigations.

Deagan, Kathleen A.
1983 *Spanish St. Augustine: The Archaeology of a Colonial Creole Community.* New York: Academic Press.
1995 *Puerto Real: The Archaeology of a Sixteenth-Century Spanish Town in Hispaniola.* Gainesville: University Press of Florida.
1998 Transculturation and Spanish American Ethnogenisis: The Archaeological Legacy of the Quincentenary. In *Studies in Culture Contact: Interaction, Culture Change, and Archaeology,* edited by James G. Cusick, pp. 23–43. Carbondale: Southern Illinois University Press.

Dean, Caroline, and Dana Leibsohn
2003 Hybridity and Its Discontents: Considering Visual Culture in Colonial Spanish America. *Colonial Latin American Review* 12(1):5–35.

De Benedetto, G. E., Pasquale Acquafredda, Maurizio Masieri, G. Quarta, Luigia Sabbatini, P. G. Zambonin, M. S. Tite, and Marc Walton
2004 Investigation on Roman Lead Glaze from Canosa: Results of Chemical Analyses. *Archaeometry* 46(4):615–624.

de Certeau, Michel
1984 *The Practice of Everyday Life.* Berkeley: University of California Press.

Deer, William A., Robert A. Howie, and Jack Zussman
1966 *An Introduction to the Rock Forming Minerals.* London: Longman.

Dobres, Marcia-Anne
  2000   *Technology and Social Agency.* Oxford: Blackwell.
Dobres, Marcia-Anne, and Christopher R. Hoffman
  1994   Social Agency and the Dynamics of Prehistoric
          Technology. *Journal of Archaeological Method
          and Theory* 1(3):211–257.
Duff, Andrew I.
  2002   *Western Pueblo Identities: Regional Interaction,
          Migration and Transformation.* Tucson: Univer-
          sity of Arizona Press.
Ehrhardt, Kathleen L.
  2005   *European Metals in Native Hands: Rethinking
          Technological Change, 1640–1683.* Tuscaloosa:
          University of Alabama Press.
Epstein, Jeremiah F.
  1991   Cabeza de Vaca and the Sixteenth-Century
          Copper Trade in Northern Mexico. *American
          Antiquity* 56(3):474–482.
Fenn, Thomas R., Barbara J. Mills, and Maren Hopkins
  2006   The Social Contexts of Glaze Paint: Ceramic
          Production and Consumption in the Silver
          Creek Area. In *The Social Life of Pots: Glaze
          Wares and Cultural Dynamics in the Southwest
          AD 1250–1680,* edited by Judith A. Habicht-
          Mauche, Suzanne L. Eckert, and Deborah L.
          Huntley, pp. 60–85. Tucson: University of
          Arizona Press.
Ferguson, Charles A., J. Michael Timmons,
Frank J. Pazzaglia, Karl E. Karlstrom, G. R. Osburn,
and Paul W. Bauer
  1999   Geology of Sandia Park Quadrangle, Bernalillo
          and Sandoval Counties, New Mexico. *Open-file
          Report* GM1. Soccoro: New Mexico Bureau of
          Mines and Mineral Resources.
Ferguson, Leland G.
  1992   *Uncommon Ground: Archaeology and Colonial
          African America, 1650–1800.* Washington, D.C.:
          Smithsonian Institution Press.
Ferguson, T. J., and E. Richard Hart
  1985   *A Zuni Atlas.* Norman: University of Okla-
          homa Press.
Finlay, J. R.
  1922   *Report of Appraisal of Mining Properties of
          New Mexico.* Santa Fe: New Mexico State Tax
          Commission.
Flint, Richard, and Shirley C. Flint
  2005   *Documents of the Coronado Expedition,
          1539–1542: "They Were Not Familiar with
          His Majesty, nor Did They Wish to be His
          Subjects."* Dallas: Southern Methodist Uni-
          versity Press.

Flores, Ramón Sanchez
  1994   Technology of Mining in Colonial Mexico:
          Installations, Tools, Artifacts and Machines
          Used in the Patio Process, Sixteenth to Eigh-
          teenth Centuries. In In Quest of Mineral
          Wealth: Aboriginal and Colonial Mining and
          Metallurgy in Spanish America, edited by
          Alan K. Craig and Robert C. West, pp. 93–108.
          Geoscience and Man, Vol. 33. Baton Rouge:
          Louisiana State University.
Ford, Richard I.
  1992   *An Ecological Analysis Involving the Popula-
          tion of San Juan Pueblo, New Mexico. The
          Evolution of North American Indians.* New
          York: Garland.
Gage, John
  1999   *Color and Culture: Practice and Meaning from
          Antiquity to Abstraction.* Berkeley: University of
          California Press.
Gerhard, Peter
  1993   *The North Frontier of New Spain,* revised edition.
          Norman: University of Oklahoma Press.
Goh, Siew Wei, Alan N. Buckley, and Robert N. Lamb
  2006   Copper (II) Sulfide? *Minerals Engineering*
          19(2):204–208.
Graeber, David
  2001   *Toward an Anthropological Theory of Value:
          The False Coin of Our Own Dreams.* New York:
          Palgrave.
Graves, William M., and Suzanne L. Eckert
  1998   Decorated Ceramic Distributions and Ideo-
          logical Developments in the Northern and
          Central Rio Grande Valley, New Mexico. In
          Migration and Reorganization: The Pueblo
          IV Period in the American Southwest, edited
          by Katherine A. Spielmann, pp. 263–284.
          Anthropological Research Papers Vol. 51.
          Tempe: Arizona State University.
Graves, William M., and Katherine A. Spielmann
  2000   Leadership, Long-Distance Exchange, and
          Feasting in the Protohistoric Rio Grande.
          In *Alternative Leadership Strategies in the
          Prehispanic Southwest,* edited by Barbara J.
          Mills, pp. 45–59. Tucson: University of Ari-
          zona Press.
Grinberg, D. M. K. de
  1996   Técnicas minero-metalúrgicas en Mesoamérica.
          In *Mesoamérica y Los Andes,* edited by Mayán
          Cervantes, pp. 427–471. México, D.F.: Centro
          de Investigaciones y Estudios Superiores en
          Antropología Social.

Habicht-Mauche, Judith A.
1993   The Pottery from Arroyo Hondo Pueblo, New Mexico: Tribalizationand Trade in the Northern Rio Grande. *Arroyo Hondo Archaeological Series* No. 8. Santa Fe: School of American Research Press.
2006   The Social History of the Southwestern Glaze Wares. In *The Social Life of Pots: Glaze Wares and Cultural Dynamics in the Southwest AD 1250–1680,* edited by Judith A. Habicht-Mauche, Suzanne L. Eckert and Deborah L. Huntley, pp. 4–16. Tucson: University of Arizona Press.

Habicht-Mauche, Judith A., Stephen T. Glenn, Homer Milford, and A. Russell Flegal
2000   Isotopic Tracing of Prehistoric Rio Grande Glaze-Paint Production and Trade. *Journal of Archaeological Science* 27(8):709–713.

Habicht-Mauche, Judith A., Suzanne L. Eckert, and Deborah L. Huntley, editors
2006   *The Social Life of Pots: Glaze Wares and Cultural Dynamics in the Southwest AD 1250–1680.* Tucson: University of Arizona Press.

Hammond, George P., and Agapito Rey
1953   *Don Juan de Oñate, Colonizer of New Mexico 1595–1628.* Albuquerque: University of New Mexico Press.
1966   *The Rediscovery of New Mexico, 1580–1594.* Albuquerque: University of New Mexico Press.

Harley, R. D.
1982   *Artists' Pigments c. 1600–1835: A Study in English Documentary Sources,* second edition. London: Butterworth Scientific.

Hedquist, Saul L.
2017   A Colorful Past: Turquoise and Social Identity in the Late Prehispanic Western Pueblo Region, AD 1275–1400. Doctoral dissertation, School of Anthropology, University of Arizona, Tucson.

Hedquist, Saul L., Alyson M. Thibodeau, John Welch, and David J. Killick
2017   Canyon Creek Revisited: New Investigations of a Late Prehispanic Turquoise Mine (Arizona, USA). *Journal of Archaeological Science* 87:44–58.

Herbert, E. W.
1981   The West African Copper Trade in the 15th and 16th Centuries. In *Precious Metals in the Age of Expansion: Papers of the XIVth International Congress of the Historical Sciences,* edited by Hermann Kellenbenz, pp. 119–130. Stuttgart: Klett-Cotta.

Herhahn, Cynthia L.
2006   Inferring Social Interactions from Pottery Recipes: Rio Grande Glaze Paint Composition and Cultural Transmission. In *The Social Life of Pots: Glaze Wares and Cultural Dynamics in the Southwest, AD 1250–1680,* edited by Judith A. Habicht-Mauche, Suzanne L. Eckert, and Deborah L. Huntley, pp. 177–196. Tucson: University of Arizona Press.

Herskovits, Melville J.
1958   *Acculturation: A Study of Culture Contact.* Gloucester: Peter Smith.

Hodge, Frederick W., George P. Hammond, and Agapito Rey, editors
1945   *Fray Alonso de Benevides' Revised Memorial of 1634.* Albuquerque: University of New Mexico Press.

Holmyard, E. J.
1957   *Alchemy.* New York: Dover.

Hoover, Herbert C., and Lou H. Hoover
1950   *Georgius Agricola's De Re Metallica.* New York: Dover.

Hosler, Dorothy
1994   *The Sounds and Colors of Power: The Sacred Metallurgical Technology of Ancient West Mexico.* Cambridge: MIT Press.

Hu-DeHart, Evelyn
1981   *Missionaries, Miners, and Indians.* Tucson: University of Arizona Press.

Huntley, Deborah L., Katherine A. Spielmann, Judith A. Habicht-Mauche, Cynthia L. Herhahn, and A. Russell Flegal
2007   Local Recipes or Distant Commodities? Lead Isotope and Chemical Compositional Analysis of Glaze Paints from the Salinas Pueblos, New Mexico. *Journal of Archaeological Science* 34:1135–1147.

Judd, Neil M.
1954   *The Material Culture of Pueblo Bonito.* Washington, D.C.: Smithsonian Institution.

Keane, Webb
2001   Money Is No Object: Materiality, Desire, and Modernity in an Indonesian Society. In *The Empire of Things: Regimes of Value and Material Culture,* edited by Fred R. Myers, pp. 65–90. Santa Fe: School of American Research.

Keller, Charles M., and Janet D. Keller
1996   *Cognition and Tool Use: The Blacksmith at Work.* New York: Cambridge University Press.

Kidder, Alfred Vincent
1932   The Artifacts of Pecos. *Phillips Academy Papers of the Southwestern Expedition* No. 6. New

Haven: Yale University Press, and London: Oxford University Press.

Killick, David J., and Thomas R. Fenn

2012   Archaeometallurgy: The Study of Preindustrial Mining and Metallurgy. *Annual Review of Anthropology* 41:559–575.

Kingery, W. David

1993   Technological Systems and Some Implications with Regard to Continuity and Change. In *History from Things: Essays on Material Culture,* edited by Steven Lubar and W. D. Kingery, pp. 215–230. Washington, D.C.: Smithsonian Institution Press.

Kingery, W. David, and W. H. Gourdin

1976   Examination of Furnace Linings from Rothenberg Site #590 in Wadi Zaghra. *Journal of Field Archaeology* 3:351–353.

Knapp, Arthur B., Vincent C. Pigott, and Eugenia W. Herbert, editors

1998   *Social Approaches to an Industrial Past: The Archaeology and Anthropology of Mining.* New York: Routledge.

Kohler, Timothy A., Matthew. W. Van Pelt, and Lorene Y. Yap

2000   Reciprocity and Its Limits: Considerations for a Study of the Prehispanic Pueblo World. In *Alternative Leadership Strategies in the Prehispanic Southwest,* edited by Barbara J. Mills, pp. 180–206. Tucson: University of Arizona Press.

Kopytoff, Igor

1986   The Cultural Biography of Things. In *The Social Life of Things: Commodities in Cultural Perspective*, edited by Arjun Appadurai, pp. 64–91. Cambridge: Cambridge University Press.

Lambert, Marjorie F.

1954   *Paa-ko, Archaeological Chronicle of an Indian Village in North Central New Mexico.* Santa Fe: School of American Research.

Lechtman, Heather

1977   Style in Technology: Some Early Thoughts. In *Material Culture: Styles, Organization, and Dynamics of Technology*, edited by Heather Lechtman and Robert S. Merrill, pp. 3–20. St. Paul: American Ethnological Society.

1984   Andean Value System and the Development of Prehistoric Metallurgy. *Technology and Culture* 25:1–36.

1999   Afterword. In *The Social Dynamics of Technology: Practice, Politics and Word Views*, edited by Marcia-Anne Dobres and Christopher R.

Hoffman, pp. 223–232. Washington, D.C.: Smithsonian Institution Press.

Lemonnier, Pierre

1993   Elements for an Anthropology of Technology. *Museum of Anthropology Anthropological Papers* 88. Ann Arbor: University of Michigan.

Leroi-Gourhan, André

1993   *Gesture and Speech.* Translated from the French by Anna Bostock Berger. Cambridge: MIT Press.

Lightfoot, Kent G.

1995   Culture Contact Studies: Redefining the Relationship between Prehistoric and Historical Archaeology. *American Antiquity* 60:199–217.

Lightfoot, Kent G., Antoinette Martinez, and Ann M. Schiff

1998   Daily Practice and Material Culture in Pluralistic Social Settings: An Archaeological Study of Culture Change and Persistence from Fort Ross, California. *American Antiquity* 63(2):199–222.

Lockhart, James, and Stuart B. Schwartz

1983   Early Latin America: A History of Colonial Spanish America and Brazil. *Latin American Studies* 46. Cambridge: Cambridge University Press.

Lomawaima, Hartman H.

1989   Hopification, a Strategy for Cultural Preservation. In Archaeological and Historical Perspectives on the Spanish Borderlands West, edited by D. H. Thomas, pp. 93–99. *Columbian Consequences*, Vol. I. Washington, D.C.: Smithsonian Institution Press.

Lycett, Mark T.

1995   *Archaeological Implications of European Contact: Demography, Settlement, and Land Use in the Middle Rio Grande Valley, New Mexico.* Doctoral dissertation, University of New Mexico, Albuquerque.

1997   Preliminary Report of Archaeological Surface Documentation and Test Excavations at LA 162, Bernalillo County, New Mexico, conducted by Northwestern University Archaeological Field Studies Program, between 17 June and 8 August, 1996, under permit SP-269. On file, Department of Anthropology, University of Chicago, Chicago.

1998   Report of Archaeological Excavations at LA 162, Bernalillo County, New Mexico, conducted by the University of Chicago Archaeological Field Studies Program, between 21 June and 19 August 1997, under permit SE-120. On file, New Mexico State Historic Preservation Division, Santa Fe.

Lycett, Mark T. (continued)

1999   Report of Archaeological Excavations at LA 162, Bernalillo County, New Mexico, conducted by the University of Chicago Archaeological Field Studies Program, between 21 June and 18 August 1998, under permit SE-134. On file, Department of Anthropology, University of Chicago, Chicago.

2000   Report of Archaeological Excavations at LA 162, Bernalillo County, New Mexico, conducted by the University of Chicago Archaeological Field Studies Program, between 21 June and 12 August 1999, under permit SE-144. On file, New Mexico State Historic Preservation Division, Santa Fe.

2001   Report of Archaeological Excavations at LA 162, Bernalillo County, New Mexico, conducted by the University of Chicago Archaeological Field Studies Program, between 21 June and 17 August 2000, under permit SE-156. On file, New Mexico State Historic Preservation Division, Santa Fe.

2002   Transformations of Place: Occupational History and Differential Persistence in Seventeenth-Century New Mexico. In *Archaeologies of the Pueblo Revolt: Identity, Meaning, and Renewal in the Pueblo World,* edited by Robert W. Preucel, pp. 61–75. Albuquerque: University of New Mexico Press.

2003   Report of Archaeological Excavations at LA 162, Bernalillo County, New Mexico, conducted by the University of Chicago Archaeological Field Studies Program, between June 15 and August 1, 2002. On file, New Mexico State Historic Preservation Division, Santa Fe.

2004   Report of Archaeological Excavations at LA 162, Bernalillo County, New Mexico, conducted by the University of Chicago Archaeological Field Studies Program, between June 18 and August 1, 2003. On file, New Mexico State Historic Preservation Division, Santa Fe.

2005   On the Margins of Peripheries: The Consequences of Differential Incorporation in the Colonial Southwest. In *The Postclassic to Spanish-era Transition in Mesoamerica: Archaeological Perspectives,* edited by Susan Kepecs and Rani Alexander, pp. 97–115. Albuquerque: University of New Mexico Press.

Maldonado, Blanca E.

2006   *Preindustrial Copper Production at the Archaeological Zone of Itziparátzico, a Tarascan Location in Michoacán, México.* Doctoral dissertation, Pennsylvania State University, University Park.

Maniatis, Y., and M. S. Tite

1981   Technological Examination of Neolithic-Bronze Age Pottery from Central and Southeast Europe and from the Near East. *Journal of Archaeological Science* 8:59–76.

Marrow, Baker H.

1992   *A Harvest of Reluctant Souls: The Memorial of Fray Alonso Benavides 1630.* Niwot: University Press of Colorado.

Mauss, Marcel

1979   Les techniques du corps. In *Sociology and Psychology: Essays of Marcel Mauss,* pp. 97–123. Translated by B. Brewster. London: Routledge and Kegan Paul.

Mayer, Vincent J.

1974   The Black on New Spain's Northern Frontier: San Jose de Parral 1631 to 1641. *Occasional Papers of the Center of Southwest Studies* 2. Durango, Colorado: Center of Southwest Studies.

Meek, Wilbur T.

1948   *The Exchange Media of Colonial Mexico.* New York: King's Crown Press.

Mera, H. P.

1933   A Proposed Revision of the Rio Grande Glaze Paint Sequence. *Laboratory of Anthropology Technical Series* No. 5. Santa Fe: Museum of New Mexico.

Milford, Homer E., and M. E. Swick

1995   Historic Survey of the Los Cerrillos Area and Its Mining History. Cultural Resource Survey for Real de los Cerrillos Project, Santa Fe County, New Mexico, vol. 1. *New Mexico Abandoned Mine Land Bureau Report* 1994-2. Santa Fe: New Mexico Mining and Minerals Division.

Miller, Daniel

1987   *Material Culture and Mass Consumption.* Oxford: Basil Blackwell.

Mills, Barbara J.

2002   Acts of Resistance: Zuni Ceramics, Social Identity, and the Pueblo Revolt. In *Archaeologies of the Pueblo Revolt: Identity, Meaning, and Renewal in the Pueblo World,* edited by Robert W. Preucel, pp. 85–98. Albuquerque: University of New Mexico Press.

2004   The Establishment and Defeat of Hierarchy: Inalienable Possessions and the History of Collective Prestige Structures in the Pueblo Southwest. *American Anthropologist* 106(2):238–251.

Mindeleff, Victor
    1886   A Study of Pueblo Architecture: Tusayan and Cibola. *Eighth Annual Report of the Bureau of American Ethnology.* Washington, D.C.: Smithsonian Institution.

Mirti, Piero, and Patrizia Davit
    2004   New Developments in the Study of Ancient Pottery by Colour Measurement. *Journal of Archaeological Science* 31:741–751.

Mobley-Tanaka, Jeanette L.
    2002   Crossed Cultures, Crossed Meanings: The Manipulation of Ritual Imagery in Early Historic Pueblo Resistance. In *Archaeologies of the Pueblo Revolt: Identity, Meaning, and Renewal in the Pueblo World,* edited by Robert W. Preucel, pp. 77–84. Albuquerque: University of New Mexico Press.

Morrison, Kathleen D., Nicole Arendt, and Nicole Barger
    2002   Vegetation History of the San Pedro Valley: Pollen Evidence for Anthropogenic Change. Poster presented at the 67th Annual Meeting of the Society for American Archaeology, Denver, Colorado.

Motomura, Akira
    1997   New Data on Minting, Seigniorage, and the Money Supply in Spain (Castile), 1597–1643. *Explorations in Economic History* 34:331–367.

Myers, Fred R.
    2001   Introduction: The Empire of Things. In *The Empire of Things: Regimes of Value and Material Culture,* edited by F. R. Myers, pp. 3–64. Santa Fe: School of American Research Press.

Nelson, Katherine, and Judith A. Habicht-Mauche
    2006   Lead, Paint, and Pots: Rio Grande Intercommunity Dynamics from a Glaze Ware Perspective. In *The Social Life of Pots: Glaze Wares and Cultural Dynamics in the Southwest, AD 1250–1680,* edited by Judith A. Habicht-Mauche, Suzanne L. Eckert, and Deborah L. Huntley, pp. 197–215. Tucson: University of Arizona Press.

Nelson, Nels C.
    1914   Pueblo Ruins of the Galisteo Basin, New Mexico. *Anthropological Papers of the American Museum of Natural History* 15. New York: American Museum of Natural History.

Nesse, William D.
    2000   *Introduction to Mineralogy.* New York: Oxford University Press.

Northrop, Stuart A.
    1996   *Minerals of New Mexico,* third edition, revised by Florence A. La Bruzza. Albuquerque: University of New Mexico Press.

Nriagu, Jerome O.
    1993   Legacy of Mercury Pollution. *Nature* 363:589.

Ortiz, Alfonso
    1969   *The Tewa World: Space, Time, Being and Becoming in a Pueblo Society.* Chicago: University of Chicago Press.
    1994   The Dynamics of Pueblo Cultural Survival. In *North American Indian Anthropology: Essays on Society and Culture,* edited by Raymond J. DeMallie and Alfonso Ortiz, pp. 278–306. Norman: University of Oklahoma Press.

Ostler, James, Marian E. Rodee, and Milford Nahohai
    1996   *Zuni: A Village of Silversmiths.* Albuquerque: University of New Mexico Press.

Parsons, Elsie C.
    1966   *Pueblo Indian Religion.* Lincoln: University of Nebraska Press.

Pauketat, Timothy R.
    2000   The Tragedy of the Commoners. In *Agency in Archaeology,* edited by Marcia-Ann Dobres and John E. Robb, pp. 113–129. London: Routledge.
    2001   A New Tradition in Archaeology. In *The Archaeology of Traditions: Agency and History Before and After Columbus,* edited by Timothy R. Pauketat, pp. 1–16. Gainesville: University Press of Florida.

Pierce, Donna
    2006   Hide Paintings in New Mexico: New Archival Evidence. In *Transforming Images: New Mexican Santos in-between Worlds,* edited by Claire Farago and Donna Pierce, pp. 138–144. University Park: Pennsylvania State University Press.

Platt, Tristan
    2000   The Alchemy of Modernity: Alonso Barba's Copper Cauldrons and the Independence of Bolivian Metallurgy (1790–1890). *Journal of Latin American Studies* 32(1):1–54.

Plog, Stephen
    2003   Exploring the Ubiquitous Through the Unusual: Color Symbolism in Pueblo Black-on-white Pottery. *American Antiquity* 68(4): 665–718.

Preucel, Robert W., editor
    2002   *Archaeologies of the Pueblo Revolt: Identity, Meaning, and Renewal in the Pueblo World.* Albuquerque: University of New Mexico Press.

Probert, Alan
    1969   Bartolome de Medina: The Patio Process and the Sixteenth-Century Silver Crisis. *Journal of the West* 8:90–124.

Pruna, P. M.

1989 Apuntes sobre la minería del cobre en Cuba en el siglo XVII. *Revista de la Biblioteca Nacional José Martí* 31(1):167–185.

Ramenofsky, Ann F., and C. David Vaughan

2003 Jars Full of Shiny Metal: Analyzing Barrionnuevo's Visit to Yuque. In *The Coronado Expedition: From the Distance of 460 Years*, edited by Richard Flint and Shirley C. Flint, pp. 116–139. Albuquerque: University of New Mexico Press.

Reff, Daniel T.

1991 *Disease, Depopulation, and Culture Change in Northwestern New Spain, 1518–1764*. Salt Lake City: University of Utah Press.

Reimer, Paula J., and others

2013 IntCal13 and Marine13 Radiocarbon Age Calibration Curves 0–50,000 Years cal BP. *Radiocarbon* 55(4):1869–1887.

Rothschild, Nan A.

2003 *Colonial Encounters in a Native American Landscape: The Spanish and Dutch in North America*. Washington, D.C.: Smithsonian Books.

Rovira, S.

1995 New Native Metallurgical Technology after Hispanic Contact in Peru. In *Trade and Discovery: The Scientific Study of Artefacts from Post-Medieval Europe and Beyond*, edited by Duncan R. Hook and David R. M. Gaimster, pp. 299–308. *Occasional Paper* No. 109, London: British Museum.

Rubertone, Patricia E.

1989 Archaeology, Colonialism, and 17th-century Native America: Towards an Alternative Interpretation. In *Conflict in the Archaeology of Living Traditions*, edited by Robert Layton, pp. 31–45. London: Unwin Hyman.

2000 The Historical Archaeology of Native Americans. *Annual Review of Anthropology* 29:425–446.

Salazar-Soler, Carmen

1997 Álvaro Alonso Barba: Teorias de la antiguedad, alquimia y creencias prehispanicas en las ciencias de la tierra en el Nuevo Mundo. In *Entre dos Mundos: Fronteras Culturales y Agentes Mediadores*, edited by Berta A. Queija and Serge Gruzinski, pp. 269–296. Sevilla: Consejo Superior de Investigaciones Cientificas.

Sanchez-Crispin, A.

1994 The Territorial Organization of Metallic Mining in New Spain. In In Quest of Mineral Wealth: Aboriginal and Colonial Mining and Metallurgy in Spanish America, edited by Alan K. Craig and Robert C. West, pp. 155–170. *Geoscince and Man* Vol. 33. Baton Rouge: Louisiana State University, Geoscience Publications.

Scholes, France V.

1930 The Supply Service of the New Mexico Missions in the Seventeenth Century. *New Mexico Historical Review* V(1):93–115.

1942 Troublous Times in New Mexico: 1659–1670. *Publications in History* 11. Albuquerque: Historical Society of New Mexico.

Scott, James C.

1990 *Domination and the Arts of Resistance (Hidden Transcripts)*. New Haven: Yale University Press.

Sheridan, Thomas E.

1992 The Limits of Power: The Political Ecology of the Spanish Empire in the Greater Southwest. *Antiquity* 66:153–157.

Sheridan, Thomas E., Stewart B. Koyiyemptewa, Anton Daughters, Dale S. Brenneman, T.J. Ferguson, Leigh Kumanwisiwma, and Lee Wayne Lomayestewa, editors

2015 *Moquis and Kastiilam: Hopis, Spaniards, and the Trauma of History*. Tucson: University of Arizona Press.

Simmons, Marc, and Frank Turley

1980 *Southwestern Colonial Ironwork: the Spanish Blacksmithing Tradition from Texas to California*. Santa Fe: Museum of New Mexico.

Simpson, Lesley B.

1937 The Medicine of the Conquistadores: An American Pharmacopoea of 1536. *Osiris* 3:142–164.

Singleton, Theresa A.

1998 Cultural Interaction and African American Identity in Plantation Archaeology. In Studies in Culture Contact: Interaction, Culture Change, and Archaeology, edited by James G. Cusick, pp. 172–189. *Occasional Paper* No. 25. Carbondale, Illinois: Center for Archaeological Investigations.

Sisco, Anneliese G., and Cyril S. Smith

1951 *Lazarus Ercker's Treatise of Ores and Assaying: Translated from the German Edition of 1580*. Chicago: University of Chicago Press.

Smith, Cyril S.

1981 Matter versus Materials: A Historical View. In *A Search for Structure*, edited by Cyril S. Smith, pp. 112–126. Cambridge: MIT Press.

Smith, Cyril S., and Martha T. Gnudi

1959 *The Pirotechnia of Vannoccio Biringuccio: The Classic Sixteenth-Century Treatise on Metals and Metallurgy*. New York: Dover.

Snow, Dean H.
1981 Protohistoric Rio Grande Pueblo Economics: A Review of Trends. In The Protohistoric Period in the North American Southwest, AD 1450–1700, edited by David R. Wilcox and W. Bruce Masse, pp. 354–377. *Anthropological Research Papers.* Vol. 30. Tempe: Arizona State University.

Spicer, Edwin H.
1962 *Cycles of Conquest: The Impact of Spain, Mexico and the United States on the Indians of the Southwest, 1533–1960.* Tucson: University of Arizona Press.

Spielmann, Katherine A.
1998 Ritual Influences on the Development of Rio Grande Glaze A Ceramics. In Migration and Reorganization: The Pueblo IV Period in the American Southwest, edited by Katherine A. Spielmann. *Anthropological Research Paper* No. 51. Tempe: Arizona State University.
2002 Feasting, Craft Specialization, and the Ritual Mode of Production in Small-Scale Societies. *American Anthropologist* 104(1):195–207.

Stein, Stanley J., and Barbara H. Stein
2000 *Silver, Trade, and War: Spain and America in the Making of Early Modern Europe.* Baltimore: Johns Hopkins University Press.

Sunseri, Jun Usno, and Diane Gifford-Gonzalez
2002 The Paa-ko Archaeofauna: Evidence for a Creolized Animal Use. Poster presented at the 67th Annual Meeting of the Society for American Archaeology, Denver.

Thibodeau, Alyson M., Judith M. Habicht-Mauche, Deborah B. Huntley, John T. Chesley, and Joaquin Ruiz
2013 High-Precision Isotopic Analyses of Lead Ores from New Mexico by MC-ICP-MS: Implications for Tracing the Production and Exchange of Pueblo IV Glaze-Decorated Pottery. *Journal of Archaeological Science* 40:3067–3075.

Thibodeau, Alyson M., David J. Killick, Saul L. Hedquist, John T. Chesley, and Joaquin Ruiz
2015 Isotopic Evidence for the Provenance of Turquoise in the Southwestern United States. *Geological Society of America Bulletin*, 127(11/12):1617–1631.

Thomas, Nicholas
1991 *Entangled Objects: Exchange, Material Culture, and Colonialism in the Pacific.* Cambridge: Harvard University Press.
2002 Colonizing Cloth: Interpreting the Material Culture of Nineteenth-Century Oceania. In *The Archaeology of Colonialism,* edited by Claire L. Lyons and John K. Papadopoulos, pp. 182–198. Los Angeles: Getty Research Institute.

Thomas, Noah H.
2007 Colonialism, Collective Action, and the Analysis of Technological Style. *Stanford Journal of Archaeology* 5:203–223.
2011 Metals, Pigments, Ores and Assays: The Politics of Value in the Early Spanish Colony of New Mexico. In *The Archaeology of Politics: The Materiality of Political Practice and Action in the Past,* edited by Peter G. Johansen and Andrew M. Bauer, pp 56–82. Newcastle upon Tyne: Cambridge Scholars.

Thomas, Noah, and Alyson Thibodeau
2010 Early Colonial Resource Appropriation: Sourcing Copper and Lead Ores from the Seventeenth Century Metallurgical Workshop at LA 162, Bernalillo County, New Mexico. Paper presented at the 75th Annual Meeting of the Society for American Archaeology, St. Louis, Missouri.

Tite, M. S., Ian C. Freestone, R. B. Mason, J. M. M. Vendrell-Saz, Judit Molera, and Nigel Wood
1998 Lead Glazes in Antiquity—Methods of Production and Reasons for Use. *Archaeometry* 40(1):241–260.

Trigg, Heather B.
2005 *From Household to Empire: Society and Economy in Early Colonial New Mexico.* Tucson: University of Arizona Press.

Turner, Terence
1989 A Commentary. *Cultural Anthropology* 4(3): 260–264.

Vargas, Victoria D.
1995 Copper Bell Trade Patterns in the Prehispanic U.S. Southwest and Northwest Mexico. *Arizona State Museum Archaeological Series* 187. Tucson: University of Arizona.

Vaughan, C. David
2001 *Investigating Spanish Colonial Mining and Metallurgy.* Albuquerque: Archaeological Conservancy, Santa Fe: New Mexico Historic Preservation Division.
2006 *Taking the Measure of New Mexico's Colonial Miners, Mining, and Metallurgy.* Doctoral dissertation, University of New Mexico, Albuquerque.

Vivian, Gordon
1964 Gran Quivira: Excavations in a Seventeenth Century Jumano Pueblo. *Archaeological Research Series*, vol. 8. Washington, D.C., U.S. Department of the Interior, National Park Service.

Ware, John A., and Eric Blinman
  2000 Cultural Collapse and Reorganization: Origin
        and Spread of Pueblo Ritual Sodalities. In *The*
        Archaeology of Regional Interaction: Religion,
        Warfare, and Exchange across the American
        Southwest and Beyond, edited by Michelle
        Hegmon, pp. 381–410. Boulder: University
        Press of Colorado.

Warren, A. H., and Robert H. Weber
  1979 Indian and Spanish Mining in the Galisteo and
        Hagan Basins. In *Archaeology and History of*
        Santa Fe County, by Raymond Vail Ingersoll,
        pp. 7–11. Soccoro: New Mexico Geological
        Society.

Webster, Laurie D.
  1997 *Effects of European Contact on Textile Production*
        and Exchange in the North American Southwest:
        A Pueblo Case Study. Doctoral Dissertation:
        Department of Anthropology, University of
        Arizona, Tucson.
  2000 Pueblo Textile Production and Exchange. In
        Beyond Cloth and Cordage: Archaeological
        Textile Research in the Americas, edited by
        Penelope B. Drooker, pp. 179–204. Salt Lake
        City: University of Utah Press.

Weiner, Annette B.
  1985 Inalienable Wealth. *American Ethnologist*
        12(2):210–227.

West, Robert C.
  1949 The Mining Community in Northern New
        Spain: The Parral Mining District. *Ibero-*
        Americana 30. Berkeley: University of
        California.
  1973 Cultural Geography of the Modern Tarascan
        Area. *Smithsonian Institution Institute for Social*
        Anthropology Publication No. 7. Westport,
        Connecticut: Greenwood Press.
  1994a Aboriginal Metallurgy and Metalworking in
        Spanish America: A Brief Overview. In In Quest
        of Mineral Wealth: Aboriginal and Colonial
        Mining and Metallurgy in Spanish America,
        edited by Alan K. Craig and Robert C. West,
        pp. 5–20. *Geoscience and Man.* Vol. 33. Baton
        Rouge: Louisiana State University.
  1994b Early Silver Mining in New Spain, 1533–1555.
        In In Quest of Mineral Wealth: Aboriginal and
        Colonial Mining and Metallurgy in Spanish
        America, edited by Alan K. Craig and Robert C.
        West, pp. 119–136. *Geoscience and Man,* Vol. 33.
        Baton Rouge: Louisiana State University.

White, Courtney
  1996 Adobe Typology and Site Chronology: A Case
        Study from Pecos National Historical Park.
        Kiva 61(4):347–363.

Whiteley, Peter M.
  2012 Turquoise and Squash Blossom: A Pueblo
        Dialogue of the Long Run. In *Turquoise in*
        Mexico and North America: Science, Conserva-
        tion, Culture, and Collections, edited by J. C. H.
        King, M. Carocci, C. Cartwright, C. McEwan,
        and R. Stacey, pp. 145–154. London: Archetype
        Publications.

Wolf, Eric R.
  1990 Distinguished Lecture: Facing Power—Old
        Insights, New Questions. *American Anthropolo-*
        gist 92(3):586–596.

Wolf, S.
  2002 Estimation of the Production Parameters of
        Very Large Medieval Bricks from St. Urban,
        Switzerland. *Archaeometry* 44(1):37–65.

Wylie, Alison
  1989 Archaeological Cables and Tacking: The
        Implications of Practice for Bernstein's 'Options
        Beyond Objectivism and Relativism'. *Philosophy,*
        Society and Science 19:1–18.
  2000 Questions of Evidence, Legitimacy, and the
        (Dis)Union of Science. *American Antiquity*
        65(2):227–238.

Index

Page numbers in *italic* indicate illustrations.

Acapulco, 29
acculturation, 10
adobe, *plate 16*; in Eastern Terrace features, 47, 49; in Northern Exterior Area, 65, 66; partially vitrified, 76–78; in Western Terrace Features, 58–59, 60–63
Africans: in mining industry, 27, 36
agency, 5, 12, 14, 90
Agricola, 84
alum, 31
alumina, 72
anglesite, 73
animals: at Paa-ko, 40
Annunciacion Mine, 32
armaments: Spanish colonial, 22
artifact pattern analysis, 12
ash, in Northern Exterior Area, 65, 66
assays, 29, 30, 31, 82
assimilation, 10, 11
azurite, 63

Bandelier, Adolph, 37
Barba, Alvaro Alonso, 6, 84; *El arte de los metales,* 82–83
barrios: in Zacatecas, 28, 82
bells (crotals), copper, 15
Bethsheba Mine, 32

bins: masonry, 52
Blue Corn Maiden, 16
bowl furnaces: in Western Terrace, 59–62, 67
brass, 22; stable isotope ratios, *80, 81*
bronze: West Mexican production of, 22

Cabeza de Vaca, Alvar Nuñez, 15
calcite, 71, 72, 73
calcium silicates, 84
captives: in Zacatecas mines, 27
cardinal directions: colors associated with, 16–17
Castañeda de Nájera, Pedro de, 24
Central Mexico: indigenous peoples from, 36, 89
ceramics. *See* glaze ware pottery
ceremonies: Puebloan exchange system, 18
Cerrillos Hills, 1, 4, 36; lead minerals from, 16, 17–18, 32, 80; mineral assays from, 29, 30; ores from, 81, 88
cerrusite, 71, 73, 75
chalcopyrite, 63, 68, 71, 72, 81
charcoal, 4, 41, 63; in Northern Exterior Area, 65–66
charcoal preparation features, 68
Chichimec Wars, 27, 30
choice, context of, 12
Christianity, iconography of, 19

chrysocolla, 71, 72
colonial period, colonialism, 1; copper production, 22–23; material culture in, 10–11; mineral exploration, 39–30; mining, 5, 32–36; ore processing, 25, 27; at Paa-ko, 4, 40
color: Puebloan symbolism, 6, 16–17; in Spanish colonial metallurgy, 31, 83; and value, 87–88
colorados, 83
Columbus, Christopher: and Hispañola colony, 23
combustion features: in Eastern Terrace, 46, 47–49; in Northern Exterior Area, 66. *See also* furnaces
community: and mineral procurement, 16
copper, 1, 5, 59, 85, 89; in New Mexico colony, 90–91; sheet, 6, 48, 71, 78–79, 80, *plates 17, 18*; slag, 64–65, 73–75, *plates 8, 9, 10, 11*; smelting and working, 4, 82, 84, 86; Spanish colonial production of, 22–23; worked, 12, 15
copper alloys, 22, 65, 86, 89
copper carbonates, 23, 31, 68, 83, 87; in Western Terrace, 63–64
copper isotope analysis, 79, 80–81
copper ores, 65, 68, 82, 87–88, *plates 1, 2, 3, 4*; analysis of, 71, 72;

processing of, 83–84. *See also* azurite; chrysocolla; copper carbonates; malachite
copper silicates, 72
copper sulfate, 82, 83
copper sulfides, 23, 71, 72, 85
Coronado, Francisco Vásquez de, 22, 24
corrals: at Paa-ko, 37, 39
covellite, 71, 72
Culiacán (San Miguel de Culiacán), 22
culture-contact studies, 11, 12–13
cupellation, 25, 32, 48, 81, 85; evidence of, 75, 76

dates: of metallurgical facility, 41–42
de Certeau, Michel, 90, 91
diffusion, 10–11
direct historical approach, 37
Dobres, Marcia-Anne, 9
draft animals: in ore processing, 27
draft systems: in copper processing, 23

Eastern Pueblo: glaze wares in, 15–16, 32
Eastern Terrace, 41, *44,* 68, 72, 73, 85; features and surfaces in, 45–53, 67; metal refining, 75–76
East Mountain area, 1, 39
economies: Spanish colonial, 90–91
El Tuerto, 32, 82, 88
empacho, 87
encomienda, 4, 10, 89; labor pool, 23–24
energy dispersive spectroscopy (EDS), 5
entrada: Coronado's, 22
environmental data, 40
Ercker, Lazarus, 84, 85
Escalante, Phillipe de, 29–30, 82
Espejo expedition, 30, 87
Estancia Basin: salt beds from, 28
ethnic groups: in Zacatecas, 28
ethnocategories, 9
ethnography, 6
ethnohistorical research, 5

Eulate, Juan de, 88
exchange, 15, 16; Puebloan systems of, 6, 17–18

Farfan de los Godos, Marcos: exploratory expedition, 5, 31, 87
fayalitic copper slag, 73–75, *plates 8, 9*
Filipinos: in Zacatecas mining industry, 27
finances: for Parral mining industry, 29
flooding: of metallurgical facility, 43
forced-air draft: in copper processing, 23
fore hearths, 62
Fort Ross: economic relations in, 12–13
furnace bowls: in Western Terrace, 59–62, 67
furnace features, 67–68, 85; in Eastern Terrace, 49–51, 52–53; in Western Terrace, 56–62, 64

galena, 28, 68, 71, 72–73, 82, 84, *plate 5*; in lead-isotope analysis, 79, 81; in processing features, 57, 59, 62, 63
Galisteo Basin, 1, 32, 37, 39
Gallegos *relación,* 29, 30
gangue, 71, 72
Gatlin (Ariz.), copper trade at, 15
glaze, 4; minerals used in, 17–18, 32; Puebloan production of, 6, 15, 31
Glaze F pottery, *50*
glaze ware pottery, 13, 17, 19, 30; minerals used in, 6, 15–16, 32; at Paa-ko, 38, *50*
gold, 1, 22, 72, 73, 82, 83, 84
gold alloys, 89
gossan ores, 71, 81
Gran Quivira, 91
greta, 31, 87

haciendas de minas, 27, 28, 36
Hano, 39
Hawikuh, 19
healing practices, 17, 87
hegemony: interaction and, 11–12

Herskovits, Melville, 11
Hewett, Edgar Lee, 39
Hispañola, 23
historical plaza, excavations of, 39, 40
Hohokam: copper use, 15
Hopi, 30, 31
horses, 40
Hosler, Dorothy, on West Mexican copper, 15
hot and cold qualities, 17
hybridity, 11

Ibarra, Francisco de, 31
iconography: Puebloan and Spanish, 19
identity: signaling, 16
Illinois, copper working in, 12
inalienable objects, 18
indigenous populations: congregation of, 23–24; in mining industry, 27, 28, 36, 89
Inguarán, 23
iron, 15, 22, 84
iron hydroxides, 71
iron oxides, 72
iron sulfide minerals, 71
Itziparátzico region, 23

jewelry: metal, 91–92

katsina religion, 6, 16, 17
Keres speakers, 1
Kidder, A. V., 37, 38
Kingery, David W., 12
Kopytoff, Igor, 14

labor: indigenous, 36, 89; in mining industry, 23–24, 25, 27, 36
Laboratory of Anthropology, 38
La Cienega, 32, 36, 88
La Huacana, 23–24
Lambert, Marjorie, 38, 39
lead, lead minerals, 1, 4, 15, 16, 28, 82; in New Mexico, 30, 31–32; in processing features, 59, 62; Puebloan distribution of, 17–18; in refractory materials, 77–78; slag, 73, 75, *plates 12, 13*

lead glass, 84
lead isotopes: analysis of, 71, 79–*80*
lead ores, 65, 84, 88; analysis of, 71–73. *See also* galena
lead oxides, 59, 62, 75, 87
lead-zinc ore, 78, 81–82
Lechtman, Heather, 9
Lemonnier, Pierre, 9, 11
Leroi-Gourhan, Andre, 11
limestone: burned, 66
limonite, 71
liquation, 84
litharge, 28, 31, 48, 65, 75, 84, 87, *plates 14, 15*
Little Colorado drainage, 83
livestock, 27, 40
Luján, Diego Pérez de, 30, 87

macrobotanical samples, 4, 63
Magdalena district: lead minerals from, 30
magistral, 28, 82
magnetite, 73
magnetite-delafossite copper slag, 74–75, *plate 11*
malachite, 39, 63, 71, 72, 80; smelting of, 83–84
manganese oxides, 15
Manzano Mountains, 32
Mapimí, 28, 32
market systems: Pueblo IV, 17
masks: katsina, 16, 17, 18
masonry: in Eastern Terrace, 52–53; in Western Terrace, 53–55
material culture, 7, 12; in colonial contexts, 10–11; value of, 13–14
Mauss, Marcel, 8
medallions: Catholic religious, 65
medicines, 87
melilite, 75
melilite-fayalite copper slag, 74, *plate 10*
Mera, H. P., 38
merchants: in Parral, 29
mercury, 27, 31, 83
mercury amalgamation, 25, 27, 31, 82–83
metales, 14
metallography, 71

metallurgical workshop/facility, 86; construction and use of, 43–45; dates of, 41–42; excavation of, 6, 40–41; at Paa-ko, 1, 4, 37, *38. See also* Eastern Terrace; Northern Exterior Area; Northern Terrace; Western Exterior Area; Western Terrace; *various features*
metallurgists, metallurgy: Pueblo-Spanish contexts, 86–87; Spanish colonial, 82–85; West Mexican indigenous, 4, 22
metal resources: Spanish knowledge of, 22
metals, 82; evaluating, 84–85; refining, 75–76; wealth in, 91–92. *See also by type*
Mexicas, 28
Michoacán, 4; metal production in, 23, 82
microscopy: optical and electron, 5
micro-XRF, 69, 71, 72
minerals, mineral deposits: analysis of, 69, 70–71; exchange systems and, 17–18; procurement of, 1, 6, 14; Puebloan use of, 15–17; Spanish exploration for, 29–30; in Spanish value system, 18–19, 22, 31. *See also by type*
mines, 1, *3;* colonial period, 22, 32–36; in West Mexico, 82
mining communities: Spanish colonial, 32–36
mining industry, 4; New Mexico colony, 31–32, 82; New Spain, 21, *26;* in Parral, 28–29; in Zacatecas, 25, 27–28
minium, 75
missions, missionaries, 10, 19, 30, 39
Museum of New Mexico, 38

Native Americans. *See* indigenous populations; Puebloans; Tarascans; West Mexicans
negrillos, 83, 84
Nelson, Nels, research by, 37–39
New Galicia (Nuevo Galicia), 21, 22
New Mexico, New Mexico colony: 21, 24, 28, 88, 90; mineral

deposits, 29–30; Spanish mining interests in, 31–32, 36, 82
New Placers District (San Pedro District), 1, 80, 88; copper ores from, 72, 82
New Spain, 24, 83; mining industry in, 4, 25–29; trade and Tribute networks, 21–22, 88
North Division (San Pedro Viejo II), 37
Northern Exterior Area, 41, *44,* 65–66, 68
Northern Terrace, 66–67, 74
Northern Tewa, 87
North Magdalena District, 30
Northwestern University Summer Field Studies Program, 4, 40
Nueva Viscaya, mines in, 32

objects: inalienable, 18
Ohkay Owingeh (San Juan Pueblo): color symbolism at, 16–17
Old Placers District, 1, 72
Oñate, Cristóbal de, 25, 30
Oñate, Juan de, 25, 30, 82, 89, 90
Oñate family, 31
ore roasting feature: in Western Terrace, 63
ores: analysis of, 69, 71–73; colors of, 31; processing of, 83–84; samples of, 70–71(table). *See also* copper ores; lead ores
Ortiz, Alfonso: on color symbolism, 16–17
Ortiz Mountains, 1, 32

Paquimé: copper at, 15
Parral, 27, 89; mining industry in, 28–29, 82
Parsons, Elsie C., 6, 16, 18
patio process, 82; in silver ore processing, 25, 27
Pecos, 91
pigments: mineral, 31, 91; Puebloan color symbolism, 16–17; Puebloan procurement and use of, 14, 15–16
pine: ponderosa (*Pinus ponderosa*), 4
pits: in Western Terrace surface 7, 64

place: mineral procurement and production, 16
Placitas District, 1
Potosí: silver ore processing, 23
power dynamics, 8, 10, 11
precious metals, 82. *See also* gold; silver
Puebloans, 31, 88; color symbolism, 16–17; mineral exchange patterns, 17–18; mineral procurement and use, 4, 6, 14, 15–16; value system, 13, 19–20
Pueblo IV period, 6, 16, 17
Pueblo Revolt, 36
Pueblos, 1, 19, 28, 91; and Spanish mining industry, 87–88
Puerto Real, 12
pyrite, 72

quartz, 72, 73

radiocarbon dates, 41–42, 50
raids: Indian, 32
ranches, 27
rebellions: Indian, 32, 36
refractory materials, 6; refiring and analysis of, 71, 76–78
refuge, 1, 4, 39
repartimiento, 10, 23, 24, 89
resistance: power dynamics and, 11–12
Rio Grande, 1, 24
Rio Grande Glaze Ware, 16, 19, 38, 40
Rio Salado, 30
ritual production: Puebloan, 4, 6, 16–17, 18
roads: Spanish Crown-built, 29
Rodríguez-Chamuscado expedition, 29, 30, 31
roomblocks: on Northern Terrace, 66–67
Rosas, Luis de, 88
runoff: flooding from, 43

St. Augustine, 12
Salado: copper exchange, 15
Salinas Pueblos: glaze wares from, 30
salt deposits: in New Mexico, 28

San Antonio pueblo (LA 24), 1
San Cristobal Pueblo, 39
Sandia Mountains, 1, 32
San Francisco del Tuerto (LA 240), 82
San Juan Pueblo (Ohkay Owingeh): color symbolism at, 16–17
San Lazaro Pueblo, 39
San Marcos Pueblo, 29, 32, 36, 82, 88
San Pedro, 1, 37
San Pedro Arroyo, 32, 40
San Pedro mine, 82
San Pedro Mountains, 1, 32, 80, 81
San Pedro Viejo I (South Division), 37
San Pedro Viejo II (North Division), 37
Santa Bárbara Mine, 28, 32
Santa Clara del Cobre, 79
Santa Rosa Mine, 81
Santo Domingo Pueblo, 39
scanning electron microscopy with energy dispersive spectroscopy (SEM-EDS), 6, 69, 71
School of American Research, 38
SCOT. *See* Social Construction of Technology approach
SEM-EDS. *See* scanning electron microscopy with energy dispersive spectroscopy
sheet metal: copper, 4, 39, 48, 71, 91, *plates 17, 18*
silver, silver production, 1, 7, 22, 48, 73, 82, 84; Spanish colonial processing, 23, 83; in Zacatecas, 25, 27–28, 32
silver chloride ores, 28
silver sulfides, 25
slag, 63, *plates 6, 7*; analysis of, 69, 70–71; copper, 39, 64–65, 73–75, 84, *plates 8, 9, 10, 11*; lead, 48, 62, 75, *plates 12, 13*
slaves, 27, 29, 36
smelting, 25, 31, 81, 82; copper, 4, 23, 64, 83–84, 86; lead, 77–78; slag and vitrified material, 48–49
Smith, Cyril Stanley, 8, 9
smithsonite, 71, 72
Snaketown: copper trade, 15

social action, objects and, 13
Social Construction of Technology (SCOT) approach, 8
social groups: and technology, 9–10
Socorro, 29, 32
South Division (San Pedro Viejo I), 37
Southern Terrace, 43, *44. See also* Eastern Terrace; Northern Exterior Area; Western Exterior Area; Western Terrace; *various features*
Southwest Regional Cult, 16
Spain: and mineral rights, 22
Spanish colonial period, 1; economies, 90–91; metal production, 82–85; mineral explorations, 29–30; mining communities, 32–36; mining industry, 5, 22–25, 87–88; at Paa-ko, 4, 40, 86–87; tribute networks, 21–22; value systems, 13, 18–19
sphalerite, 71, 72, 73
stable isotope analyses, 71, 79–81
Style and Technology approach, 8–9
sulfide ores, 71, 72
sulfur, 31, 63, *plate 19*; in metal refining, 84, 85
sulfur-mercury theory, 83
supply caravans: to New Mexico, 29
surfaces: in Western Terrace, 55–64

Tanoan speakers, 1, 38–39
Tarahumara, 36
Tarascans, 5, 23, 28, 36, 82
Technological Choices approach, 8, 9
Technological Style approach, 8
technology, technological systems, 8, 12; social groups and, 9–10
temper: in glaze wares, 15–16
tepuzque, 89
terraces: metallurgical facility, 43
Tewa speakers, 1, 39; color symbolism, 16–17, 87
Texcocos, 28
Tijeras Canyon District, 1, 80
Tijeras Pueblo (LA 581), 1
tin, 22
Tiwa speakers, 30, 39

tlacos, 89
Tlaxcalans, 28
Tolosa, Juan de, 25, 31
Topira, 22
trade, 29, 88. *See also* exchange;
    tribute system
trench furnaces: in Eastern Terrace,
    49–51, 67
tribute networks, 21–22, 24, 88
Tuerto Pueblo (El Tuerto), 32, 82, 88
Tuerto River, 32
turquoise, 4, 15, 80

University of Chicago Field Studies
    Program, 4, 6, 39, 40–41
University of New Mexico, 38

value systems: of material culture,
    13–14; metals in, 90–92; Pueb-
    loan, 17–18, 19–20; Spanish,
    18–19, 31, 36
ventilation systems: in Eastern
    Terrace, 47–48, *51–52*

Veracruz, 29
Verde Valley (Ariz.), 30
verdigris, 31
vitrified material: adobe, 76–78, *plate
    16*; in Eastern Terrace, 46–47,
    48–49; in Western Terrace, 58–59
vitriol, 83

wage labor: in Spanish mining
    industry, 24, 25, 27, 28, 36, 89
water power: in ore processing, 28
wealth: metals as, 91–92; in Spanish
    colonial context, 14, 18–19
Western Exterior Area, 64–65, 74
Western Pueblos: mineral use, 15, 31
Western Terrace, 41, *44*, 66, 68, 72,
    85; construction of, 53–55; slag
    in, 73, 74; surfaces and features in,
    55–64, 67
West Mexicans: in mining industry,
    28, 89, 90. *See also* Tarascans
West Mexico, 82; mining and
    metallurgy in, 4, 5, 22, 23, 28, 36

White Corn Maiden, 16
wind furnaces, 23, 85
Wolf, Eric, 10
wood: access to, 4
Works Progress Administration
    (WPA), 38, 39
Wylie, Alison, 5, 7

X-ray fluorescence (XRF), 5, 6,
    69, 72, 73, 74–75, 82

Yaquis, 36
Yavapais, 31

Zacatecas, 25, 27–28, 31, 82, 89
Zacatecos, 25, 31
Zaldivar, Juan de, 25, 32, 82
Zaldivar, Vincente, 25
Zaldivar family, 29n, 31
zinc, 16, 71, 73, 78
zinc silicate, 71–72
Zuni, 16, 19, 30

ABSTRACT

This study examines archaeological features and materials related to metal production excavated from the early colonial component (AD 1598-1680) of the Pueblo of Paa-ko (LA 162), in Bernalillo County, New Mexico. Archaeological, technological, ethnohistorical, and historical data are all used in order to develop a comprehensive understanding of this rare metallurgical facility. This study investigates how economic, technical and social knowledge was communicated, contested, and transformed across the social and cultural boundaries present in early colonial New Mexico. Also examined is the way that colonial industries were shaped by the situated agency of indigenous practitioners and the effects of such agency in the resulting technology at Paa-ko. Puebloan and Early Spanish colonial constructions of economic and social value are more broadly considered.

RESUMEN

Esta investigación examina las materias arqueológicas relacionadas con la producción de metales excavados en el Pueblo de Paa-ko (LA 162), un sitio del comienzo del periodo colonial (A.D. 1598–1680), ubicado en el condado de Bernalillo, Nuevo México, en el suroeste de los Estados Unidos. Los datos arqueológicos, tecnológicos, etno-históricos e históricos son utilizados para crear un entendimiento comprensivo de esta facilidad metalúrgica que aún no son muy conocidas. Esta investigación se trata de como fue comunicado, contestado y transformado el conocimiento económico, técnico, y social, mas allá de las fronteras sociales y culturales presentes en la temporada colonial de Nuevo México. También se examina la manera en que fueron formadas las industrias coloniales por los grupos indígenas ya situados y los efectos de tales grupos en la tecnología de Paa-ko. Las construcciones de los valores económicos y sociales por los Españoles y la gente Pueblo, hoy son altamente reconocidas.

ANTHROPOLOGICAL PAPERS OF THE UNIVERSITY OF ARIZONA

1. Excavations at Nantack Village, Point of Pines, Arizona
   David A. Breternitz. 1959.

2. Yaqui Myths and Legends
   Ruth W. Giddings. 1959. Now in book form.

3. Marobavi: A Study of an Assimilated Group in Northern Sonora
   Roger C. Owen. 1959.

4. A Survey of Indian Assimilation in Eastern Sonora
   Thomas B. Hinton. 1959.

5. The Phonology of Arizona Yaqui with Texts
   Lynn S. Crumrine. 1961.

6. The Maricopas: An Identification from Documentary Sources
   Paul H. Ezell. 1963.

7. The San Carlos Indian Cattle Industry
   Harry T. Getty. 1963.

8. The House Cross of the Mayo Indians of Sonora, Mexico
   N. Ross Crumrine. 1964.

9. Salvage Archaeology in Painted Rocks Reservoir, Western Arizona
   William W. Wasley and Alfred E. Johnson. 1965.

10. An Appraisal of Tree-Ring Dated Pottery in the Southwest
    David A. Breternitz. 1966.

11. The Albuquerque Navajos
    William H. Hodge. 1969.

12. Papago Indians at Work
    Jack O. Waddell. 1969.

13. Culture Change and Shifting Populations in Central Northern Mexico
    William B. Griffen. 1969.

14. Ceremonial Exchange as a Mechanism in Tribal Integration Among the Mayos of Northwest Mexico
    Lynn S. Crumrine. 1969.

15. Western Apache Witchcraft
    Keith H. Basso. 1969.

16. Lithic Analysis and Cultural Inference: A Paleo-Indian Case
    Edwin N. Wilmsen. 1970.

17. Archaeology as Anthropology: A Case Study
    William A. Longacre. 1970.

18. Broken K Pueblo: Prehistoric Social Organization in the American Southwest
    James N. Hill. 1970.

19. White Mountain Redware: A Pottery Tradition of East-Central Arizona and Western New Mexico
    Roy L. Carlson. 1970.

20. Mexican Macaws: Comparative Osteology
    Lyndon L. Hargrave. 1970.

21. Apachean Culture History and Ethnology
    Keith H. Basso and Morris E. Opler, eds. 1971.

22. Social Functions of Language in a Mexican-American Community
    George C. Barker. 1972.

23. The Indians of Point of Pines, Arizona: A Comparative Study of Their Physical Characteristics
    Kenneth A. Bennett. 1973.

24. Population, Contact, and Climate in the New Mexico Pueblos
    Ezra B. W. Zubrow. 1974.

25. Irrigation's Impact on Society
    Theodore E. Downing and McGuire Gibson, eds. 1974.

26. Excavations at Punta de Agua in the Santa Cruz River Basin, Southeastern Arizona
    J. Cameron Greenleaf. 1975.

27. Seri Prehistory: The Archaeology of the Central Coast of Sonora, Mexico
    Thomas Bowen. 1976.

28. Carib-Speaking Indians: Culture, Society, and Language
    Ellen B. Basso, ed. 1977.

29. Cocopa Ethnography
    William H. Kelly. 1977.

30. The Hodges Ruin: A Hohokam Community in the Tucson Basin
    Isabel Kelly, James E. Officer, and Emil W. Haury, collaborators; Gayle H. Hartmann, ed. 1978.

31. Fort Bowie Material Culture
    Robert M. Herskovitz. 1978.

32. Wooden Ritual Artifacts from Chaco Canyon, New Mexico: The Chetro Ketl Collection
    R. Gwinn Vivian, Dulce N. Dodgen, and Gayle H. Hartmann. 1978.

33. Indian Assimilation in the Franciscan Area of Nueva Vizcaya
    William B. Griffen. 1979.

34. The Durango South Project: Archaeological Salvage of Two Late Basketmaker III Sites in the Durango District
    John D. Gooding. 1980.

35. Basketmaker Caves in the Prayer Rock District, Northeastern Arizona
    Elizabeth Ann Morris. 1980.

36. Archaeological Explorations in Caves of the Point of Pines Region, Arizona
    James C. Gifford. 1980.

37. Ceramic Sequences in Colima: Capacha, an Early Phase
    Isabel Kelly. 1980.

38. Themes of Indigenous Acculturation in Northwest Mexico
    Thomas B. Hinton and Phil C. Weigand, eds. 1981.

39. Sixteenth Century Maiolica Pottery in the Valley of Mexico
    Florence C. Lister and Robert H. Lister. 1982.

40. Multidisciplinary Research at Grasshopper Pueblo, Arizona
    William A. Longacre, Sally J. Holbrook, and Michael W. Graves, eds. 1982.

41. The Asturian of Cantabria: Early Holocene Hunter-Gatherers in Northern Spain
    Geoffrey A. Clark. 1983.

42. The Cochise Cultural Sequence in Southeastern Arizona
    E. B. Sayles. 1983.

43. Cultural and Environmental History of Cienega Valley, Southeastern Arizona
    Frank W. Eddy and Maurice E. Cooley. 1983.

44. Settlement, Subsistence, and Society in Late Zuni Prehistory
    Keith W. Kintigh. 1985.

45. **The Geoarchaeology of Whitewater Draw, Arizona**
    Michael R. Waters. 1986.

46. **Ejidos and Regions of Refuge in Northwestern Mexico**
    N. Ross Crumrine and Phil C. Weigand, eds. 1987.

47. **Preclassic Maya Pottery at Cuello, Belize**
    Laura J. Kosakowsky. 1987.

48. **Pre-Hispanic Occupance in the Valley of Sonora, Mexico**
    William E. Doolittle. 1988.

49. **Mortuary Practices and Social Differentiation at Casas Grandes, Chihuahua, Mexico**
    John C. Ravesloot. 1988.

50. **Point of Pines, Arizona: A History of the University of Arizona Archaeological Field School**
    Emil W. Haury. 1989.

51. **Patarata Pottery: Classic Period Ceramics of the South-central Gulf Coast, Veracruz, Mexico**
    Barbara L. Stark. 1989.

52. **The Chinese of Early Tucson: Historic Archaeology from the Tucson Urban Renewal Project**
    Florence C. Lister and Robert H. Lister. 1989.

53. **Mimbres Archaeology of the Upper Gila, New Mexico**
    Stephen H. Lekson. 1990.

54. **Prehistoric Households at Turkey Creek Pueblo, Arizona**
    Julie C. Lowell. 1991.

55. **Homol'ovi II: Archaeology of an Ancestral Hopi Village, Arizona**
    E. Charles Adams and Kelley Ann Hays, eds. 1991.

56. **The Marana Community in the Hohokam World**
    Suzanne K. Fish, Paul R. Fish, and John H. Madsen, eds. 1992.

57. **Between Desert and River: Hohokam Settlement and Land Use in the Los Robles Community**
    Christian E. Downum. 1993.

58. **Sourcing Prehistoric Ceramics at Chodistaas Pueblo, Arizona: The Circulation of People and Pots in the Grasshopper Region**
    María Nieves Zedeño. 1994.

59. **Of Marshes and Maize: Preceramic Agricultural Settlements in the Cienega Valley, Southeastern Arizona**
    Bruce B. Huckell. 1995.

60. **Historic Zuni Architecture and Society: An Archaeological Application of Space Syntax**
    T. J. Ferguson. 1996.

61. **Ceramic Commodities and Common Containers: Production and Distribution of White Mountain Red Ware in the Grasshopper Region, Arizona**
    Daniela Triadan. 1997.

62. **Prehistoric Sandals from Northeastern Arizona: The Earl H. Morris and Ann Axtell Morris Research**
    Kelley Ann Hays-Gilpin, Ann Cordy Deegan, and Elizabeth Ann Morris. 1998.

63. **Expanding the View of Hohokam Platform Mounds: An Ethnographic Perspective**
    Mark D. Elson. 1998.

64. **Great House Communities Across the Chacoan Landscape**
    John Kantner and Nancy M. Mahoney, eds. 2000.

65. **Tracking Prehistoric Migrations: Pueblo Settlers among the Tonto Basin Hohokam**
    Jeffery J. Clark. 2001.

66. **Beyond Chaco: Great Kiva Communities on the Mogollon Rim Frontier**
    Sarah A. Herr. 2001.

67. **Salado Archaeology of the Upper Gila, New Mexico**
    Stephen H. Lekson. 2002.

68. **Ancestral Hopi Migrations**
    Patrick D. Lyons. 2003.

69. **Ancient Maya Life in the Far West Bajo: Social and Environmental Change in the Wetlands of Belize**
    Julie L. Kunen. 2004.

70. **The Safford Valley Grids: Prehistoric Cultivation in the Southern Arizona Desert**
    William E. Doolittle and James A. Neely, eds. 2004.

71. **Murray Springs: A Clovis Site with Multiple Activity Areas in the San Pedro Valley, Arizona**
    C. Vance Haynes, Jr., and Bruce B. Huckell, eds. 2007.

72. **Ancestral Zuni Glaze-Decorated Pottery: Viewing Pueblo IV Regional Organization through Ceramic Production and Exchange**
    Deborah L. Huntley. 2008.

73. **In the Aftermath of Migration: Renegotiating Ancient Identity in Southeastern Arizona**
    Anna A. Neuzil. 2008.

74. **Burnt Corn Pueblo, Conflict and Conflagration in the Galisteo Basin, A.D. 1250–1325**
    James E Snead and Mark W. Allen. 2011.

75. **Potters and Communities of Practice: Glaze Paint and Polychrome Pottery in the American Southwest, A.D. 1250–1700**
    Linda S. Cordell and Judith Habicht-Mauche, eds. 2012.

76. **Los Primeros Mexicanos: Late Pleistocene and Early Holocene People of Sonora**
    Guadalupe Sánchez. 2015.

77. **The Ceramic Sequence of the Holmul Region, Guatemala**
    Michael G. Callaghan and Nina Neivens de Estrada. 2016.

78. **The Winged: An Upper Missouri River Ethno-Ornithology**
    Kaitlyn Chandler, Wendi Field Murray, María Nieves Zedeño, Samrat Clements, Robert James. 2016.

79. **Seventeenth-Century Metallurgy on the Spanish Colonial Frontier: Pueblo and Spanish Interactions**
    Noah H. Thomas. 2018.